C++ TEMPLATES AND TOOLS

C++ Templates and Tools

Scott Robert Ladd

M&T BOOKS

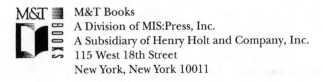

M&T Books
A Division of MIS:Press, Inc.
A Subsidiary of Henry Holt and Company, Inc.
115 West 18th Street
New York, New York 10011

Printed in the United States of America

Limits of Liability and Disclaimer of Warranty

The Author and Publisher of this book have used their best efforts in preparing the book and the programs contained in it. These efforts include the development, research, and testing of the theories and programs to determine their effectiveness.

The Author and Publisher make no warranty of any kind, expressed or implied, with regard to these programs or the documentation contained in this book. The Author and Publisher shall not be liable in any event for incidental or consequential damages in connection with, or arising out of, the furnishing, performance, or use of these programs.

```
Ladd, Scott Robert.
    C++ templates and tools / Scott Robert Ladd.
        p.  cm.
    Includes index.
    ISBN 1-55851-437-6
    1.  C++ (Computer program language)   I.  Title.
QA76.73.C153L333    1995
005.13'3--dc20                                  95-9703
                                                CIP
```

All products, names and services are trademarks or registered trademarks of their respective companies.

Editor-in-Chief: Paul Farrell
Managing Editor: Cary Sullivan
Development Editor: Michael Sprague
Production Editor: Joe McPartland
Copy Editor: Betsy Hardinger

DEDICATION

When I was young, my parents urged me to read and explore; wherever my curiosity led, they opened the way. So to them I dedicate a book and career that exists because of their encouragement and support.

Thanks, Mom & Dad!

ACKNOWLEDGEMENTS

My Lovely and talented wife, Maria, was a source of encouragement and sustenance as I worked on this book. I appreciate her listening thoughtfully to my ramblings about computer science and math; her insights are an important part of this book.

I'd also like to thank Michael Sprague and Joseph McPartland for their efforts in making this book happen.

CONTENTS

CHAPTER 2

LISTS, STACKS, AND QUEUES........................... 35

CHAPTER 3

BINARY TREES.. 91

CHAPTER 4

CHAPTER 5

CHAPTER 6

CHAPTER 7

OBJECT SETS AND FUZZY LOGIC..................... 219

CHAPTER 8

SPARSE MATRICES 247

CHAPTER 9

MATRICES AND LINEAR ALGEBRA 263

CHAPTER 10

Chapter 11

Parsing 339

Chapter 12

Data Compression 359

WHY THIS BOOK IS FOR YOU

This book is about implementing algorithms and components in C++. In addition to giving you a thorough intoduction to templates—by showing how templates work in real-world code—it includes more than 14,000 lines of C++ source code for the following tools:

❖ Numeric and object sets, implementing operations such as union, intersection, difference, and more.

❖ A powerful numeric matrix class with support for matrix multiplication, inversion, transposition, and the solution of simultaneous linear equations via both Gaussian elimination and LUP decomposition.

❖ A complete collection of container template classes, including linked lists, queues, stacks, deques, and heap-based priority queues.

❖ Binary tree template classes, including fully implemented red-black trees.

❖ A top-down, recursive descent parser that supports named variables.

❖ A class for data compression and decompression using the Huffman algorithm.

❖ A polynomial template that supports addition, subtraction, multiplication, and evaluation.

❖ Sparse matrices.

❖ Hash-table based dictionaries.

❖ An object set class for implementing fuzzy logic.

This book is intended to complement the author's other recent title, *C++ Components and Algorithms*. Although each book stands alone, the two works complement each other by providing different applications of powerful algorithms and software components.

To get the most out of this book, you should understand the basic mechanics of C++, should have written some C++ programs, and should be interested in exploring how C++ can be used in practical applications. You need Borland C++ 4.5 or another C++ 2.1-compliant compiler to use the code in this book.

INTRODUCTION

This is the first time I've written a sequel to one of my computer books—
in this case, *C++ Components and Algorithms*. My goal was to take up where
the earlier book left off, providing still more examples of how C++ can
effectively implement powerful software components. I hope you'll be
pleased with the result.

Templates have changed the way I program, not because they're
trendy but because they *work*. I resisted templates for a long time, writing
them off as another frivolous language feature that I could live without.
It wasn't until I ran into a technical "wall" that I tried templates for the
first time. Today, I can't understand how I got along so long without templates and their ability to define families of classes.

Nothing in this book is based on anyone else's class hierarchy. Borland and Microsoft spend a lot of money advertising their bulky, overwritten class libraries, hoping you'll base your applications on their proprietary code. If you're willing to be tied to a specific vendor, that's your choice. I like my code to be independent.

I don't believe in big class hierarchies. My classes work together and use each other, but they in no way form a single pyramid of interlinked classes. I find the big hierarchies to be inefficient and cumbersome; they're too big to get a handle on, and I worry about cascade effects and class landslides in all those mountains of code. And I don't see any need to create big hierarchies.

In regard to my earlier book, *C++ Components and Algorithms*: All the code therein is 100% compatible with this book, but each book stands alone. The desire for compatibility led me to include the exception handling classes and the random number generator of *Components and Algorithms* in this book. Also, the discussion in Chapter 5 of hashing algorithms is lifted from the other book. This constitutes about a dozen pages of this book that aren't original. This book does, however, extend those earlier classes to include error reporting under Windows and tables of random numbers.

Although everything herein was tested and written using Borland C++ version 4.5, it should work well with any standard C++ compiler. Some of this code is extracted from libraries that run on Sun workstations; other pieces have been compiled and run with other PC-based C++ compilers.

I've had trouble when working code no longer compiles when a vendor comes out with a new compiler version. C++ is still a growing, evolving language—and it should be treated with caution. I hope that vendors will keep backward compatibility in mind when working on new versions—and I hope readers will forgive me if I lack the prescience to anticipate future changes in compilers. Nothing bugs an author more than working on a book for months, only to have a vendor invalidate it before it sees publication!

As always, you are free to use the code herein for personal, noncommercial projects; however, I ask that you respect copyright law by contacting M&T Books before using this code in a for-profit project.

Most of all, I hope this book provides you with insights and useful code. I've enjoyed writing it, and I hope you enjoy using it.

Scott Robert Ladd
in the San Juan Mountains of Colorado
January 1995

CHAPTER 1

SIMPLE STUFF

Before delving into more complicated matters, I'll present my views on templates. This chapter also presents basic classes that I use throughout the book, including my tools for exception handling and random number generation.

FUNCTION TEMPLATES

If you want to create a set of C++ functions for performing an operation on a variety of data types, the obvious solution is to use function over-loading. For example, if I wanted functions to calculate the squares of *int* and *float* values, I could define these two functions:

```
int Square(int x)
    {
    return x * x;
    };

float Square(float x)
    {
    return x * x;
    }
```

For each data type that I want to square, I create a new *Square* function. The C++ compiler determines which function to call based on the argu-ment passed to *Square*.

```
int i = 2;
int f = 12.53;

int isq = Square(i); // call Square(int)
int fsq = Square(f); // call Square(float)
```

The similarity of these functions is—well—annoying. The actual code doesn't change; the only difference between the *Square* functions is their header. I could, of course, use a C-type macro function like this:

```
#define Square(x) (x * x)
```

A macro, however, always generates inline code. For a complex calcula-tion, it may be better to have callable functions for each data type.

   Wouldn't it be nice if I could just create one function that says, "Square any type of number," and leave it to the compiler to generate appropriate code for the data types I use? C++ offers just such a facility: function templates.

A *function template* describes a type of function rather than a specific function. Instead of creating a *Square* function for every numeric data type, I can create a function template like this:

```
template <class T>
    inline T Square(T x)
        {
        return x * x;
        };
```

A function template tells the compiler how to construct a set of similar functions. The preceding template tells the compiler, "Here's a template for a function named *Square*. It has a single argument of class *T* and returns a class *T* value. When a statement calling *Square* is encountered, generate a *Square* function that replaces *T* with the class of the argument."

For the purposes of a template, the intrinsic types (*float*, *int*, etc.) are treated as classes. For example, this piece of code:

```
int i1 = 2;
int i2 = Square(i1);
```

would cause the compiler to generate a function like this:

```
int Square(int x)
    {
    return x * x;
    }
```

The compiler generates code only for those data types used in calls to the template function. If you add a new class—for, say, complex or rational numbers—those types will *automatically* be supported by the template for *Square*. The only stipulation is that the data type used in calling a template function support the operations performed. For example, this code fragment would generate a compile-time error:

```
char * x = "Dance";
char * y = Square(x);
```

Unless you've defined the binary *operator for *char **s, this line of code will not compile.

A template may have more than one generic argument, and it can have arguments with a specific type. Here is an example:

```
template <class A, class B>
    void MyFunc(A arga, B argb, int i)
    {
    // do something
    };
```

The first two arguments in a call to *MyFunc* may have the same or different types. The third argument is always treated as an *int*. Templates generate inline functions if the function header is prefaced with the *inline* keyword.

A C++ compiler views template functions as a set of overloaded functions. It's also possible to overload a template-generated function with a nontemplate function. To resolve overloads, the compiler first looks for an exact match between a function call's arguments and existing functions; if the compiler doesn't find a match, it generates a new function from the template.

CLASS TEMPLATES

A *class template* tells the compiler how to construct a series of similar classes. I view class templates as forms, with the compiler filling in the blanks based on your template arguments.

As a tool for defining containers, class templates excel. Here's an example of a flexible record type that contains both a key value and data:

```
template <class K, class D>
    class Record
```

```
    {
public:
    Record(K kx, D dx) { Key = kx; Data = dx; }
    K GetKey() { return Key; }
    D GetData() { return Data; }
private:
    K Key;
    D Data;
};
```

When the compiler encounters a template, it creates a general definition from which it can build specific types as required. The compiler generates type-specific versions of *Record* only when it needs to; as with inline functions, a template class or function does not produce any code until it is used for a specific type. For instance, the declaration

```
Record<int, String> recis;
```

will cause the compiler to generate a *Record<int, String>* class equivalent to this:

```
class Record
    {
public:
    Record(int kx, String dx) { Key = kx; Data = dx; }
    int GetKey() { return Key; }
    String GetData() { return Data; }
private:
    int Key;
    String Data;
};
```

If I also declare a *Record<long,double>* object, the compiler generates another class definition. In other words, I can create a *Record* class for any types *K* and *D*, all based on a single common template.

Note that this power comes with the usual set of caveats. First, each class created from a template has its own static members, functions, and data members; the more classes you create from templates, the larger your programs will become. Most of your templates will be defined in header files to be included in each source module in which you use that class.

Second, templates do not, in and of themselves, generate code that can be stored in a library for later linking. A smart compiler will combine duplicate template types during linking; a less intelligent compiler may, however, leave your program containing several instances of a class. The C++ standard does not define a standard technique for "precompiling" specific template types, but some compilers have this capability.

Members defined outside the template class definition need to be templates themselves; class scope identifiers must contain template arguments:

```
template <class K, class D>
    Record<K,D>::Record(K kx, D dx)
        {
        Key = kx;
        Data = dx;
        }
```

References to the class type inside the template do not need to be qualified with template arguments, because they are implied by the template. You can derive classes from template classes; in fact, templates can be derived from other templates.

```
template <class D>
    class Object : Record<int, D>
        {
        . . .
        };
```

A *typedef* statement can define an alias for a template type, thereby eliminating the need to specify arguments in angle brackets.

```
typedef StdRecord Record<int,int>;
```

It's also possible to define a template type using another template type as an argument:

```
Record< long,Object<String,double> > rec;
```

Note the extra spaces used to keep the compiler from seeing >> as the right shift operator.

Template arguments need not be class names; template parameters may provide values. For example, most buffer implementations look something like this:

```
class Buffer
    {
    public:
        Buffer(size_t len);
        .
        .
        .
    private:
        char * data;
    };

Buffer::Buffer(size_t len)
    {
    data = new char[len];

    if (data == NULL)
        throw AnException;
    }
```

A template could provide the size of the buffer as part of the class definition, allowing the buffer to be statically allocated rather than requiring a call to new:

```
template <size_t n>
    class Buffer
        {
        public:
            Buffer();
            .
            .
            .
        private:
```

```
        char data[Len];
    };
```

The definition of a specific buffer size would look like this:

```
Buffer<128> buf;
```

Default values for template arguments let you create a default version of a class:

```
template <size_t n = 128>
    class Buffer
        {
        public:
            Buffer();
            .
            .
            .
        private:
            char data[Len];
        };

Buffer buf; // equivalent to: Buffer<128> buf;
```

THINKING ABOUT TEMPLATES

C++ didn't have templates six years ago, when I first began using it. When templates became generally available, I ignored them. Support for templates was far from universal; even today, some versions of big-name compilers still ignore templates. Only in the last year or so have templates become prevalent across platforms and compilers.

I can't blame compiler vendors for taking time to implement templates. The concept is simple: A template defines a type of class or function from which specific classes or functions can be defined. However, in the bowels of a compiler, templates can create incredible headaches. I know more than one C++ compiler author who have grumbled and growled about implementing templates.

From an application programmer's perspective, however, the compiler writer's troubles are largely a moot point. Templates are here, they work well in most compilers, and everyone is eager to use them. After several years of C++ programming, I had created a large personal library of C++ code—about 200,000 lines' worth—and none of it used templates. I'm not one to tear apart working code just to add a new language feature; my class library originated long before templates were available to me.

So what made me begin using templates? Curiosity. I was playing around with a simulation program, indulging a hobby. I realized that several of my classes had exactly the same format and function but different data formats. This being my own project, and with a new, template-supporting Borland compiler in hand, I dug into templates to see how well they worked.

Templates reduced the source code for my simulation program by almost one-third without any noticeable change in performance. The code was easier to read, too. That experience inspired me to try rewriting one of my messier class sets using templates. As projects came and went, I began including templates more often than not, and my old library underwent a slow transformation.

I didn't plan for templates to become a central part of my class designs; it happened because templates worked so well. For example, my other book on class libraries, *C++ Components and Algorithms*, included 15,000 lines of nontemplate code in its first edition. Rewriting the book for the second edition, I employed templates—and increased the number of classes and algorithms while reducing the source code to only 10,000 lines. I've had similar experiences with other projects.

EXCEPTIONS

An intelligent data structure knows enough about itself to know when something has gone wrong. Useful diagnostics must be displayed somewhere, either on the screen or in a file. Programs require different output mechanisms for various environments, such as command-line DOS, windowed DOS, and Microsoft Windows. I want my classes to be platform-independent, so I created a very simple base class that defines the output of text and an error level:

```
enum DiagLevel
    {
    DIAG_MSG,
    DIAG_WARNING,
    DIAG_ERROR,
    DIAG_FATAL
    };

class DiagOutput
    {
    public:
        virtual void DisplayMsg
          (
          const char * msg,
          DiagLevel level = DIAG_MSG
          ) = 0;
    };
```

DiagOutput is a virtual base class from which I derive specific classes for various environments. For MS-DOS command-line programs, for example, I created this class:

```
class DiagOutDOS : public DiagOutput
    {
    public:
        DiagOutDOS
          (
          ostream & strm
          );

        virtual void DisplayMsg
          (
          const char * msg,
```

```
        DiagLevel level = DIAG_MSG
        );

    private:
        ostream & outstrm;
    };

inline DiagOutDOS::DiagOutDOS
    (
    ostream & strm
    )
    : outstrm(strm)
    {
     // otherwise empty
    }
```

You provide a stream object when creating a *DiagOutDOS* object; usually,
I use the standard streams *cerr* or *cout*. I implemented the *DisplayMsg*
function as follows:

```
void DiagOutDOS::DisplayMsg
    (
    const char * msg,
    DiagLevel level
    )
    {
    switch (level)
        {
        // note that DIAG_MSG does not display a header!
        case DIAG_WARNING:
            outstrm << "Warning: ";
            break;
        case DIAG_ERROR:
            outstrm << "ERROR: ";
            break;
        case DIAG_FATAL:
            outstrm << "FATAL ERROR: ";
        }

    outstrm << msg;
```

```
    if (level != DIAG_MSG)
        {
        outstrm << endl << "Press any key to ";

        if (level == DIAG_WARNING)
            outstrm << "continue.";
        else
            outstrm << "TERMINATE this program.";

        while (!kbhit());        // wait for keypress
        if (!getch()) getch(); // clear input character
        }

    outstrm << endl;

    if (level >= DIAG_ERROR)
        exit(EXIT_FAILURE);
    }
```

If the error level is *DIAG_MSG* (the default), *DisplayMsg* simply displays the string and returns. For a *DIAG_WARNING* message, *DisplayMsg* also stops and waits for the user to press a key before it returns. *DIAG_ERROR* and *DIAG_FATAL* messages cause *DisplayMsg* to terminate the program. Several variations on this theme exist; this is how I usually handle problems in a command-line program.

For Microsoft Windows, my *DiagOutWin* class displays messages in message boxes. Here's its definition:

```
class DiagOutWin : public DiagOutput
    {
    public:
        DiagOutWin
            (
            const char * t
            );

        ~DiagOutWin();

        virtual void DisplayMsg
            (
```

```
        const char * msg,
        DiagLevel level = DIAG_MSG
        );

public:
    char * Title;
};
```

DiagOutWin reflects the added features of the Windows environment. When creating a *DiagOutWin* object, a constructor parameter specifies the title of any message boxes. Usually, the title will be the name of the program. Because the *Title* data member is dynamically allocated, *DiagOutWin* requires a destructor to free that memory.

```
inline DiagOutWin::DiagOutWin
    (
    const char * t
    )
    {
    Title = strdup(t);
    }

inline DiagOutWin::~DiagOutWin()
    {
    if (Title != NULL)
        delete Title;
    }
```

This is the default implementation of *DiagOutWin*'s *DisplayMessage* function:

```
void DiagOutWin::DisplayMsg
    (
    const char * msg,
    DiagLevel level
    )
    {
    UINT style;
    UINT sound;
    int response;
    char text[256];
```

```
// copy message to output buffer
strncpy(text,msg,128);

// set values specific to error severity
switch (level)
    {
    case DIAG_FATAL:
        sound = MB_ICONSTOP;
        style = MB_OK;
        strcat(text,"\nPROGRAM WILL TERMINATE!");
        break;
    case DIAG_ERROR:
        sound = MB_ICONEXCLAMATION;
        style = MB_YESNO;
        strcat(text,"\nClick 'Yes' to terminate program, "
                    "or 'No' to continue");
        break;
    case DIAG_WARNING:
    case DIAG_MSG:
        sound = MB_ICONASTERISK;
        style = MB_OK;
    }

// match icon to sound
style |= sound;

// sound off and display message
MessageBeep(sound);
response = MessageBox(NULL,text,Title,style);

// check for termination
switch (level)
    {
    case DIAG_ERROR:
        if (response == IDNO)
            break;
    case DIAG_FATAL:
        PostQuitMessage(1); // boom-boom
        // program should never reach this point!
    }
}
```

Again, the Windows-based class is more complicated than the DOS equivalent. For Windows, I create different message box attributes based on the severity of the message. For *DIAG_ERROR* messages, I include **Yes** and **No** buttons in the message box that give the user choices in terminating or continuing the program. *DIAG_FATAL* messages always cause the application to stop.

The *ExceptionBase* Class

My exception and diagnostic classes write their messages through a *DiagOutput* object that is appropriate to an application's environment. This makes my diagnostic classes platform-independent; the application is responsible for handling output. It's up to you how you want your errors processed; *DiagOutput* classes provide the flexibility to customize error handling without the need to make changes to diagnostic classes. All my exception types are based on this class:

```
class ExceptionBase
    {
    public:
        virtual ~ExceptionBase();
        virtual void Explain(DiagOutput & out) = 0;
    };

ExceptionBase::~ExceptionBase()
    {
    // does nothing
    }
```

The virtual destructor is a piece of good programming style. It ensures that the proper destructor call is made for any object type derived from *ExceptionBase*. Most *ExceptionBase* objects won't need a destructor—that's why *ExceptionBase*'s destructor is not pure—but for those exception objects that need destruction, the virtual designation is vital.

The virtual *Explain* function displays a text description of the problem through a *DiagOutput* object. Classes derived from *ExceptionBase* should implement a problem-specific version of *Explain*.

The *DiagnosticBase* Class

Another basic class defines the common features that I use when debugging data structures and complex classes:

```
class DiagnosticBase
    {
    public:
        virtual void Dump(DiagOutput & out) = 0;
        virtual void ShowInternals(DiagOutput & out) = 0;
        virtual Boolean CheckIntegrity() = 0;
    };
```

DiagnosticBase is an abstract base class that defines the functions I use for analyzing an object. *Dump* displays the contents of an object; for example, to debug an array class, *Dump* would output the elements of the array. *ShowInternals* should output control information, such as the number of elements in an array and pointers to the array elements.

CheckIntegrity is a self-diagnostic that returns *BOOL_TRUE* if everything with the object is ok, and *BOOL_FALSE* if it finds something wrong. Implementing this function can be tricky, because you have to be sure that you've implemented your checks correctly. It's been proven that software can never verify software, because any software can have bugs—including verification software! I suggest that *CheckIntegrity* be implemented to look for blatantly obvious faults; trying to be too thorough only makes opportunities for errors in verification.

I didn't combine *ExceptionBase* and *DiagnosticBase* because most exceptions will be simple. *DiagnosticBase* is designed to provide detailed information on the internal structure of a complex object. Combining the two classes would be overkill for most exceptions.

RANDOM NUMBER GENERATION

Here's an example of a simple class that introduces the way in which I describe and implement classes throughout this book.

A random number is just that: a number whose value cannot be predicted in advance of its existence. Although the human mind has been known to be unpredictable, it isn't very good at generating a completely unrelated set of numbers. Try creating a list of 20 random integers selected from the range 1 through 100, inclusive. Are those numbers really random? And wouldn't it be tedious if you had to generate a thousand or a million random numbers?

Computers are supposed to be good at reducing tedious numeric operations. Unfortunately, computers perform calculations using algorithms, and truly random numbers cannot be generated by an algorithm. By definition, an algorithm is a specific sequence of operations that produces a predictable output for a given set of parameters. In the case of random numbers, the last thing we want is something predictable!

The best we can do with a computer is to create an algorithm that *appears* to generate a random sequence of numbers. The numbers aren't really random—a human being with a sharp mind or a calculator could predict the numbers in the sequence by following the algorithm. But the sequence of numbers is difficult to follow, and someone looking at the values would not be able to see any algorithmic pattern to them. For practical applications, pseudo-random numbers suffice.

Choosing an Algorithm

In general, a pseudo-random number generator begins with a *seed value* that begins the sequence. A set of mathematical operations is performed on the seed, generating a value that is reported as a pseudo-random number. That return value is then used as the next seed value.

Researchers have devoted copious time to inventing and analyzing pseudo-random number generators. The goal of this research has been to produce the most unpredictable sequence of values. Designing a good random number generator involves solving two problems:

❖ Increasing the size of the repetition cycle. As the algorithm is applied, the seed will eventually return to its starting value, and

23

the values will start repeating themselves. An algorithm that repeats after generating a million numbers is more useful than a generator that repeats itself every hundred numbers.

❖ Avoiding predictability. A random number generator that always returns values with the same last digit is worthless. An algorithm that generates only odd numbers is equally useless.

Although there are many fancy and complicated algorithms that generate pseudo-random numbers, one of the most commonly used algorithms is also one of the simplest. First introduced by D. Lehmer in 1951, the *linear congruential* method involves only two mathematical operations. Here's a basic implementation of a random number generator for *unsigned shorts*:

```
unsigned short seed = 1u;

unsigned short randshort()
    {
    const unsigned short k1 = 9821u;
    const unsigned short k2 = 1u;

    seed = seed * k1 + k2;

    return seed;
    }
```

Note that this algorithm relies on truncation after an overflow in a calculation. When *seed* is multiplied by *k1*, it will often overflow, generating a value that is larger than can be held by an *unsigned short*. On most PC-type computers, the extra high-order bits of *seed* will be dropped, in effect performing a *seed % USHRT_MAX* operation. This algorithm will not work on a machine that generates an exception when overflow occurs; in such a case, you'll need to change the algorithm to prevent overflow.

How did I select the constants *k1* and *k2*? Although volumes have been written on the subject, Donald Knuth provided the best analysis in volume 2 of his series The *Art of Computer Programming*. Knuth suggests that *k1* should be a "moderately sized" number less than the maximum random value, with no pattern to its digits, and ending in 21. In other words, setting *k1* to 2 or 100 would not make for a good generator. As for *k2*, Knuth states that it must be an odd number, preferably 1.

The underlying numerical analysis that led Knuth to select these values is outside the scope of this book. I suggest that you look up his three-volume series; the best programmers consider them to be the bibles of their profession.

So we have a pseudo-random number generator, right? Wrong! Alas, *randshort* has a nontrivial bug. The first 20 values it generates are:

```
 9822, 58407, 44076,  5117, 53482, 41219, 61464, 51385,
24886, 21663, 22468, 64053, 49986, 47867, 12080, 17521,
41742, 20503, 33372,   877, 27802, 20467,  7496, 21289,
19430, 46735, 35828,  4005, 11506, 16363,  6752, 54497,
48062, 26631, 54412, 65245, 25674, 27363, 34424, 43417
```

On the surface, these numbers don't look related. They do, however, follow a pattern: Odd and even values alternate! Unfortunately, fiddling with the values of *seed*, *k1*, or *k2* will only change the pattern of alternation. The problem is endemic to the algorithm.

Is the linear congruential method useless? Certainly not; we merely need to expand our algorithm to avoid the problem:

```
unsigned long seed = 1ul;

unsigned short randshort2()
    {
    const unsigned long k1 = 5709421ul;
    const unsigned long k2 = 1ul;

    seed = seed * k1 + k2;

    return (unsigned short)(seed >> 16L);
    }
```

The pattern in *randshort2*'s values is located in the lowest bits of *seed*. I eliminated this problem by using *unsigned longs* in the calculations, returning the upper 16 bits of *seed* as *randshort2*'s result.

The algorithm above assumes that a *long* is 32 bits and a *short* is 16 bits. This holds true for all PCs and workstations I have used. The shift values and other constants could be defined so that they are adjusted automatically based on the actual sizes of *shorts* and *longs*.

Starting from a given *seed* value, *randshort2* will always generate the same sequence of values. A function to set the *seed* value can be useful:

```
void setseed(unsigned long newseed)
    {
    seed = newseed;
    }
```

Setting the *seed* to an unpredictable value, such as the system time, generates an unpredictable set of values:

```
setseed((unsigned long)time(NULL));
```

The ANSI C standard defines the *rand* and *srand* functions, which directly correspond to *randshort2* and *seed*—right down to the use of a linear congruential algorithm.

A Class for Random Numbers.

Hold it! If ANSI C defines a random number generator, why did I go through this discussion? Why not use the ANSI functions?

I've found that C++ classes can often provide a better way of accomplishing a task normally performed via stand-alone functions. From a software engineering standpoint, *rand* and *srand* have several faults:

❖ A program must explicitly call *srand* to initialize the *seed*. If *srand* isn't called, the default value of *seed* will be used, and every execution of the program will generate the same sequence of pseudo-random numbers.

❖ Because *srand* and *rand* are two separate functions, *seed* is defined as a global variable. Good programmers avoid global variables, even those that can be hidden using the *static* keyword.

❖ Because there is only one *seed* value, only one sequence of pseudo-random numbers is generated in a program. Often, I like to have separate random number generators for different parts of a program.

❖ The ANSI *rand* function returns values between 0 and *UINT_MAX*. In most cases, I want to retrieve random values that are within a specific range, say from 1 to 100.

A class can solve all these problems. Here's the definition of my *RandGen* class:

```
class RandGen
    {
    protected:
        // used to set default seed argument from system time
        static unsigned long TimeSeed()
            {
            return (unsigned long)time(NULL);
            }

    public:
        // constructor
        RandGen
            (
            unsigned long initSeed = TimeSeed()
            );

        // set seed value
        void SetSeed
            (
            unsigned long newSeed = TimeSeed()
            );

        // get a psuedo-random number from 0 to (lim - 1)
        unsigned short operator ()
            (
            unsigned short lim
            );

    private:
        unsigned long Seed;
    };
```

The *RandGen* class encapsulates everything having to do with generating a pseudo-random number sequence. It also demonstrates some unconventional C++ programming techniques.

When a *RandGen* object is created, the constructor assigns a value to *Seed*. I wanted *Seed* to be automatically initialized by the system clock. The ANSI *time* function returns the current time, and I simply included a call to *time* as a default parameter in the prototypes for the constructor and *SetSeed* functions. I implemented the constructor and *SetSeed* inline:

```
inline RandGen::RandGen
    (
    unsigned long initSeed
    )
    {
    Seed = initSeed;
    }

inline void RandGen::SetSeed
    (
    unsigned long newSeed
    )
    {
    Seed = newSeed;
    }
```

The actual generator function is implemented via the parenthesis operators. Within the parentheses, a value can be supplied; a number between 0 and *lim* will be returned.

```
unsigned short RandGen::operator ()
    (
    unsigned short lim
    )
    {
    // get next seed value
    Seed = Seed * 5709421UL + 1UL;

    // return value from 0 to (lim - 1)
    return (unsigned short)((Seed >> 16UL) % lim);
    }
```

I used the modulus operator % to limit the returned value to between 0 and *lim*. This example program demonstrates how a *RandGen* object is used:

```
#include "randgen.h"
#include "iostream.h"

#define TAB_CHAR '\t'

int main()
    {
    RandGen rg1; // use the default, time-based seed
    RandGen rg2(1701); // explicitly set the seed

    // print 20 random numbers
    for (int i = 0; i < 20; ++i)
        cout << TAB_CHAR << rg1() << TAB_CHAR << rg2() << endl;

    return 0;
    }
```

The program will display two columns, each containing of 20 pseudo-random numbers. The first column will contain different numbers for each run of the program; however, the second column will always display the same sequence, because it uses a fixed seed value.

As C++ classes go, *RandGen* is nothing fancy. It does, however, provide capabilities not found in the ANSI function library. In later chapters, you'll see how I use *RandGen* objects in statistical analysis and simulations.

RANDOM NUMBER TABLES

Generating random numbers one-by-one is fine for some applications; for other problems, however, it can be advantageous to have a set of pre-generated random values. Back in the days before computers, math books often contained tables of random numbers; you simply started at the beginning of the list and moved sequentially through it as you needed numbers.

Some algorithms work well with tables of random numbers. If, for example, an inner loop constantly requests random values, calling *RandGen*'s () function will slow processing with constant multiplications and divisions. By pregenerating a table, the inner loop can quickly read an extant value.

The genetic algorithms of Chapter 12 provide a case in point. A genetic algorithm uses random numbers in refining its process; by providing a table containing suitable random values, a genetic algorithm can precalculate a set of random values. That need led me to create *RandTable*, a class that uses *RandGen* to build random number tables.

```
template <size_t Size, unsigned short Limit>
    class RandTable : private RandGen
        {
        public:
            // constructors
            RandTable
                (
                unsigned long seed = TimeSeed()
                );

            RandTable
                (
                const RandTable<Size,Limit> & table
                );

            // assignment
            void operator =
                (
                const RandTable<Size,Limit> & table
                );

            // get next value
            unsigned short Number();

        private:
            size_t Index;
            unsigned short Values[Size];

            // initialize an array
```

```
    void Initialize();
};
```

RandTable is a template derived from RandGen; it has two parameter arguments: the number of values in the table and a limit for those values. The table is an array named *Values*, which contains numbers between 0 and *Limit* -1. The *Index* data member points to the element of *Values* that will be returned by the *Number* function.

Upon construction, a *RandTable* fills the *Value* array with random numbers by calling *Initialize*.

```
template <size_t Size, unsigned short Limit>
    inline RandTable<Size,Limit>::RandTable
        (
        unsigned long seed
        )
        : RandGen(seed)
        {
        Initialize();
        }

template <size_t Size,unsigned short Limit>
    void RandTable<Size,Limit>::Initialize()
        {
        for (size_t n = 0; n < Size; ++n)
            Values[n] = RandGen::operator () (Limit);

        Index = 0;
        }
```

Index begins at zero; when the *Number* routine returns a value from the table, it also increments *Index*. When Index reaches the end of the table, *Number* calls *Initialize* to reload *Values* with a new set of random numbers.

```
template <size_t Size,unsigned short Limit>
    unsigned short RandTable<Size,Limit>::Number()
        {
        unsigned short result = Values[Index];
```

```
            ++Index;

            if (Index == Size)
                Initialize();

            return result;
            }
```

Just for the record, the copy constructor and assignment operator look like this:

```
template <size_t Size,unsigned short Limit>
    inline RandTable<Size,Limit>::RandTable
        (
        const RandTable<Size,Limit> & table
        )
        {
        Index  = table.Index;
        memcpy(Values,table.Values,
                sizeof(unsigned short) * Size);
        }

// assignment
template <size_t Size,unsigned short Limit>
    inline void RandTable<Size,Limit>::operator =
        (
        const RandTable<Size,Limit> & table
        )
        {
        Index  = table.Index;
        memcpy(Values,table.Values,
                sizeof(unsigned short) * Size);
        }
```

RandTable demonstrates that templates can be useful, with applications far beyond the creation of container classes. By including the size of the table in the template argument, I can create a static *Values* array without having to allocate dynamic memory. You'll see me use this technique in other classes throughout this book.

APPLICATION

The base classes for diagnotics reside in **diagnose.h** and **diagnose.cpp**; *DiagOutDOS* is in the **diagdos.h** and **diagdos.cpp** files, and *DiagOutWin* is located in the files **diagwin.h** and **diagwin.cpp**.

The complete source code for *RandGen* can be found in the file **randgen.h** and **randgen.cpp**, both of which are found on the accompanying source diskette. The *RandTable* class is completely implemented in the file **rantable.h**. The module **tbrand.cpp** tests the random number generators, and nearly every module includes an example of exception handling.

CHAPTER 2

LISTS, STACKS, AND QUEUES

In the abstract world of programming theory, templates are known as *parameterized types*. A parameter defines the specific type being manipulated by a template, which is why templates were originally thought of as tools for building container classes. In this chapter, I present several container classes, including lists, stacks, queues, and deques.

REPRESENTING CONTAINERS

A *container* is an object that holds other objects. Most programs employ containers to organize data in some fashion. C++ provides only one type of built-in container, the *array*, which contains a fixed number of objects. Implementation of more complicated containers is left to the programmer.

I've implemented more types of containers than I care to remember. Templates allowed me to create a single definition of a container type from which the compiler constructs actual type-specific classes at compile time. This eliminates the need to define specific classes for each type, and templates eliminate the need to define "generic" container types using void pointers and memory allocation tricks.

My current library generally provides two versions of each container type. The traditional implementation of containers uses dynamically allocated memory; for each item in the container, a node is created via *new*, and it is linked via pointers to other nodes.

Implementing containers with dynamic memory has the advantage of flexibility; the number of items a container can hold is limited only by the amount of available dynamic memory. On the other hand, each node must contain pointers along with data—and adding that overhead to the built-in overhead of dynamic memory allocation can be both slow and memory-intensive.

There is another choice, although I haven't seen it presented very often. Containers can be implemented with arrays and indexes in place of dynamic memory and pointers. For most of the fundamental container types, such as singly linked lists, stacks, and queues, using an array is shorter and faster than using a dynamic memory implementation.

For each of the following container types, I present both dynamic memory- and array-based versions. The dynamic types allocate memory, allowing any number of items to be included in a container. The array-based containers require a template parameter to specify the maximum number of elements that the containers can hold.

The pros and cons will lead you to decide which implementation of a container to use. Because they allocate memory at run time, dynamic containers may throw exceptions if *new* cannot allocate the required memory. Memory allocation problems will not occur at run time with an array-based container, because it uses a statically generated array.

Containers can be either associative or inclusive. An associative container holds pointers to objects created elsewhere, and an inclusive container creates copies of the objects stored. Using templates, you define an associative container by declaring the template type as a pointer or reference; use an explicit object type for inclusive containers.

Choose carefully the type of data stored, because each has trade-offs. Storing pointers or references forces the assumption that those pointers remain valid throughout the life of the container. Creating an object, storing its pointer in a container, and then destroying the object could leave you with dangling pointers and program bugs. On the other hand, storing copies of objects uses more memory than storing pointers uses.

Watch out for default objects and the side effects of the copy constructor. When you're storing pointers, constructors are never called to create new objects. A dynamic container will invoke a constructor only when you add a new node; an array-based container will automatically call the default constructor to initialize the elements of the array. Because of this, array-based container may hold only objects that have a default constructor.

Associative array-based containers are the fastest; inclusive dynamic containers, the slowest. The choice of dynamic versus array and associative versus inclusive should be made based on performance and the need to protect data integrity.

One further note: My containers are not polymorphic. My original class library built all my containers on a single base class, which is the way recommended by many pundits of object orientation. I didn't like it. First, the similarities between the container types were relatively trivial. A stack is not a linked list, in that a stack's *push* and *pop* have different semantics from a list's *append* and *get*. And I never have used a "generic" container; I've never seen the point or need.

If I'm processing data, I know whether I'm using a queue or a stack—and because there I didn't use polymorphic containers, I abandoned them. Looking at my current classes, you'll see that they have very little in common. Each has a role to play, and those roles are not interchangeable.

EXCEPTIONS

I created a single system for handling exceptions thrown by a variety of container types. The *ContainerEx* class, derived fom *ExceptionBase*, provides the basic exception type. The *ContainerEx* constructor requires an argument of the enumerated type *ContainerError*, which specifies a specific problem.

```
enum ContainerError
    {
    CX_ALLOC,
    CX_NULL,
    CX_ARRAYALLOC,
    CX_NULLARRAY,
    CX_NOTREADY,
    CX_OVERFLOW
    };

class ContainerEx : public ExceptionBase
    {
    public:
        ContainerEx
            (
            ContainerError err
            )
            {
            Error = err;
            }

        ContainerError WhatsWrong()
            {
            return Error;
```

```
        }

    virtual void Explain
        (
        DiagOutput & diag
        );

private:
    ContainerError Error;
};
```

The implementation of *ContainerEx::Explain* includes a *switch* statement
to display different messages for each *ContainerError* value.

```
void ContainerEx::Explain
    (
    DiagOutput & diag
    )
    {
    switch (Error)
        {
        case CX_ALLOC:
            diag.DisplayMsg("Cont: Memory allocation failed",
                            DIAG_ERROR);
            break;
        case CX_NULL:
            diag.DisplayMsg("Cont: Attempt to use empty list",
                            DIAG_WARNING);
            break;
        case CX_ARRAYALLOC:
            diag.DisplayMsg("Cont: Failed to allocate array",
                            DIAG_WARNING);
            break;
        case CX_NULLARRAY:
            diag.DisplayMsg("Cont: Can't copy from NULL array",
                            DIAG_WARNING);
            break;
        case CX_NOTREADY:
            diag.DisplayMsg("Cont: Work pointer not initialized",
                            DIAG_WARNING);
            break;
        case CX_OVERFLOW:
```

```
        diag.DisplayMsg("Cont: Overflowed capacity",
                        DIAG_ERROR);
    }
}
```

In subsequent chapters, you'll see that I use a similar style in creating exception types.

SIMPLE LISTS

The most basic container beyond a simple array is the *linked list*. The list is empty to begin, and new items automatically go at the end of the list. That system orders a list's contents from oldest to newest. The first item in a list is the *head*; the last item is the *tail*. A node is the *parent* of the *child* node it is linked to; the head has no parent, and the tail has no children. Because each node points to only one other node, this type of list is often called a *singly linked list*.

The most common list implementations use a series of nodes, each of which contains an object and a pointer to the next node in the list. Thus, you can move forward through the list, following the chain of nodes. Inserting the items A, B, C, and D (in that order) into a new linked list will create four nodes, with node A pointing to B, node B pointing to C, and node C pointing to D. Node D points nowhere (NULL).

Searching a list is a linear process; begin at the first node and follow the chain until you find what you're looking for. Deleting an item is more complicated: Search through the list for an item, keeping track of its parent, and then link its parent to its child.

Generally, a list is for storage; as with an array, it's unlikely that you'll be deleting any elements. I don't implement a delete function in my basic lists; if I need to make complex changes in a list, I prefer to use a *doubly linked list*. Doubly linked trees, the basis of more complex structures called *trees*, will be discussed in Chapter 3.

Following the list from head to tail involves the manipulation of an internal pointer, or index, that indicates the currently selected element.

This internal pointer can be set to the head of the list or incremented; when it reaches the tail element, the pointer can go no further unless the list is defined as circular. A *circular* list assumes that its head points to its tail, effectively creating a continuous loop of items.

Based on the concepts above, I defined two singly linked list classes: one dynamic and the other array-based. I'll describe the dynamic class first.

Dynamic Linked List

Here is the definition of *SListDyanmic*:

```
template <class T>
    class SListDynamic
        {
        public:
            // constructors
            SListDynamic
                (
                Boolean circ = BOOL_FALSE
                );

            // copy constructor
            SListDynamic
                (
                const SListDynamic<T> & slst,
                Boolean shallow = BOOL_FALSE
                );

            // construct from array
            SListDynamic
                (
                const T * array,
                size_t no
                );

            // destructor
            ~SListDynamic();

            // assignment operator (deep copy)
            void operator =
```

```
        (
        const SListDynamic<T> & slst
        );

    // conversion to array operator
    operator T * ();

    // append new items
    void Append
        (
        const T & item
        );

    void Append
        (
        const T * array,
        size_t no
        );

    void Append
        (
        const SListDynamic<T> & slst
        );

    // remove all items from the list
    void Erase();

    // get current item
    T Get();

    // TRUE if current item is last item
    Boolean AtTail();

    // set current item to head of list
    void ToHead();

    // move to next item in list
    Boolean ToNext();

    // interrogate list
    size_t  GetCount();
    Boolean IsShallow();
```

```
      Boolean IsCircular();

protected:
    // type defining a node in the list
    struct Node
        {
        T Data;
        Node * Next;
        };

    size_t Count; // # of items in list
    Node * Head;  // first item
    Node * Tail;  // last item
    Node * Work;  // current item

    Boolean Shallow;  // Is this a shallow copy?
    Boolean Circular; // is this a circular list?

    // internal utility functions
    void DeepCopy
        (
        const SListDynamic<T> & slst
        );

    void ShallowCopy
        (
        const SListDynamic<T> & slst
        );

    void SetNull();
    };
```

The *Node* structure defines an element in the list; it contains a data item and a pointer to the next item in the list. The data elements of the class include a count of elements, a pointer to the head node, a pointer to the tail node, and a "work" pointer that points to the node that can be examined by the *Get* member function.

Most of my classes define private utility functions that perform tasks common to several public functions. For example, the copy constructor and assignment operator need to copy the contents of one list into another. Several functions need to set the data members to a "null," or empty, condition. In the latter case, I defined the private *SetNull* function:

```
template <class T>
    inline void SListDynamic<T>::SetNull()
        {
        Head  = NULL;
        Tail  = NULL;
        Work  = NULL;
        Count = 0;
        }
```

When you're duplicating a dynamic data structure, the copy can be either deep or shallow. A *deep* copy creates an entirely new structure, complete with independent copies of all data and internal values. A *shallow* copy, by contrast, creates a new structure that uses the same data as the source structure uses.

In the case of *SListDynamic*, *DeepCopy* creates an entirely new list by allocating new nodes that contain copies of data from the source list. Once created, a list created with *DeepCopy* has no connection to or influence over the original list.

```
template <class T>
    void SListDynamic<T>::DeepCopy
        (
        const SListDynamic<T> & slst
        )
        {
        if (slst.Count == 0)
            return;

        Node * n = slst.Head;

        do  {
            Append(n->Data);
            n = n->Next;
            }
        while (n != NULL);
```

```
Work = Head;
Shallow  = BOOL_FALSE;
Circular = slst.Circular;
}
```

ShallowCopy is much simpler; its only job is to copy the source list's data members. A copy made via *ShallowCopy* produces a new list that manipulates the same data as the original it copied. This can be dangerous, because changes made by a shallow copy will not be reflected in the original list, and vice versa. However, a shallow copy requires less memory and is created faster than is a deep copy.

```
template <class T>
    inline void SListDynamic<T>::ShallowCopy
        (
        const SListDynamic<T> & slst
        )
        {
        Head  = slst.Head;
        Tail  = slst.Tail;
        Work  = slst.Work;
        Count = slst.Count;
        Shallow  = BOOL_TRUE;
        Circular = slst.Circular;
        }

template <class T>
    inline void SListDynamic<T>::SetNull()
        {
        Head  = NULL;
        Tail  = NULL;
        Work  = NULL;
        Count = 0;
        }
```

The default constructor creates an empty list. Its only parameter is a Boolean value that states whether the new list is circular. A default parameter assigns *BOOL_FALSE* to *circ* so that this function can act as the default (no argument) constructor.

```
inline SListDynamic<T>::SListDynamic
        (
        Boolean circ
        )
        {
        SetNull();
        Shallow  = BOOL_FALSE;
        Circular = circ;
        }
```

The copy constructor has two parameters: a reference to the list being copied and a Boolean flag that determines the type of copy made. A shallow copy is made only when the parameter *shallow* is explicitly set to *BOOL_TRUE*; when *shallow* is *BOOL_FALSE*—the default—the constructor calls *DeepCopy*.

```
template <class T>
    SListDynamic<T>::SListDynamic
        (
        const SListDynamic<T> & slst,
        Boolean shallow
        )
        {
        if (shallow)
            ShallowCopy(slst);
        else
            {
            SetNull();
            DeepCopy(slst);
            }
        }
```

I created a third constructor that creates a list with elements taken from an array. The first parameter is the address of the array's first element, and the second parameter states the number of elements to be copied. The constructor then loops through the array, calling *Append* to add each input value to the list.

```
template <class T>
    SListDynamic<T>::SListDynamic
```

```
(
const T * array,
size_t no
)
{
SetNull();

Circular = BOOL_FALSE;
Shallow  = BOOL_FALSE;

if ((array == NULL) || (no == 0))
    throw ContainerEx(CX_NULLARRAY);

const T * aptr = array;

for (size_t n = 0; n < no; ++n)
    {
    Append(*aptr);
    ++aptr;
    }
}
```

The assignment operator is simply a call to *DeepCopy*. Because an assignment operator may have only one parameter, I couldn't specify the type of copy, as I did with the copy constructor. I chose to automatically perform a *DeepCopy*, the safest alternative.

```
template <class T>
    inline SListDynamic<T>::~SListDynamic()
        {
        Erase();
        }
```

The destructor simply calls the *Erase* function to delete all entries in the list before the object is destroyed.

```
template <class T>
    inline SListDynamic<T>::~SListDynamic()
        {
        Erase();
        }
```

A useful, if somewht nontraditional, function is the conversion operator that creates an array from a list. This is incredibly useful in some cases; for example, when I want to write a linked list to a file, I convert it to an array, which can then be easily and quickly written. Note that in creating the array, a copy constructor will be called to duplicate items in the list.

```
template <class T>
    SListDynamic<T>::operator T * ()
        {
        if (Count == 0)
            return NULL;

        T * result = new T [Count];

        if (result == NULL)
            throw ContainerEx(CX_ARRAYALLOC);

        Node * temp = Head;
        T    * aptr = result;

        while (temp != NULL)
            {
            *aptr = temp->Data;
            ++aptr;
            temp = temp->Next;
            }

        // note: caller must delete this array!
        return result;
        }
```

Three functions append items to a list. The first appends a single item of type *T*; the second appends the elements of an array, and the third *Append* function concatenates two lists.

```
template <class T>
    void SListDynamic<T>::Append
        (
        const T & item
        )
        {
```

```
        Node * n = new Node;

        if (n == NULL)
            throw ContainerEx(CX_ALLOC);

        n->Data = item;
        n->Next = NULL;

        if (Tail == NULL)
            {
            Head = n;
            Tail = n;
            Work = n;
            }
        else
            {
            Tail->Next = n;
            Tail = n;
            }

        ++Count;
        }

template <class T>
    void SListDynamic<T>::Append
        (
        const T * array,
        size_t no
        )
        {
        if ((array == NULL) || (no == 0))
            throw ContainerEx(CX_NULLARRAY);

        const T * aptr = array;

        for (size_t n = 0; n < no; ++n)
            {
            Append(*aptr);
            ++aptr;
            }
        }

template <class T>
```

```
void SListDynamic<T>::Append
    (
    const SListDynamic<T> & slst
    )
    {
    const Node * n = slst.Head;

    while (n != NULL)
        {
        Append(n->Data);
        n = n->Next;
        }
    }
```

Erase loops through the list, deleting all members, essentially resetting a list to the "empty" state.

```
template <class T>
    void SListDynamic<T>::Erase()
        {
        if (!Shallow)
            {
            Work = Head;

            while (Work != NULL)
                {
                Head = Work->Next;
                delete Work;
                Work = Head;
                }
            }

        SetNull();
        Shallow = BOOL_FALSE;
        }
```

To examine the elements in the list, I created four functions. *ToHead* sets *Work* to point to the head item in the list.

```
template <class T>
    inline void SListDynamic<T>::ToHead()
```

```
    {
    Work = Head;
    }
```

A call to *Get* returns the item stored in the node currently pointed to by *Work.*

```
template <class T>
    T SListDynamic<T>::Get()
        {
        if (Count == 0)
            throw ContainerEx(CX_NULL);

        if (Work == NULL)
            throw ContainerEx(CX_NOTREADY);

        return Work->Data;
        }
```

ToNext moves *Work* to the next item in the list, if there is one. When *Work* equals *Tail*, calling *ToNext* generates an exception—unless the list is circular, in which case *Work* is set to *Head.*

```
template <class T>
    Boolean SListDynamic<T>::ToNext()
        {
        if (Count == 0)
            throw ContainerEx(CX_NULL);

        if (Work == NULL)
            throw ContainerEx(CX_NOTREADY);

        if (Work == Tail)
            {
            if (Circular)
                Work = Head;
            else
                return BOOL_FALSE;
            }
        else
```

```
        Work = Work->Next;

    return BOOL_TRUE;
    }
```

AtTail simply returns true if *Work* equals *Tail,* and false if it does not.

```
template <class T>
    inline Boolean SListDynamic<T>::AtTail()
        {
        if (Work == Tail)
            return BOOL_TRUE;
        else
            return BOOL_FALSE;
        }
```

The final set of functions return various values defining the nature of a list.

```
template <class T>
    inline size_t SListDynamic<T>::GetCount()
        {
        return Count;
        }

template <class T>
    inline Boolean SListDynamic<T>::IsShallow()
        {
        return Shallow;
        }

template <class T>
    inline Boolean SListDynamic<T>::IsCircular()
        {
        return Circular;
        }
```

By using a template, I've created a dynamic linked list that can hold any type of data.

Array-Based Linked List

My array-based list has basically the same features as its dynamic cousin,
but it is much shorter in definition and quicker in execution.

```
template <class T, size_t Limit>
    class SList
        {
        public:
            // constructors
            SList
                (
                Boolean circ = BOOL_FALSE
                );

            // copy constructor
            SList
                (
                const SList<T,Limit> & slst
                );

            // construct from array
            SList
                (
                const T * array,
                size_t no
                );

            // destructor
            ~SList();

            // assignment operator (deep copy)
            void operator =
                (
                const SList<T,Limit> & slst
                );

            // conversion to array operator
            operator T * ();
```

```
// append new items
void Append
    (
    const T & item
    );

void Append
    (
    const T * array,
    size_t no
    );

void Append
    (
    const SList<T,Limit> & slst
    );

// remove all items from the list
void Erase();

// get current item
T Get();

// TRUE if current item is last item
Boolean AtTail();

// set current item to head of list
void ToHead();

// move to next item in list
Boolean ToNext();

// interrogate list
size_t  GetCount();
size_t  GetLimit();
Boolean IsCircular();

protected:
    size_t Count;       // # of items in list
    size_t Work;        // currently selected element
    T Data[Limit];      // elements in list

    Boolean Circular;   // is this a circular list?
```

```
        // internal utility functions
        void DeepCopy
            (
            const SList<T,Limit> & slst
            );
    };
```

SListDynamic's implementation required nearly 300 lines of code; for the array-based *SList*, I needed a bit over 200 lines of C++ to implement the same functionality.

The *Data* array holds the list's elements, and *Count* keeps track of how many items have been stored. The template-defined constant *Limit* defines the size of *Data*. *Work* contains the index of the currently select-ed elements. The head of the list is always *Data* element 0, and the tail element is always one less than *Count*; therefore, *SList* doesn't need data elements for head or tail.

SList needs only one private function, *DeepCopy*. A shallow copy is meaningless because *Slist* doesn't allocate memory or use pointers. *DeepCopy* 's main task is to duplicate the *Data* array from the source list.

```
template <class T, size_t Limit>
    void SList<T,Limit>::DeepCopy
        (
        const SList<T,Limit> & slst
        )
        {
        Count = slst.Count;
        Work  = slst.Work;

        for (size_t n = 0; n < Count; ++n)
            Data[n] = slst.Data[n];

        Circular = slst.Circular;
        }
```

Most of *SList*'s functions correspond to the functions I defined for *SListDynamic*, and the constructors are no exception. However, without needing to allocate memory or worry about shallow copies, *SList*'s constructors and assignment operator are simpler than those for *SListDynamic.*

```cpp
template <class T, size_t Limit>
    inline SList<T,Limit>::SList
        (
        Boolean circ
        )
        {
        Count    = 0;
        Work     = 0;
        Circular = circ;
        }

template <class T, size_t Limit>
    inline SList<T,Limit>::SList
        (
        const SList<T,Limit> & slst
        )
        {
        DeepCopy(slst);
        }

template <class T, size_t Limit>
    SList<T,Limit>::SList
        (
        const T * array,
        size_t no
        )
        {
        if ((array == NULL) || (no == 0))
            throw ContainerEx(CX_NULLARRAY);

        Count = 0;
        Work  = 0;
        Circular = BOOL_FALSE;

        const T * aptr = array;

        for (size_t n = 0; n < no; ++n)
            {
            Append(*aptr);
            ++aptr;
```

```
        }
    }

template <class T, size_t Limit>
    inline void SList<T,Limit>::operator =
        (
        const SList<T,Limit> & slst
        )
        {
        Erase();
        DeepCopy(slst);
        }
```

The destructor merely calls *Erase*; the compiler will generate code to automatically destroy the objects in *Data*.

```
template <class T, size_t Limit>
    inline SList<T,Limit>::~SList()
        {
        Erase();
        }
```

Creating an array from an *SList* is a matter of copying *Data*'s elements into an allocated array. Note that this conversion operator allocates *result* but cannot delete it later. Deleting *result* requires the calling function to track and delete any arrays created by *operator T * ()*.

```
template <class T, size_t Limit>
    SList<T,Limit>::operator T * ()
        {
        if (Count == 0)
            return NULL;

        T * result = new T [Count];

        if (result == NULL)
            throw ContainerEx(CX_ARRAYALLOC);

        for (size_t n = 0; n < Count; ++n)
            result[n] = Data[n];
```

```
// note: caller must delete this array!
return result;
}
```

Count keeps track of the number of elements in the list and is used to find the tail element when new items are appended.

```
template <class T, size_t Limit>
    void SList<T,Limit>::Append
        (
        const T & item
        )
        {
        if (Count == Limit)
            throw ContainerEx(CX_OVERFLOW);

        Data[Count] = item;

        ++Count;
        }
```

SList's Append(array,no) and *Append(SList)* functions use the single-item *Append* function to add a set of items to the list.

```
template <class T, size_t Limit>
    void SList<T,Limit>::Append
        (
        const T * array,
        size_t no
        )
        {
        if ((array == NULL) || (no == 0))
            throw ContainerEx(CX_NULLARRAY);

        const T * aptr = array;

        for (size_t n = 0; n < no; ++n)
            {
            Append(*aptr);
            ++aptr;
            }
```

```
        }

template <class T, size_t Limit>
    void SList<T,Limit>::Append
        (
        const SList<T,Limit> & slst
        )
        {
        for (size_t n = 0; n < slst.Count; ++n)
            Append(slst.Data[n]);
        }
```

Examining an *SList*'s elements uses the same semantics as used for *SListDyanmic.*

```
template <class T, size_t Limit>
    T SList<T,Limit>::Get()
        {
        if (Count == 0)
            throw ContainerEx(CX_NULL);

        if (Work == Count)
            throw ContainerEx(CX_NOTREADY);

        return Data[Work];
        }

template <class T, size_t Limit>
    inline Boolean SList<T,Limit>::AtTail()
        {
        if (Work == Count)
            return BOOL_TRUE;
        else
            return BOOL_FALSE;
        }

template <class T, size_t Limit>
    inline void SList<T,Limit>::ToHead()
        {
        Work = 0;
        }
```

```
template <class T, size_t Limit>
    Boolean SList<T,Limit>::ToNext()
        {
        if (Count == 0)
            throw ContainerEx(CX_NULL);

        if (Work == Count)
            throw ContainerEx(CX_NOTREADY);

        ++Work;

        if (Work == Count)
            {
            if (Circular)
                Work = 0;
            else
                return BOOL_FALSE;
            }

        return BOOL_TRUE;
        }
```

Finally, a set of functions will return various *SList* parameters.

```
template <class T, size_t Limit>
    inline size_t SList<T,Limit>::GetCount()
        {
        return Count;
        }

template <class T, size_t Limit>
    inline size_t SList<T,Limit>::GetLimit()
        {
        return Limit;
        }

template <class T, size_t Limit>
    inline Boolean SList<T,Limit>::IsCircular()
        {
        return Circular;
        }
```

I tend to use *SList* more than *SListDynamic*, because *SList* is much faster. However, both are useful, and when I don't know how many list elements I'll need, *SListDynamic* is a superior choice. In programming, one-size-fits-all solutions are rare; a good programmer builds for a variety of needs.

STACKS

A *stack* is a list wherein new items become the head, thus "pushing" down the other items in the list. Instead of traveling through a stack element-by-element, information is retrieved from a stack by *popping* the top item—removing it from the list. Items *pushed* onto a stack are popped in reverse order. If I push the numbers 1, 2, 3, and 4 onto a stack in that order and then pop the top item, I will receive 4 and the list will contain 3, 2, and 1. Popping again retrieves 3, leaving 2 and 1 in the stack.

The major difference between a stack and a list lies in how they store and access elements. Unlike a list, which allows you to look at all its elements, a stack lets you retrieve only the last item you stored. And when you pop an item, it is deleted from the stack, reducing the stack size by one.

In essence, using a stack is like traveling backward in history. Several advanced algorithms rely on stacks, as you'll see later in this book.

Dynamic Stacks

My dynamic stack class is defined this way:

```
template <class T>
    class StackDynamic
        {
        public:
            StackDynamic();

            StackDynamic
                (
                const StackDynamic<T> & stk
                );
```

```
        ~StackDynamic();

        void operator =
            (
            const StackDynamic<T> & stk
            );

        void Push
            (
            const T & item
            );

        T Pop();

        void Erase();

        size_t GetCount();
    protected:
        struct Node
            {
            T Data;
            Node * Below;
            };

        Node * Head;
        size_t Count;

        // utility functions
        void DeepCopy
            (
            const StackDynamic<T> & stk
            );
    };
```

The data elements closely parallel those in *Slist*; a stack is, for all intents and purposes, a singly linked list that has limited requirements for storing and retrieving data. The *Node* structure defines a stack element, and *Head* points to the top node in the list. *Count* keeps the total number of elements in the stack.

The only private function is *DeepCopy,* which creates a duplicate of an existing *StackDynamic.* Stacks in application programs generally don't contain a large number of data items, and I've yet to find a need for making shallow copies.

```
template <class T>
    void StackDynamic<T>::DeepCopy
        (
        const StackDynamic<T> & stk
        )
        {
        if (stk.Count == 0)
            {
            Head = NULL;
            Count = 0;
            return;
            }

        Head = new Node;

        if (Head == NULL)
            throw ContainerEx(CX_ALLOC);

        Node * source = stk.Head;
        Node * dest   = Head;

        while (1)
            {
            dest->Data = source->Data;

            ++Count;

            if (source->Below != NULL)
                {
                dest->Below = new Node;

                if (dest->Below == NULL)
                    throw ContainerEx(CX_ALLOC);

                dest = dest->Below;
                source = source->Below;
                }
```

```
        else
            {
            dest->Below = NULL;
            break;
            }
        }
    }
```

As with my other container classes, I define an *Erase* function for *Stack*. It uses a loop to call *Pop*, which removes items until the stack is empty.

```
template <class T>
    void StackDynamic<T>::Erase()
        {
        while (Count)
            Pop();
        }
```

The base constructor, copy constructor, and assignment operator are straightforward.

```
template <class T>
    inline StackDynamic<T>::StackDynamic()
        {
        Count = 0;
        Head  = NULL;
        }

template <class T>
    inline StackDynamic<T>::StackDynamic
        (
        const StackDynamic<T> & stk
        )
        {
        Count = 0;
        DeepCopy(stk);
        }

template <class T>
    void StackDynamic<T>::operator =
        (
```

```
const StackDynamic<T> & stk
)
{
Erase();
DeepCopy(stk);
}
```

The destructor is simple, too.

```
template <class T>
    inline StackDynamic<T>::~StackDynamic()
        {
        Erase();
        }
```

The *Push* function places the new item at the head of the list, linking the new head to the old one. Note that *StackDynamic* doesn't keep track of the tail element. The tail can be recognized because it has no child.

```
template <class T>
    void StackDynamic<T>::Push(const T & item)
        {
        Node * newhead = new Node;

        if (newhead == NULL)
            throw ContainerEx(CX_ALLOC);

        newhead->Below = Head;
        newhead->Data  = item;

        Head = newhead;

        ++Count;
        }
```

Pop is the opposite of *Push*—*Pop* retrieves the data stored in *Head* and then replaces *Head* with its child.

```
template <class T>
    T StackDynamic<T>::Pop()
```

```
{
if (Head == NULL)
    throw ContainerEx(CX_NULL);

T result = Head->Data;

Node * newhead = Head->Below;

delete Head;

Head = newhead;

-Count;

return result;
}
```

The remaining function is *GetCount*, which has an obvious purpose.

```
template <class T>
    inline size_t StackDynamic<T>::GetCount()
        {
        return Count;
        }
```

Array-Based Stacks

The equivalent array-based stack looks like this:

```
template <class T, size_t Limit>
    class Stack
        {
        public:
            Stack();

            Stack
                (
                const Stack<T,Limit> & stk
                );
```

```
        void operator =
            (
            const Stack<T,Limit> & stk
            );

        void Push
            (
            const T & item
            );

        T Pop();

        void Erase();

        size_t GetCount();
        size_t GetLimit();

    protected:
        T Data[Limit];

        size_t Count;

        // utility functions
        void DeepCopy
            (
            const Stack<T,Limit> & stk
            );
    };
```

Without the need to allocate memory and track points, *Stack* is far simpler than *StackDynamic*. *Stack* defines only two data elements: *Data*, (the array of elements) and *Count*, which tracks the number of active elements in *Data*. Like *SList*, *Stack*'s template includes a *Limit* parameter that declares the size of the *Data* array.

The *DeepCopy* function is responsible for copying *Data* elements from one *Stack* to another. *Erase* resets *Count* to zero, effectively declaring the list to be empty.

```
template <class T, size_t Limit>
    void Stack<T,Limit>::DeepCopy
        (
```

```
            const Stack<T,Limit> & stk
            )
            {
            Count = stk.Count;

            for (size_t n = 0; n < Limit; ++n)
                Data[n] = stk.Data[n];
            }

template <class T, size_t Limit>
    inline void Stack<T,Limit>::Erase()
        {
        Count = 0;
        }
```

The constructor, destructor, and assignment operator need little elaboration.

```
template <class T, size_t Limit>
    inline Stack<T,Limit>::Stack()
        {
        Count = 0;
        }

template <class T, size_t Limit>
    inline Stack<T,Limit>::Stack
        (
        const Stack<T,Limit> & stk
        )
        {
        DeepCopy(stk);
        }

template <class T, size_t Limit>
    inline void Stack<T,Limit>::operator =
        (
        const Stack<T,Limit> & stk
        )
        {
        DeepCopy(stk);
        }
```

In pushing items on the stack, *Push* simply adds them at the end of the array. Instead of *Data[0]* being the head of the list, it is the tail, with the head at *Data[Count - 1].* This is very quick; were it not for the possibility of an exception, *Push* could be implemented inline.

```
template <class T, size_t Limit>
    void Stack<T,Limit>::Push(const T & item)
        {
        if (Count == Limit)
            throw ContainerEx(CX_OVERFLOW);

        ++Count;

        Data[Count - 1] = item;
        }
```

Pop is the opposite of *Push,* returning the value of the last element stored in *Data.*

```
template <class T, size_t Limit>
    T Stack<T,Limit>::Pop()
        {
        if (Count == 0)
            throw ContainerEx(CX_NULL);

        —Count;

        return Data[Count];
        }
```

GetCount and *GetLimit* return various aspects of a *Stack.*

```
template <class T, size_t Limit>
    inline size_t Stack<T,Limit>::GetCount()
        {
        return Count;
        }

template <class T, size_t Limit>
    inline size_t Stack<T,Limit>::GetLimit()
```

```
    {
    return Limit;
    }
```

Most applications work with fixed stacks, because, unlike lists, stacks tend to be limited in size. Elements come and go as items are pushed and popped. In some cases, knowing the size of a data set allows you to determine the maximum size you'll need for your stacks. I use the array-based *Stack* more than the dynamic version, especially when working with intrinsic types or objects with simple constructors.

QUEUES

Like a stack, a *queue* is another variation on how a list can store and retrieve information. A queue appends new items to the end of the list and retrieves items from the head. The last item stored is the last item retrieved. Thus, if I store 1, 2, 3, and 4 in a queue, I'll retrieve them in the order 1, 2, 3, 4. You can think of a queue as you would a line at a checkout stand or movie theater; the last person in line is the last one served.

Dynamic Queues

To implement a template for dynamic queues, I created this class:

```
template <class T>
    class QueueDynamic
        {
        public:
            QueueDynamic();

            QueueDynamic
                (
                const QueueDynamic<T> & stk
                );

            ~QueueDynamic();
```

```
        void operator =
            (
            const QueueDynamic<T> & stk
            );

        void Push
            (
            const T & item
            );

        T Pop();

        void Erase();

        size_t GetCount();
    protected:
        struct Node
            {
            T Data;
            Node * Next;
            };

        Node * Head;
        Node * Tail;
        size_t Count;

        // utility functions
        void DeepCopy
            (
            const QueueDynamic<T> & stk
            );
    };
```

I won't go into great detail explaining the various basic functions; they should, by now, be self-explanatory. In general, *QueueDynamic* is similar to *StackDynamic* with the exception of the storage semantics.

```
template <class T>
    void QueueDynamic<T>::DeepCopy
        (
        const QueueDynamic<T> & que
```

```
)
{
if (que.Count == 0)
    {
    Head = NULL;
    Tail = NULL;
    Count = 0;
    return;
    }

Head = new Node;

if (Head == NULL)
    throw ContainerEx(CX_ALLOC);

Tail = Head;

Node * source = que.Head;

while (1)
    {
    Tail->Data = source->Data;

    ++Count;

    if (source->Next != NULL)
        {
        Tail->Next = new Node;

        if (Tail->Next == NULL)
            throw ContainerEx(CX_ALLOC);

        Tail = Tail->Next;
        source = source->Next;
        }
    else
        {
        Tail->Next = NULL;
        break;
        }
    }
}
```

```
template <class T>
    inline QueueDynamic<T>::QueueDynamic()
        {
        Count = 0;
        Head  = NULL;
        Tail  = NULL;
        }

template <class T>
    inline QueueDynamic<T>::QueueDynamic
        (
        const QueueDynamic<T> & que
        )
        {
        Count = 0;
        DeepCopy(que);
        }

template <class T>
    inline QueueDynamic<T>::~QueueDynamic()
        {
        Erase();
        }

template <class T>
    void QueueDynamic<T>::operator =
        (
        const QueueDynamic<T> & que
        )
        {
        Erase();
        DeepCopy(que);
        }

template <class T>
    void QueueDynamic<T>::Erase()
        {
        while (Count)
            Pop();
        }

template <class T>
    inline size_t QueueDynamic<T>::GetCount()
```

```
{
return Count;
}
```

A call to *Queue*'s *Push* function adds new items to the tail of the list, just as does the *Append* procedure from the *SListDynamic* class.

```
template <class T>
    void QueueDynamic<T>::Push(const T & item)
        {
        Node * newtail = new Node;

        if (newtail == NULL)
            throw ContainerEx(CX_ALLOC);

        newtail->Next = NULL;
        newtail->Data = item;

        if (Tail != NULL)
            Tail->Next = newtail;
        else
            Head = newtail;

        Tail = newtail;

        ++Count;
        }
```

Using *Pop* will do exactly what *StackDynamic*'s *Pop* did, by retrieving the data in the *Head* node and then replacing that node with its successor.

```
template <class T>
    T QueueDynamic<T>::Pop()
        {
        if (Head == NULL)
            throw ContainerEx(CX_NULL);

        T result = Head->Data;

        Node * newhead = Head->Next;
```

```
delete Head;

Head = newhead;

—Count;

return result;
}
```

Array-Based Queues

An array-based queue isn't as simple as an array-based stack. Because both ends of the list change, both a head and a tail index must be managed.

```
template <class T, size_t Limit>
    class Queue
        {
        public:
            Queue();

            Queue
                (
                const Queue<T,Limit> & que
                );

            void operator =
                (
                const Queue<T,Limit> & que
                );

            void Push
                (
                const T & item
                );

            T Pop();

            void Erase();
```

```
        size_t GetCount();
        size_t GetLimit();

    protected:
        T Data[Limit];

        size_t Count;
        size_t Head;
        size_t Tail;

        // utility functions
        void DeepCopy
            (
            const Queue<T,Limit> & que
            );
    };
```

Again, the core functions look so similar to those of past array-based classes that I won't go into detail beyond presenting them.

```
template <class T, size_t Limit>
    void Queue<T,Limit>::DeepCopy
        (
        const Queue<T,Limit> & que
        )
        {
        Count = que.Count;
        Head  = que.Head;
        Tail  = que.Tail;

        for (size_t n = 0; n < Limit; ++n)
            Data[n] = que.Data[n];
        }

template <class T, size_t Limit>
    inline Queue<T,Limit>::Queue()
        {
        Count = 0;
        Head  = 0;
        Tail  = 0;
        }
```

```
template <class T, size_t Limit>
    inline Queue<T,Limit>::Queue
        (
        const Queue<T,Limit> & que
        )
        {
        DeepCopy(que);
        }

template <class T, size_t Limit>
    inline void Queue<T,Limit>::operator =
        (
        const Queue<T,Limit> & que
        )
        {
        DeepCopy(que);
        }

template <class T, size_t Limit>
    inline void Queue<T,Limit>::Erase()
        {
        Count = 0;
        }

template <class T, size_t Limit>
    inline size_t Queue<T,Limit>::GetCount()
        {
        return Count;
        }

template <class T, size_t Limit>
    inline size_t Queue<T,Limit>::GetLimit()
        {
        return Limit;
        }
```

Unlike other array-based list types, in array-based queues neither head nor tail is in a fixed location within *Data*. As *Push* adds new items, it increments the *Tail* index; once *Tail* reaches the end of *Data*, it may (if the array is not full) wrap around the index 0.

```
template <class T, size_t Limit>
    void Queue<T,Limit>::Push(const T & item)
        {
        if (Count == Limit)
            throw ContainerEx(CX_OVERFLOW);

        if (Count == 0)
            {
            Tail = 0;
            Head = 0;
            Data[0] = item;
            }
        else
            {
            ++Tail;

            if (Tail == Limit)
                Tail = 0;

            Data[Tail] = item;
            }

        ++Count;
        }
```

When *Pop* retrieves data from the head of the queue, the *Head* index is incremented to the next item. Like *Tail*, *Head* may wrap around the end of the *Data* array.

```
template <class T, size_t Limit>
    T Queue<T,Limit>::Pop()
        {
        if (Count == 0)
            throw ContainerEx(CX_NULL);

        T result = Data[Head];

        —Count;

        if (Count != 0)
            {
            ++Head;
```

```
        if (Head == Limit)
            Head = 0;
        }

    return result;
    }
```

By allowing the indexes to wrap the array, I make available the full capacity of the *Data* array, no matter how many pushes and pops have been made.

As with stacks, I tend to use the array-based *Queue* over the dynamic implementation. *Queue*'s limited overhead and fast processing make it a better choice than *QueueDynamic*, which is superior only when storing complex objects or when I can't predetermine the queue size.

DEQUES

There's one more beast in my list menagerie: the deque (pronounced dee-Q). A *deque* is a list that combines the attributes of stacks and queues by allowing items to be pushed and popped at either the head or the tail. In my *C++ Components and Algorithms* book, I implemented a deque under the fanciful name of "Quack." The deques presented here are more robust than my previous "Quack", and they're consistent with the other classes presented herein.

Dynamic Deques

By nature, the *DequeDynamic* class looks like a combination of *StackDynamic* and *QueueDynamic*.

```
template <class T>
    class DequeDynamic
        {
        public:
            DequeDynamic();

            DequeDynamic
```

```
        (
        const DequeDynamic<T> & deq
        );

    ~DequeDynamic();

    void operator =
        (
        const DequeDynamic<T> & deq
        );

    void PushTop
        (
        const T & item
        );

    void PushBtm
        (
        const T & item
        );

    T PopTop();
    T PopBtm();

    void Erase();

    size_t GetCount();

protected:
    struct Node
        {
        T Data;
        Node * Prev;
        Node * Next;
        };

    Node * Head;
    Node * Tail;
    size_t Count;

    // utility functions
    void DeepCopy
        (
```

```
        const DequeDynamic<T> & deq
        );
    };
```

The only unusual thing about a *Deque* is that each node has links to both
parent and child. This is like the doubly linked list of Chapter 3,
although the limited operations of a deque make its implementation
more direct. The parent pointer is used only by the *PopBtm* function,
which must replace the tail with its predecessor.

As with the *Queue* classes, I'll won't belabor the obvious implementations of constructors and utility functions. The meat of the story is in the
Push and *Pop* functions.

```
template <class T>
    void DequeDynamic<T>::DeepCopy
        (
        const DequeDynamic<T> & deq
        )
        {
        if (deq.Count == 0)
            {
            Head = NULL;
            Tail = NULL;
            Count = 0;
            return;
            }

        Node * n = deq.Head;

        do  {
            PushBtm(n->Data);
            n = n->Next;
            }
        while (n != NULL);
        }

template <class T>
    inline DequeDynamic<T>::DequeDynamic()
        {
        Count = 0;
        Head  = NULL;
```

```
        Tail  = NULL;
        }

template <class T>
    inline DequeDynamic<T>::DequeDynamic
        (
        const DequeDynamic<T> & deq
        )
        {
        Count = 0;
        DeepCopy(deq);
        }

template <class T>
    inline DequeDynamic<T>::~DequeDynamic()
        {
        Erase();
        }

template <class T>
    void DequeDynamic<T>::operator =
        (
        const DequeDynamic<T> & deq
        )
        {
        Erase();
        DeepCopy(deq);
        }

template <class T>
    void DequeDynamic<T>::Erase()
        {
        while (Count)
            PopTop();
        }

template <class T>
    inline size_t DequeDynamic<T>::GetCount()
        {
        return Count;
        }
```

Pushing an item at the top of a deque with *PushTop* involves replacing *Head* with a new node.

```
template <class T>
    void DequeDynamic<T>::PushTop(const T & item)
        {
        Node * newhead = new Node;

        if (newhead == NULL)
            throw ContainerEx(CX_ALLOC);

        newhead->Prev = NULL;
        newhead->Next = Head;
        newhead->Data = item;

        Head = newhead;

        ++Count;
        }
```

PopTop acts like the *StackDynamic Pop* function by retrieving the information stored in the *Head* node and then replacing *Head* with its successor.

```
template <class T>
    T DequeDynamic<T>::PopTop()
        {
        if (Head == NULL)
            throw ContainerEx(CX_NULL);

        T result = Head->Data;

        Node * newhead = Head->Next;

        delete Head;

        Head = newhead;

        —Count;

        if (Head != NULL)
            Head->Prev = NULL;
```

```
    return result;
    }
```

PushBtm places a new item at the end of the list, creating a new *Tail* node.

```
template <class T>
    T DequeDynamic<T>::PopTop()
        {
        if (Head == NULL)
            throw ContainerEx(CX_NULL);

        T result = Head->Data;

        Node * newhead = Head->Next;

        delete Head;

        Head = newhead;

        —Count;

        if (Head != NULL)
            Head->Prev = NULL;

        return result;
        }
```

And finally, *PopBtm* pulls an item off the deque by replacing *Tail* with its predecessor.

```
template <class T>
    T DequeDynamic<T>::PopBtm()
        {
        if (Head == NULL)
            throw ContainerEx(CX_NULL);

        T result = Tail->Data;

        Node * newtail = Tail->Prev;

        delete Head;
```

```
Tail = newtail;
Tail->Next = NULL;

—Count;

return result;
}
```

Array-Based Deques

Array-based deques require tricky handling of indexes, because both *Head* and *Tail* can wrap either end of the *Data* array. Whenever a new node is added, I check to see whether *Count* has reached *Limit*; if it has, I generate an exception. If, however, the deque isn't full, I decrement *Head* or increment *Tail*. *Head* and *Tail* move in opposite directions, so I know I can safely wrap around either end of the array without running over valuable data.

Here is the array-based *Deque* class, in its entirety:

```
template <class T, size_t Limit>
    class Deque
        {
        public:
            Deque();

            Deque
                (
                const Deque<T,Limit> & deq
                );

            ~Deque();

            void operator =
                (
                const Deque<T,Limit> & deq
                );

            void PushTop
                (
```

```
                const T & item
                );

            void PushBtm
                (
                const T & item
                );

            T PopTop();
            T PopBtm();

            void Erase();

            size_t GetCount();

        protected:
            T Data[Limit];
            size_t Head;
            size_t Tail;
            size_t Count;

            // utility functions
            void DeepCopy
                (
                const Deque<T,Limit> & deq
                );
        };

template <class T, size_t Limit>
    void Deque<T,Limit>::DeepCopy
        (
        const Deque<T,Limit> & deq
        )
        {
        Count = deq.Count;
        Head  = deq.Head;
        Tail  = deq.Tail;

        for (size_t n = 0; n < Limit; ++n)
            Data[n] = deq.Data[n];
        }

template <class T, size_t Limit>
```

```
    inline Deque<T,Limit>::Deque()
        {
        Count = 0;
        Head  = 0;
        Tail  = 0;
        }

template <class T, size_t Limit>
    inline Deque<T,Limit>::Deque
        (
        const Deque<T,Limit> & deq
        )
        {
        Count = 0;
        DeepCopy(deq);
        }

template <class T, size_t Limit>
    inline Deque<T,Limit>::~Deque()
        {
        Erase();
        }

template <class T, size_t Limit>
    void Deque<T,Limit>::operator =
        (
        const Deque<T,Limit> & deq
        )
        {
        Erase();
        DeepCopy(deq);
        }

template <class T, size_t Limit>
    void Deque<T,Limit>::PushTop(const T & item)
        {
        if (Count == Limit)
            throw ContainerEx(CX_OVERFLOW);

        if (Count == 0)
            {
            Tail = 0;
            Head = 0;
```

```
                        Data[0] = item;
                        }
                else
                        {
                        if (Head == 0)
                            Head = Limit - 1;
                        else
                            —Head;

                        Data[Head] = item;
                        }

                ++Count;
                }

template <class T, size_t Limit>
    void Deque<T,Limit>::PushBtm(const T & item)
        {
        if (Count == Limit)
            throw ContainerEx(CX_OVERFLOW);

        if (Count == 0)
            {
            Tail = 0;
            Head = 0;
            Data[0] = item;
            }
        else
            {
            ++Tail;

            if (Tail == Limit)
                Tail = 0;

            Data[Tail] = item;
            }

        ++Count;
        }

template <class T, size_t Limit>
    T Deque<T,Limit>::PopTop()
        {
```

```
        if (Count == 0)
            throw ContainerEx(CX_NULL);

        T result = Data[Head];

        —Count;

        if (Count != 0)
            {
            ++Head;

            if (Head == Limit)
                Head = 0;
            }

        return result;
        }

template <class T, size_t Limit>
    T Deque<T,Limit>::PopBtm()
        {
        if (Count == 0)
            throw ContainerEx(CX_NULL);

        T result = Data[Tail];

        —Count;

        if (Count != 0)
            {
            if (Tail == 0)
                Tail = Limit - 1;
            else
                —Tail;
            }

        return result;
        }

template <class T, size_t Limit>
    inline void Deque<T,Limit>::Erase()
        {
        Count = 0;
```

```
    }

template <class T, size_t Limit>
    inline size_t Deque<T,Limit>::GetCount()
        {
        return Count;
        }
```

APPLICATION

The exception types are located in the files **contx.h** and **contx.cpp**. *SListDynamic* and *SList* are implemented in **slist.h**, and you'll find the stack classes in **stack.h**. The file **queue.h** contains the Queue classes, and **deque.h** holds the *Deque* classes. In the sample application, look at **tblist.cpp** for examples of working with these list classes.

CHAPTER 3

BINARY TREES

Applications often require that data be accessed in a sequence, such as alphabetical order. A tree structure may be the perfect choice when your program must automatically store data in sorted order.

BINARY TREES

All trees consist of *nodes* that contain keys. Nodes have *links* to other nodes, and the type of tree being constructed defines the structure of the links between nodes. Links are one-way; they connect *parent* nodes to *child* nodes. All trees have a single *root* node, to which all other nodes are linked. Any node lacking links is known as a *leaf* node. These definitions will become clearer when you view the figures in the pages to come.

A *binary tree* is the simplest type of tree structure. Each node in a binary tree contains a key and two links; one link connects to all nodes with lesser keys, and the other link connects to all nodes with greater keys. If there are no lesser or greater nodes, the link contains a sentinel value marking it as a *null link*.

Searching

I use diagrams in which nodes are boxes containing their key value. For simplicity, the examples use single-letter keys. Links are shown by lines connecting the lower left- and right-hand corners of a parent node to the center top of a child node. Lesser nodes are linked on the left; greater nodes are linked on the right.

Figure 3.1 shows an example of a binary tree. K is the root of the tree, and it is the parent of G and M. Notice that a node can be both a parent and a child; G is a child of K and the parent of D and H. The nodes containing the A, E, H, N, and S keys are leaf nodes.

The algorithm for finding a key in a binary tree begins by comparing the search key to the key stored in the root node. If the keys don't match, the algorithm follows the links to other nodes in the tree based on the relationship between the search key and the keys in the nodes. For example, if the search key is less than the root key, we follow the left link to the next node; if the search key is greater than the root key, we follow the right link. The newly selected node is now treated just as the root was, by comparing the search key against the node key and selecting the next search node. If the link to be followed does not connect to a child node, the search key is not in the tree.

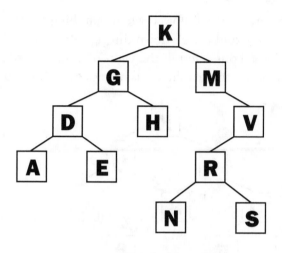

FIGURE 3.1 A BINARY TREE

Figure 3.2 uses arrows to show the links followed in searching for the key E in the example binary tree. E is less than the root node key K, so we move follow the left link. E is less than G, so again we follow the left link. E is greater than D, and we follow the right link to the node that contains E.

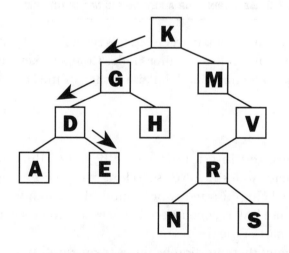

FIGURE 3.2 SEARCHING FOR E IN A BINARY TREE

Figure 3.3 shows the procedure followed when searching for the key T. The search begins at the root and travels down through the tree until it reaches the S node. T would be connected to the right of S—if it were in the tree! When a null link is found, the search key is not resident in the tree.

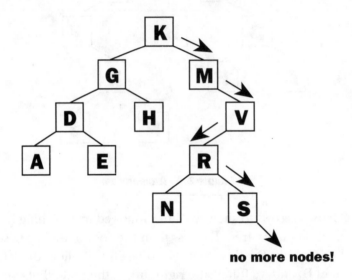

FIGURE 3.3 SEARCHING FOR A KEY THAT IS NOT IN THE TREE

You probably noticed that a binary tree search is recursive. Start at the root node, compare keys, and select another node. Compare keys and select another node—and so on until a null link is reached or the key is found.

Insertion

The first node inserted into a binary tree becomes the root node. Inserting subsequent nodes involves searching the tree for the proper location. If the key being inserted is not found, the search will end at a null link. When a null link is encountered, a new leaf node is constructed and linked to that part of the tree.

Figure 3.4 assumes that insertion begins with an empty tree and shows the results of inserting each of the keys C, A, R, K, D, and U, in that order.

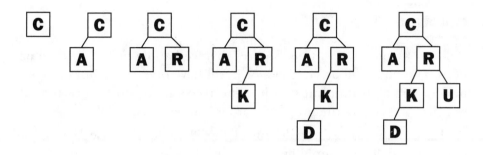

FIGURE 3.4 BINARY TREE INSERTION

The first key inserted, C, becomes the root node. A is less than C, so it is attached to the left of C; R is greater than C, so it links to C's right side. K is greater than C but less than R, placing it left of R. D is greater than C and less than R and K, so it is attached to K's left link. U is greater than C and R, and it is linked to R's right side.

Figure 3.5 shows the tree after adding the keys P, B, E, N, X, Z, and S. You may notice that more nodes are greater than the root, giving the tree a lopsided appearance. For now, we'll ignore this problem; I'll address it later in the chapter.

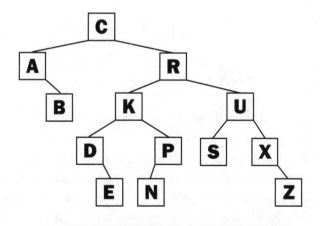

FIGURE 3.5 THE RESULT OF INSERTING MORE NODES

Deletion

Deleting a node from a tree requires that we handle one of three situations: The node will be childless, or it will have one or two links to child nodes. The algorithm must adjust the tree's nodes to ensure that all remaining keys have the proper, in-order connections.

Figure 3.6 shows the deletion of the H node. Because H is a leaf node, it is deleted simply by setting the link from its parent to null. Deleting a leaf node does not require us to change the organization of other nodes.

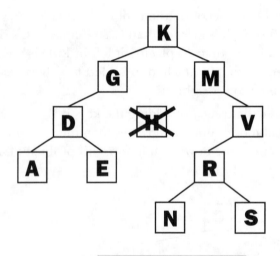

FIGURE 3.6 DELETING A LEAF NODE

When a parent node is deleted from a binary tree, all its child nodes must be relinked to the tree.

Figure 3.7 shows how a parent with a single child is deleted from a binary tree. The deleted node is replaced by its child; in this case, G is replaced by D. All children of a node have the same relationship to the node's parent as does the node, so replacing a deleted node with its child maintains the integrity of the tree's organization.

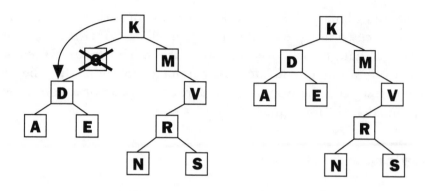

FIGURE 3.7 DELETING A PARENT NODE WITH ONE CHILD

When deleting a two-child node from the tree, we need to use a more complicated algorithm, as shown in Figure 3.8. The deleted node is replaced by its immediate successor, which is defined as the node that immediately follows the deleted node in sequence. In Figure 3.8, N immediately follows M and is therefore its successor. The data stored in N—such as the key value—is transferred to the deleted node (M). All of M's links remain intact. Once the successor node has replaced the deleted node, the algorithm deletes the original successor node from the tree. The relationship of the keys remains intact.

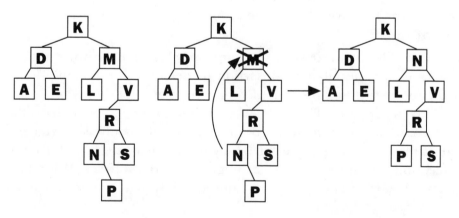

FIGURE 3.8 DELETING A PARENT NODE WITH TWO CHILDREN

Implementing binary trees with a C++ class was not as complicated as one might expect. By using templates, I've defined a set of classes that allow any type of data to be stored in binary trees. The *BinaryTree* class is defined with a single template class parameter that identifies the data type being stored. The type must support comparison operators, assignment, and default (no argument) construction.

Iterators

An *iterator* is an object through which you can examine the contents of another object. A pointer to the elements of an array is one type of iterator that's built into C++. An iterator class is usually a friend of the container class, and the iterator usually acts as a pointer to an element of the container it is associated with. More than one iterator can exist contemporaneously, allowing different sections of a program to examine the same container in different ways.

For a binary tree, an iterator would point to a node in the tree. I define the dereferencing operator * to return the data pointed to by a node. Increment and decrement operators would "move" the iterator to the next or previous element of the tree, and other functions set an iterator to the first or last tree element. This approach allows an iterator to traverse the tree from end to end, in order and in reverse order.

A problem will arise if an iterator references a node that is changed by manipulation—insertion or deletion, for example—of a tree. To prevent that problem, I've incorporated the theory of "locks" into my binary trees. The creation of an iterator object increments the lock count; when an iterator is destroyed, the lock count is decremented. If the lock count is greater than zero, a binary tree will throw an exception for an operation that might potentially affect an iterator. Thus, while iterators exist, items cannot be inserted or deleted from a binary tree.

BINARY TREE EXCEPTIONS

I've defined an enumerated type and a class for handling exceptions that are thrown from binary trees. The enumerated type defines the types of error that might occur in a binary tree:

```
enum TreeError
    {
    BTX_ALLOC,
    BTX_NOTFOUND,
    BTX_LOCKVIOLATION,
    BTX_LOCKMAX,
    BTX_LOCKZERO
    };
```

The class *TreeEx* defines an exception object to be thrown whenever a problem occurs. When creating a new *TreeEx* object, you provide a *TreeError* value to indicate the type of error.

```
class TreeEx : public ExceptionBase
    {
    public:
        TreeEx
            (
            TreeError err
            )
            {
            Error = err;
            }

        TreeError WhatsWrong()
            {
            return Error;
            }

        virtual void Explain
            (
```

```
        DiagOutput & out
        );

    private:
        TreeError Error;
    };
```

WhatsWrong reports the error type, and *Explain* is the polymorphic function that displays the error message.

```
void TreeEx::Explain(DiagOutput & out)
    {
    switch (Error)
        {
    case BTX_ALLOC:
        out.DisplayMsg("Can't alloc memory for tree",
                       DIAG_ERROR);
        break;
    case BTX_NOTFOUND:
        out.DisplayMsg("Tree look-up failed",
                       DIAG_WARNING);
        break;
    case BTX_LOCKVIOLATION:
        out.DisplayMsg("Attempt change in locked tree",
                       DIAG_WARNING);
        break;
    case BTX_LOCKMAX:
        out.DisplayMsg("Too many lock increments for tree",
                       DIAG_WARNING);
        break;
    case BTX_LOCKZERO:
        out.DisplayMsg("Too many lock decrements for tree",
                       DIAG_WARNING);
        break;
    default:
        out.DisplayMsg("Unknown tree exception",
                       DIAG_FATAL);
        }
    }
```

NODE STRUCTURE

A template defines the appropriate structure for nodes in a binary tree.

```
template <class D>
    struct TreeNode
        {
        // links
        TreeNode<D> * Less;
        TreeNode<D> * More;
        TreeNode<D> * Parent;

        // contents
        D Data;

        // constructor
        TreeNode
            (
            const D & item,
            TreeNode<D> * sentinel
            );

        TreeNode(); // creates a sentinel node

        // copy constructor
        TreeNode
            (
            const TreeNode<D> & node
            );

        // assignment operator
        void operator =
            (
            const TreeNode<D> & node
            );
        };
```

The *Less* member points to a child node containing a lesser key; the *More* member points to a child node containing a greater key. The *Parent* pointer is a backward link to the node's parent. Deletion of nodes from the tree is greatly simplified when a link provides the address of the parent node. *Key* identifies the information stored in *Data*.

Null nodes are indicated by *Less* or *More* pointers set to special node called a *sentinel*. The *sentinel* could be *NULL*, which is the way most binary trees indicate empty nodes. In the case of more advanced binary tree types, such as the red-black trees shown later in this chapter, the sentinel is a special node that points to itself. As you'll see later, using a sentinel node can simplify the implementation of red-black trees.

The default *TreeNode* constructor creates a sentinel node that points to itself. For a sentinel, the data element is meaningless. Because *Data* is static, it must be initialized through a constructor call; for a sentinel node, *Data* is generated through a default constructor. This requires the data type stored in a node to support a default (no argument) constructor. Standard arrays also require a default constructor; in general, it is good practice to define a default constructor for any class.

```
template <class D>
    TreeNode<D>::TreeNode()
        : Data()
        {
        Parent = this;
        Less   = this;
        More   = this;
        }
```

The default *TreeNode* constructor is used only to create a sentinel node; *BinaryTree* generates all other nodes with a constructor that requires a data parameter and a sentinel pointer.

```
template <class D>
    TreeNode<D>::TreeNode
        (
        const D & item,
        TreeNode<D> * sentinel
        )
        : Data(item)
        {
```

```
Parent = sentinel;
Less   = sentinel;
More   = sentinel;
}
```

The *TreeNode* copy constructor duplicates an existing node, and the assignment operator copies one *TreeNode* to another.

```
template <class D>
    TreeNode<D>::TreeNode
        (
        const TreeNode<D> & node
        )
        : Data(node.Data)
        {
        Parent = node.Parent;
        Less   = node.Less;
        More   = node.More;
        }

template <class D>
    void TreeNode<D>::operator =
        (
        const TreeNode<D> & node
        )
        {
        Parent = node.Parent;
        Less   = node.Less;
        More   = node.More;
        Data   = node.Data;
        }
```

The binary tree class manages *TreeNodes* directly, creating them dynamically and managing their pointers and internal data.

BINARYTREE CLASS

The *BinaryTree* class defines three data members: the *Root* pointer to the root node, a *Sentinel* node, and a function pointer named *WalkFunc* that is used in listing the entries in a tree. The function pointer locates a function that has a type *D* parameter, matching the parameter passed to the *Walk* member function.

```
template <class D>
    class BinaryTree
        {
        friend
            class BinaryTreeIterator<D>;

        public:
            // constructor
            BinaryTree();

            BinaryTree
                (
                const BinaryTree<D> & tree
                );

            // destructor
            ~BinaryTree();

            // assignment operator
            void operator =
                (
                const BinaryTree<D> & tree
                );

            // store an item
            void Insert
                (
                const D & item
                );

            // delete an item
            Boolean Delete
                (
                const D & item
                );

            // walk entire tree, calling function for nodes
            void Walk
```

```
    (
    void (* func)(const D & item)
    );

  // examine lock count
  unsigned int  GetLockCount();

  // retrieve pointer to sentinel
  const TreeNode<D> * GetSentinel();

protected:
  TreeNode<D> * Root;      // root node
  TreeNode<D> * Sentinel;  // sentinel node

  unsigned int LockCount;  // number of iterator locks

  // function called during traverse
  void (*WalkFunc)(const D & item);

  // function to create and delete nodes
  TreeNode<D> * CreateNode
      (
      const D & item
      );

  void DeleteNode
      (
      TreeNode<D> * node
      );

  // internal insert function
  TreeNode<D> * InternalInsert
      (
      const D & item
      );

  // recursive copy function
  void RecursiveCopy
      (
      TreeNode<D> * node
      );

  // recursive traversal function
```

```
void RecurseWalk
    (
    TreeNode<D> * node
    );

// recursive deletion function
void RecursiveDelete
    (
    TreeNode<D> * node
    );

// find minimum node
TreeNode<D> * Minimum
    (
    TreeNode<D> * node
    );

// find maximum node
TreeNode<D> * Maximum
    (
    TreeNode<D> * node
    );

// find successor node
TreeNode<D> * Successor
    (
    TreeNode<D> * node
    );

// find predecessor node
TreeNode<D> * Predecessor
    (
    TreeNode<D> * node
    );

// find node containing specific item
TreeNode<D> * Search
    (
    const D & item
    );
};
```

LockCount tracks the number of iterators created; functions such as *Delete* will throw an exception if they are called for a *BinaryTree* with a *LockCount* greater than zero. *LockCount* is changed only by the *BinaryTreeIterator* class.

Utility Functions

A dozen protected utility functions provide basic services for a *BinaryTree*.

I placed the creation and deletion of nodes in the functions *CreateNode* and *DeleteNode* rather than embed calls to *new* and delete in various functions. This places exception handling for memory allocation in a single location.

```
template <class D>
    TreeNode<D> * BinaryTree<D>::CreateNode
        (
        const D & item
        )
        {
        TreeNode<D> * z = new TreeNode<D>(item, Sentinel);

        if (z == NULL)
            throw TreeEx(BTX_ALLOC);

        return z;
        }

template <class D>
    void BinaryTree<D>::DeleteNode
        (
        TreeNode<D> * node
        )
        {
        delete node;
        }
```

Three recursive utility functions process all nodes in a given subtree by passing the *Less* and *Greater* pointers to themselves. To process the entire tree, pass these functions the *Root* node.

RecursiveCopy duplicates a tree. The copy constructor and assignment operator call *RecursiveCopy* with the *Root* node of the tree that is being duplicated. The function then adds those nodes recursively to the destination tree.

```
template <class D>
    void BinaryTree<D>::RecursiveCopy
        (
        TreeNode<D> * node
        )
        {
        if (node != Sentinel)
            {
            Insert(node->Data);
            RecursiveCopy(node->Less);
            RecursiveCopy(node->More);
            }
        }
```

The destructor calls *RecursiveDelete* with the *Root* node. *RecursiveDelete* recursively deletes the subtrees before deleting the node itself.

```
template <class D>
    void BinaryTree<D>::RecursiveDelete
        (
        TreeNode<D> * node
        )
        {
        if (node != Sentinel)
            {
            RecursiveDelete(node->Less);
            RecursiveDelete(node->More);
            DeleteNode(node);
            }
        }
```

Walk assigns its function pointer parameter to the *WalkFunc* data member; then it calls *RecurseWalk* with the *Root* node. *RecurseWalk* first recursively processes the *Less* subtree; then it calls *WalkFunc* for the current node, followed by a call to itself for the *More* subtree.

```
template <class D>
    void BinaryTree<D>::Walk
        (
        void (* func)(const D & item)
        )
        {
        WalkFunc = func;
        RecurseWalk(Root);
        }

template <class D>
    void BinaryTree<D>::RecurseWalk
        (
        TreeNode<D> * node
        )
        {
        if (node != Sentinel)
            {
            RecurseWalk(node->Less);
            WalkFunc(node->Data);
            RecurseWalk(node->More);
            }
        }
```

The *Minimum, Maximum, Predecessor,* and *Successor* utility functions find, respectively, the first, last, previous, and next items in a binary tree by following the links between nodes.

```
// find minimum node
template <class D>
    TreeNode<D> * BinaryTree<D>::Minimum
        (
        TreeNode<D> * node
        )
        {
        while (node->Less != Sentinel)
            node = node->Less;

        return node;
        }

// find maximum node
```

```
template <class D>
    TreeNode<D> * BinaryTree<D>::Maximum
        (
        TreeNode<D> * node
        )
        {
        while (node->More != Sentinel)
            node = node->More;

        return node;
        }

// find successor node
template <class D>
    TreeNode<D> * BinaryTree<D>::Successor
        (
        TreeNode<D> * node
        )
        {
        TreeNode<D> * x, * y;

        if (node->More != Sentinel)
            return Minimum(node->More);
        else
            {
            x = node;
            y = node->Parent;

            while ((y != Sentinel) && (x == y->More))
                {
                x = y;
                y = y->Parent;
                }
            }

        return y;
        }

// find predecessor node
template <class D>
    TreeNode<D> * BinaryTree<D>::Predecessor
        (
        TreeNode<D> * node
```

```
)
{
TreeNode<D> * x, * y;

if (node->Less != Sentinel)
    return Maximum(node->Less);
else
    {
    x = node;
    y = node->Parent;

    while ((y != Sentinel) && (x == y->Less))
        {
        x = y;
        y = y->Parent;
        }
    }

return y;
}
```

Finally, the *Search* utility function finds the node that contains a specific data item. Beginning at the root, *Search* follows the node links by comparing the requested item against node contents. If *Search* finds a *Sentinel* node, it has reached the end of the tree; it then returns *Sentinel* to indicate that the item was not found.

```
template <class D>
    TreeNode<D> * BinaryTree<D>::Search
        (
        const D & item
        )
        {
        TreeNode<D> * n = Root;

        while ((n != Sentinel) && (n->Data != item))
            {
            if (item < n->Data)
                n = n->Less;
            else
                n = n->More;
```

```
        }

    return n;
    }
```

Constructors and Destructors

The default constructor creates a *Sentinel* node and creates an empty tree by setting *Count* to 0 and *Root* to *Sentinel*.

```
template <class D>
    BinaryTree<D>::BinaryTree()
        {
        Sentinel  = new TreeNode<D>;

        if (Sentinel == NULL)
            throw TreeEx(BTX_ALLOC);

        Root      = Sentinel;
        LockCount = 0;
        }
```

The destructor calls *RecursiveDelete* to destroy all nodes and the *Sentinel*.

```
template <class D>
    BinaryTree<D>::~BinaryTree()
        {
        if (LockCount > 0)
            throw TreeEx(BTX_LOCKVIOLATION);

        RecursiveDelete(Root);
        }
```

The copy constructor and assignment operator duplicate the members of an existing tree using the *RecursiveCopy* utility.

```
template <class D>
    BinaryTree<D>::BinaryTree
```

```
        (
        const BinaryTree<D> & tree
        )
        {
        Sentinel = new TreeNode<D>(*(tree.Sentinel));

        if (Sentinel == NULL)
            throw TreeEx(BTX_ALLOC);

        Root      = Sentinel;
        LockCount = 0;

        RecursiveCopy(tree.Root);
        }

template <class D>
    void BinaryTree<D>::operator =
        (
        const BinaryTree<D> & tree
        )
        {
        if (LockCount > 0)
            throw TreeEx(BTX_LOCKVIOLATION);

        Sentinel = new TreeNode<D>(*(tree.Sentinel));

        if (Sentinel == NULL)
            throw TreeEx(BTX_ALLOC);

        RecursiveDelete(Root);
        Root = Sentinel;
        RecursiveCopy(tree.Root);

        delete Sentinel;
        }
```

Each tree creates a unique *Sentinel* to prevent conflicts with other trees. A conflict could arise if two separate threads of a program contained *BinaryTrees* that manipulated a common *Sentinel*. To the greatest extent possible, objects should be independent and self-contained.

Insertion and Deletion

The *InternalInsert* function performs a standard binary tree insertion and returns the address of the new node. The basic *BinaryTree* class can insert a new node simply by calling *InternalInsert* and ignoring the return value; red-black trees, however, perform operations to rebalance a tree after each new node is inserted.

After it creates a node, *InternalInsert* searches the tree for the data value. If a match is found, the new node replaces the existing one using the original links and parent. Otherwise, the search ends at a sentinel where the new node is added.

```
template <class D>
    TreeNode<D> * BinaryTree<D>::InternalInsert
        (
        const D & item
        )
        {
        if (LockCount > 0)
            throw TreeEx(BTX_LOCKVIOLATION);

        TreeNode<D> * z = CreateNode(item);
        TreeNode<D> * y = Sentinel;
        TreeNode<D> * x = Root;

        while (x != Sentinel)
            {
            y = x;

            if (z->Data < x->Data)
                x = x->Less;
            else
                x = x->More;
            }

        z->Parent = y;

        if (y == Sentinel)
            Root = z;
```

```
else
    {
    if (z->Data < y->Data)
        y->Less = z;
    else
        y->More = z;
    }

return z;
}
```

The inline *Insert* function calls *InternalInsert* and returns, ignoring the returned node pointer.

```
template <class D>
    void BinaryTree<D>::Insert
        (
        const D & item
        )
        {
        InternalInsert(item);
        }
```

Deleting an item involves the removal of nodes with zero, one, or two links. Subtle differences in deletion algorithms prevented me from creating an efficient "internal delete" function that works for all binary trees.

```
template <class D>
    Boolean BinaryTree<D>::Delete
        (
        const D & item
        )
        {
        if (LockCount > 0)
            throw TreeEx(BTX_LOCKVIOLATION);

        // find node
        TreeNode<D> * z = Search(item);

        if (z == Sentinel)
            return BOOL_FALSE;
```

```
TreeNode<D> * y, * x;

// find node to splice out
if ((z->Less == Sentinel) || (z->More == Sentinel))
    y = z;
else
    y = Successor(z);

// find child with which to replace y
if (y->Less != Sentinel)
    x = y->Less;
else
    x = y->More;

// splice child onto parent
if (x != Sentinel)
    x->Parent = y->Parent;

if (y->Parent == Sentinel)
    Root = x; // replace root
else
    {
    // splice in child node
    if (y == y->Parent->Less)
        y->Parent->Less = x;
    else
        y->Parent->More = x;
    }

// if needed, save y data
if (y != z)
    z->Data = y->Data;

// free memory
DeleteNode(y);

return BOOL_TRUE;
}
```

Delete begins by searching for the key. If the key isn't found, *Delete* returns *BOOL_FALSE*, indicating that it didn't perform any deletions. Otherwise, *node* is deleted and the tree is adjusted. If the deleted node is the only node, *Delete* leaves an empty tree. If the node has only one child, that child replaces the deleted node—becoming the new root if the root node is being deleted. Otherwise, the node has two children and it is swapped with its immediate successor.

Interrogators

Two interrogation functions return, respectively, a *BinaryTree*'s lock count and the sentinel pointer.

```
template <class D>
    inline size_t BinaryTree<D>::GetLockCount()
        {
        return LockCount;
        }

template <class D>
    inline const TreeNode<D> * BinaryTree<D>::GetSentinel()
        {
        return Sentinel;
        }
```

ITERATORS

The *BinaryTreeIterator* class is defined largely in terms of functions provided by *BinaryTree*.

```
template <class D>
    class BinaryTreeIterator
        {
        public:
            BinaryTreeIterator
                (
                BinaryTree<D> & bt
                );

            BinaryTreeIterator
                (
```

```
            BinaryTreeIterator<D> & iter
            );

        ~BinaryTreeIterator();

        void operator =
            (
            BinaryTreeIterator<D> & iter
            );

        void Smallest();
        void Largest();

        void operator ++ ();
        void operator - ();

        D operator * ();

    protected:
        BinaryTree<D> & Tree;
        TreeNode<D>    * Node;
    };
```

Each iterator contains a reference, *Tree*, to the tree it is traversing and a pointer, *Node*, to the currently selected node.

In creating a new *BinaryTreeIterator*, a program must provide a reference to a *BinaryTree*. The constructor increments the tree's lock count and sets the *Node* pointer to the smallest element in the tree.

```
template <class D>
    BinaryTreeIterator<D>::BinaryTreeIterator
        (
        BinaryTree<D> & bt
        )
        : Tree(bt)
        {
        if (Tree.LockCount == UINT_MAX)
            throw TreeEx(BTX_LOCKMAX);

        ++Tree.LockCount;
```

```
Smallest();
}
```

The copy constructor and assignment operator duplicate the contents of
an existing iterator.

```
template <class D>
    BinaryTreeIterator<D>::BinaryTreeIterator
        (
        BinaryTreeIterator<D> & iter
        )
        : Tree(iter.Tree)
        {
        if (Tree.LockCount == UINT_MAX)
            throw TreeEx(BTX_LOCKMAX);

        ++Tree.LockCount;

        Node = iter.Node;
        }

template <class D>
    void BinaryTreeIterator<D>::operator =
        (
        BinaryTreeIterator<D> & iter
        )
        {
        Tree = iter.Tree;

        if (Tree.LockCount == 0)
            throw TreeEx(BTX_LOCKZERO);

        -Tree.LockCount;

        if (Tree.LockCount == UINT_MAX)
            throw TreeEx(BTX_LOCKMAX);

        ++Tree.LockCount;

        Node = iter.Node;
        }
```

The destructor ensures that *Tree*'s lock count is decremented when the program destroys an iterator.

```
template <class D>
    BinaryTreeIterator<D>::~BinaryTreeIterator()
        {
        if (Tree.LockCount == 0)
            throw TreeEx(BTX_LOCKZERO);

        -Tree.LockCount;
        }
```

The remaining functions move *Node* through *Tree*'s elements using the private functions built into *BinaryTree*.

```
template <class D>
    void BinaryTreeIterator<D>::Smallest()
        {
        Node = Tree.Minimum(Tree.Root);
        }

template <class D>
    void BinaryTreeIterator<D>::Largest()
        {
        Node = Tree.Maximum(Tree.Root);
        }

template <class D>
    void BinaryTreeIterator<D>::operator ++ ()
        {
        Node = Tree.Successor(Node);
        }

template <class D>
    void BinaryTreeIterator<D>::operator - ()
        {
        Node = Tree.Predecessor(Node);
        }
```

In keeping with the nomenclature of pointers, I use the increment and decrement operators to move an iterator forward and backward, respectively, in the tree. The * operator returns the data contained in *Node*.

```
template <class D>
    D BinaryTreeIterator<D>::operator * ()
        {
        if (Node == Tree.GetSentinel())
            throw TreeEx(BTX_NOTFOUND);
        else
            return Node->Data;
        }
```

BINARY TREE LIMITATIONS

Binary trees sort information as it is inserted, making them very useful for applications in which dynamic information must be organized. Binary trees, however, have deficiencies.

Figure 3.9 shows a tree constructed from the keys C, A, R, K, D, U, P, B, E, N, X, Z, and S, inserted in that order. The tree has two nodes left of the root and 10 nodes to its right. Searching for a key greater than C can require as many as five comparisons, which is certainly less than optimal.

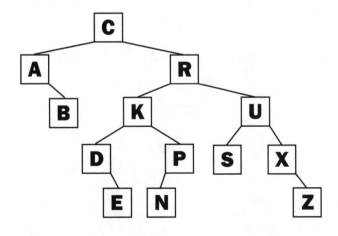

FIGURE 3.9 AN UNBALANCED BINARY TREE

A tree is balanced when it has an equal number of nodes on each side of its root. For example, inserting the same set of keys in a different order will result in a perfectly balanced tree.

Figure 3.10 shows the keys inserted in the order NCUBADEKRPSXZ. N is a good root value, because it is near the median value of all keys. C was a bad root value, because it tended toward one end of the range of values.

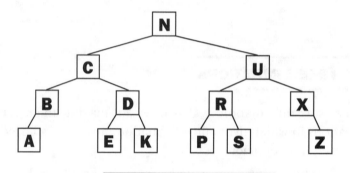

FIGURE 3.10 A BALANCED BINARY TREE

Figure3.11 shows a binary tree generated from the keys A, B, C, D, E, and F. Because each subsequent node is greater than its predecessor, the binary tree degenerates into a linked list. A search on a linked list is inefficient, and all benefits of a binary tree are lost.

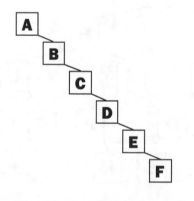

FIGURE 3.11 A DEGENERATE BINARY TREE

Sorted and almost-sorted data is common, and computer scientists have developed several schemes—such as QuickSort—for lessening the impact of sorted data. Balancing and nearly balancing binary trees require sophisticated rearrangement of the tree as nodes are added and deleted.

RED-BLACK TREES

Red-black trees use a marking technique to ensure that portions of the tree do not become massively unbalanced with other parts of the tree. Each red-black tree node contains a color marker, which can be either "red" or "black." All red-back nodes follow this set of rules:

1. Every node is either red or black.

2. Every leaf (sentinel) node is considered black.

3. If a node is red, its children are black.

4. All paths from a node to descendant leaves will contain the same number of black nodes.

The number of black nodes in any path is that path's "black height." The rules above ensure that a red-black tree is approximately balanced; no path through the tree can be more than twice as long as its sibling path.

For the most part, red-black trees operate exactly like standard binary trees; only insertion and deletion change substantially, because they need to maintain the four color rules I specified previously. Red-black trees, then, should be derived from *BinaryTrees*.

Red-black nodes contain a color indicator not found in standard binary nodes. The most effective way I've found to do this is by creating a template for an auxiliary data structure, *RBData*, that combines a data item and a color indicator.

```
enum RBColor { BLACK, RED };

template <class D>
```

```
struct RBData
    {
    RBColor Color;
    D       RealData;

    RBData()
        : RealData()
        {
        Color = BLACK;
        }

    RBData
        (
        const D & item
        )
        {
        RealData = item;
        Color = BLACK;
        }

    int operator <
        (
        const RBData & rbd
        )
        const
        {
        return (RealData < rbd.RealData);
        }

    int operator >
        (
        const RBData & rbd
        )
        const
        {
        return (RealData > rbd.RealData);
        }

    int operator ==
        (
        const RBData & rbd
        )
```

```
        const
        {
        return (RealData == rbd.RealData);
        }

    int operator !=
        (
        const RBData & rbd
        )
        const
        {
        return (RealData == rbd.RealData);
        }
    };
```

At first glance, this implementation may seem strange. Why didn't I derive a new "red black node" class from *TreeNode*? In fact, my original implementation did just that, creating a *RedBlackNode* class that added a color value to *TreeNode*. This approach, however, didn't solve a nasty problem: *TreeNode* defines the *Less*, *More*, and *Parent* members as pointers to *TreeNode<D>*. in the *RedBlackTree* functions, I needed to constantly cast those pointers to *RedBlackNode<D>* pointers. Not only was this messy, but it was also error-prone. By using the *RBData* structure, I extended *TreeNode* without having to create a new type.

RED-BLACK TREE CLASS

Then I derived the *RedBlackTree* class from *BinaryTree < RBData<D> >*.

```
template <class D>
    class RedBlackTree : public BinaryTree< RBData<D> >
        {
        public:
            // constructor
            RedBlackTree();

            RedBlackTree
```

```
            (
            const RedBlackTree<D> & tree
            );

        // assignment operator
        void operator =
            (
            const RedBlackTree<D> & tree
            );

        // store an item
        void Insert
            (
            const D & item
            );

        // delete an item
        Boolean Delete
            (
            const D & item
            );

    protected:
        // tree adjustment utilities
        void RotateLeft
            (
            TreeNode< RBData<D> > * node
            );

        void RotateRight
            (
            TreeNode< RBData<D> > * node
            );

        void DeleteFixup
            (
            TreeNode< RBData<D> > * node
            );
    };
```

RedBlackTree adds to *BinaryTree* those functions needed to handle the organization of the tree.

Constructors and Destructors

The constructors, destructors, and assignment operators simply provide shells for calling their *BinaryTree* equivalents.

```
template <class D>
    inline RedBlackTree<D>::RedBlackTree()
        : BinaryTree< RBData<D> >()
        {
        // placeholder
        }

template <class D>
    inline RedBlackTree<D>::RedBlackTree
        (
        const RedBlackTree<D> & tree
        )
        : BinaryTree< RBData<D> >(tree)
        {
        // placeholder
        }

template <class D>
    void RedBlackTree<D>::operator =
        (
        const RedBlackTree<D> & tree
        )
        {
        BinaryTree< RBData<D> >::operator = (tree);
        }
```

Utility Functions

RotateLeft and *RotateRight* exchange (in opposite directions) the two subtrees of a node.

```
template <class D>
    void RedBlackTree<D>::RotateLeft
```

```
        (
        TreeNode< RBData<D> > * node
        )
        {
        TreeNode< RBData<D> > * y = node->More;

        // turn y's left subtree into node's right subtree
        node->More = y->Less;

        if (y->Less != Sentinel)
            y->Less->Parent = node;

        // link node's parent to y
        y->Parent = node->Parent;

        if (node->Parent == Sentinel)
            Root = y;
        else
            {
            if (node == node->Parent->Less)
                node->Parent->Less = y;
            else
                node->Parent->More = y;
            }

        // put node on y's left
        y->Less = node;
        node->Parent = y;
        }

template <class D>
    void RedBlackTree<D>::RotateRight
        (
        TreeNode< RBData<D> > * node
        )
        {
        TreeNode< RBData<D> > * y = node->Less;

        // turn y's right subtree into node's left subtree
        node->Less = y->More;

        if (y->More != Sentinel)
            y->More->Parent = node;
```

```
// link node's parent to y
y->Parent = node->Parent;

if (node->Parent == Sentinel)
    Root = y;
else
    {
    if (node == node->Parent->More)
        node->Parent->More = y;
    else
        node->Parent->Less = y;
    }

// put node on y's right
y->More = node;
node->Parent = y;
}
```

DeleteFixup adjusts the tree after a node has been deleted. In essence, it travels down through the tree, rotating nodes until the red-black tree conditions are met.

```
template <class D>
    void RedBlackTree<D>::DeleteFixup
        (
        TreeNode< RBData<D> > * node
        )
        {
        TreeNode< RBData<D> > * w, * x = node;

        while ((x != Root) && (x->Data.Color == BLACK))
            {
            if (x == x->Parent->Less)
                {
                w = x->Parent->More;

                if (w->Data.Color == RED)
                    {
                    w->Data.Color = BLACK;
                    x->Parent->Data.Color = RED;
                    RotateLeft(x->Parent);
                    w = x->Parent->More;
```

```
            }

      if ((w->Less->Data.Color == BLACK)
      && (w->More->Data.Color == BLACK))
          {
          w->Data.Color = RED;
          x = x->Parent;
          }
      else
          {
          if (w->More->Data.Color == BLACK)
             {
             w->Less->Data.Color = BLACK;
             w->Data.Color = RED;
             RotateRight(w);
             w = x->Parent->More;
             }

          w->Data.Color = x->Parent->Data.Color;
          x->Parent->Data.Color = BLACK;
          w->More->Data.Color = BLACK;
          RotateLeft(x->Parent);
          x = Root;
          }
      }
else
    {
    w = x->Parent->Less;

    if (w->Data.Color == RED)
        {
        w->Data.Color = BLACK;
        x->Parent->Data.Color = RED;
        RotateRight(x->Parent);
        w = x->Parent->Less;
        }

    if ((w->More->Data.Color == BLACK)
    && (w->Less->Data.Color == BLACK))
        {
        w->Data.Color = RED;
        x = x->Parent;
        }
```

```
        else
            {
            if (w->Less->Data.Color == BLACK)
                {
                w->More->Data.Color = BLACK;
                w->Data.Color = RED;
                RotateLeft(w);
                w = x->Parent->Less;
                }

            w->Data.Color = x->Parent->Data.Color;
            x->Parent->Data.Color = BLACK;
            w->Less->Data.Color = BLACK;
            RotateRight(x->Parent);
            x = Root;
            }
        }
    }

    x->Data.Color = BLACK;
    }
```

When a black node is deleted from the tree, it causes any path containing the removed node to have one fewer black node—possibly violating the red-black tree conditions. The problem is corrected by pretending that an extra "black" node is connected to x; this artificial "blackness" is moved toward the root until a red node is found or the root is encountered. If a red node is found, it is colored black; if the loop reaches the root, the blackness is simply discarded.

Insertion and Deletion

The insert function begins by calling *InternalInsert* to insert a new node into the tree. Then the *Insert* function moves up the tree, rotating subtrees to restore the red-black tree conditions.

```
template <class D>
    void RedBlackTree<D>::Insert
        (
        const D & item
```

```
)
{
RBData<D> rbitem(item);

TreeNode< RBData<D> > * x = InternalInsert(rbitem);
TreeNode< RBData<D> > * y;

x->Data.Color = RED;

while ((x != Root) && (x->Parent->Data.Color == RED))
    {
    if (x->Parent == x->Parent->Parent->Less)
        {
        y = x->Parent->Parent->More;

        if (y->Data.Color == RED)
            {
            x->Parent->Data.Color = BLACK;
            y->Data.Color = BLACK;
            x->Parent->Parent->Data.Color = RED;
            x = x->Parent->Parent;
            }
        else
            {
            if (x == x->Parent->More)
                {
                x = x->Parent;
                RotateLeft(x);
                }

            x->Parent->Data.Color = BLACK;
            x->Parent->Parent->Data.Color = RED;
            RotateRight(x->Parent->Parent);
            }
        }
    else
        {
        y = x->Parent->Parent->Less;

        if (y->Data.Color == RED)
            {
            x->Parent->Data.Color = BLACK;
```

```
                y->Data.Color = BLACK;
                x->Parent->Parent->Data.Color = RED;
                x = x->Parent->Parent;
                }
        else
            {
            if (x == x->Parent->Less)
                {
                x = x->Parent;
                RotateRight(x);
                }

            x->Parent->Data.Color = BLACK;
            x->Parent->Parent->Data.Color = RED;
            RotateLeft(x->Parent->Parent);
            }
        }
    }

    Root->Data.Color = BLACK;
    }
```

Delete is almost—but not quite—identical to the *BinaryTree::Delete* function. The assignment of *y*'s parent as *x*'s parent is automatic; if *x* points to
Sentinel, Sentinel's parent pointer now points to *y*'s parent. If *y* is black, a
call to *DeleteFixup* adjusts the tree based on *x*. At that call, *x* is the node
that was *y*'s sole child before *y* was spliced out of the tree—or *x* is the
Sentinel if *y* had no children. In any case, *x*'s parent pointer will reference
the parent of *y*, allowing *DeleteFixup* to treat *x* in a generic fashion.

```
template <class D>
    Boolean RedBlackTree<D>::Delete
        (
        const D & item
        )
        {
        if (LockCount > 0)
            throw TreeEx(BTX_LOCKVIOLATION);

        // find node
```

```
TreeNode< RBData<D> > * z = Search(item);

if (z == Sentinel)
    return BOOL_FALSE;

TreeNode< RBData<D> > * y, * x;

// find node to splice out
if ((z->Less == Sentinel) || (z->More == Sentinel))
    y = z;
else
    y = Successor(z);

// find child with which to replace y
if (y->Less != Sentinel)
    x = y->Less;
else
    x = y->More;

// splice child onto parent
x->Parent = y->Parent;

if (y->Parent == Sentinel)
    Root = x; // replace root
else
    {
    // splice in child node
    if (y == y->Parent->Less)
        y->Parent->Less = x;
    else
        y->Parent->More = x;
    }

// if needed, save y data
if (y != z)
    z->Data = y->Data;

// adjust tree under red-black rules
if (y->Data.Color == BLACK)
    DeleteFixup(x);

// free memory
```

```
DeleteNode(y);

return BOOL_TRUE;
}
```

Why didn't I implement *Insert* and *Delete* as virtual functions, making *BinaryTree* and *RedBlackTree* polymorphic? It wasn't possible! Because the underlying parent *BinaryTree* has used an *RBData<D>* type for its item type, its *Insert(RBData<D>)* and *Delete(RBData<D>)* functions do not match the *Insert(D)* and *Delete(D)* functions in *RedBlackTree*.

RED-BLACK TREE ITERATORS

Because the data elements in a *RedBlackTree* reside within *RBData* structures, I created a new type of iterator to add the required extra level of indirection to *BinaryTreeIterator*.

```
template <class D>
    class RBTreeIterator : public BinaryTreeIterator< RBData<D> >
        {
        public:
            RBTreeIterator
                (
                RedBlackTree<D> & bt
                );

            RBTreeIterator
                (
                RBTreeIterator<D> & iter
                );

            void operator =
                (
                RBTreeIterator<D> & iter
                );

            D operator * ();
```

```
        };

template <class D>
    RBTreeIterator<D>::RBTreeIterator
        (
        RedBlackTree<D> & bt
        )
        : BinaryTreeIterator< RBData<D> >(bt)
        {
        // placeholder
        }

template <class D>
    RBTreeIterator<D>::RBTreeIterator
        (
        RBTreeIterator<D> & iter
        )
        : BinaryTreeIterator< RBData<D> >(iter)
        {
        // placeholder
        }

template <class D>
    void RBTreeIterator<D>::operator =
        (
        RBTreeIterator<D> & iter
        )
        {
        BinaryTreeIterator< RBData<D> >::operator = (iter);
        }

template <class D>
    D RBTreeIterator<D>::operator * ()
        {
        if (Node == Tree.GetSentinel())
            throw TreeEx(BTX_NOTFOUND);
        else
            return Node->Data.RealData;
        }
```

APPLICATION

You'll find the binary tree classes in **bintree.h**, and the exception types in **treex.h** and **treex.cpp**. I implemented the red-black tree classes in the file **rbtree.h**. Look in the **tbtree.cpp** module for examples of working with both binary and red-black trees.

CHAPTER 4

PRIORITY QUEUES AND HEAPS

One of the most useful algorithmic tools is the *priority queue*, in which items are extracted in order of a key value. Scheduling applications, for example, use priority queues to automatically organize data in order of creation time or priority. In simulation programs, a priority queue ensures that events occur in a specified order, even when new events join the queue.

PRIORITY QUEUES AND HEAPS

In most cases, a priority queue is implemented as a *heap*. A *binary* heap—usually just called a heap—is an array of elements organized like a binary tree. Each array element corresponds to a tree node, and every level in the tree is completely filled before elements are added to the next level. The first array element is the root, and it always contains the largest value in the heap.

Simple math can be used to calculate the indexes of parent and child nodes. For element i,

```
Parent index = i / 2
Less child   = 2 * i
More child   = 2 * i + 1
```

What makes heaps useful is that they satisfy a heap property: Every node is less than or equal to its parent. The largest element is stored in the root, and subtrees contain progressively smaller values. For example, Figure 4.1 shows a heap containing twelve characters.

X	T	O	G	S	M	N	A	E	R	A	I
0	1	2	3	4	5	6	7	8	9	10	11

FIGURE 4.1 THE HEAP CONTAINING TWELVE LETTERS

Operations on heaps include creation, insertion of new nodes, and the extraction of the largest (root) value. Inserting a new value involves a simple search through the tree, moving the new key upward from the root until the heap condition is met.

Whenever the heap changes, something must be done to adjust it so that the heap property is maintained. This involves recursively exchanging larger child values with smaller parent nodes until the parent is larger than its children. This process is known by a number of names; I prefer to use the term *heapify*, which I've found in several texts.

140

Extracting the largest value from a heap is simple: Return the data in the heap's first element and then swap the last item in the heap into the first element. This reduces the size of the heap by one and requires the heapify process to be invoked. Thus, as elements are removed from a heap, the highest value "sifts" down to the root. In this context, a heap acts as a priority queue, and the two can be considered equivalent.

HEAP EXCEPTIONS

I define an enumerated type that identifies the types of errors that might occur in a *Heap*.

```
enum HeapError
    {
    HPX_NULLARRAY,
    HPX_FULL,
    HPX_UNDERFLOW
    };
```

When something goes wrong, the *Heap* class throws an exception object of type *HeapEx*, as defined here:

```
class HeapEx : public ExceptionBase
    {
    public:
        HeapEx
            (
            HeapError err
            )
            {
            Error = err;
            }

        HeapError WhatsWrong()
            {
            return Error;
            }
```

```
        virtual void Explain
            (
            DiagOutput & out
            );

    private:
        HeapError Error;
    };
```

The *Explain* function displays an appropriate error message for a *HeapEx*.

```
void HeapEx::Explain(DiagOutput & out)
    {
    switch (Error)
        {
        case HPX_NULLARRAY:
            out.DisplayMsg("Can't create heap from NULL array",
                            DIAG_ERROR);
            break;
        case HPX_FULL:
            out.DisplayMsg("Heap is full",
                            DIAG_WARNING);
            break;
        case HPX_UNDERFLOW:
            out.DisplayMsg("Heap underflow",
                            DIAG_WARNING);
        default:
            out.DisplayMsg("Unknown heap exception",
                            DIAG_FATAL);
        }
    }
```

HEAP CLASS

My definition of a heap looks like this:

```
template <class D, size_t Levels>
    class Heap
        {
        public:
```

```
// constructors
Heap();

Heap
    (
    const Heap & h
    );

Heap
    (
    const D * array,
    size_t no
    );

// assignment operator
void operator =
    (
    const Heap & h
    );

// insert new item
void Insert
    (
    const D & item
    );

// look at maximum item
D Maximum();

// return and remove maximum item
D ExtractMax();

// interrogation functions
size_t GetCount();
size_t GetLimit();

protected:
    D Data[(1 << Levels) - 1];
    const size_t Limit;
    size_t Count;

    // computer child and parent indexes
    size_t LessIdx
        (
```

```
                size_t idx
                );

        size_t MoreIdx
            (
            size_t idx
            );

        size_t ParentIdx
            (
            size_t idx
            );

        // adjust to meet heap conditions
        void Heapify
            (
            size_t idx
            );
    };
```

This template is a bit odd. Instead of defining the number of possible elements, it defines the number of tree "levels" allowed. Because each level in a heap tree is filled before the next level is used, the array must contain complete levels.

A single-level heap contains one node, a two-level heap contains three nodes, and a four-level heap contains 15 nodes. In other words, the number of elements required is 2 raised to the power of the number of levels, minus 1. A seven-level tree, for example, requires a 127-element array.

The simplest way to calculate such a value is to shift one left by the number of levels and then subtract 1. That value, stored in the *Limit* constant, defines the number of elements in the *Data* array. *Count* keeps track of the number of elements stored in a *Heap*.

INDEXING FUNCTIONS

Three private inline functions calculate the indexes of parent and child nodes for a given index.

```
// computer child and parent indexes
template <class D, size_t Levels>
    inline size_t Heap<D,Levels>::LessIdx
        (
        size_t idx
        )
        {
        return ((idx + 1) * 2) - 1;
        }

template <class D, size_t Levels>
    inline size_t Heap<D,Levels>::MoreIdx
        (
        size_t idx
        )
        {
        return ((idx + 1) * 2);
        }

template <class D, size_t Levels>
    inline size_t Heap<D,Levels>::ParentIdx
        (
        size_t idx
        )
        {
        return ((idx + 1) / 2) - 1;
        }
```

Today's "smart" compilers will convert these multiplications into shifts, making these functions quite speedy.

Constructors and Assignment

The default constructor creates an empty heap.

```
template <class D, size_t Levels>
    Heap<D,Levels>::Heap()
        : Limit((1u << Levels) - 1)
        {
        Count = 0;
        }
```

The copy constructor duplicates the parameters and array elements of an existing heap.

```
// copy constructor
template <class D, size_t Levels>
    Heap<D,Levels>::Heap
        (
        const Heap & h
        )
        : Limit(h.Limit)
        {
        Count = h.Count;

        // copy source elements
        for (size_t n = 0; n < Count; ++n)
            Data[n] = h.Data[n];
        }
```

A third constructor creates a new heap from an existing array. As with any operations involving C-style arrays, this constructor will produce bogus results if the *no* parameter does not correspond to the number of elements in *array*. The constructor does verify that *array* points to something (although it can't be certain that it points to the correct data) and makes sure that the requested number of levels can hold *no* elements.

```
// copy from array constructor
template <class D, size_t Levels>
    Heap<D,Levels>::Heap
        (
        const D * array,
        size_t no
        )
        : Limit((1u << Levels) - 1)
        {
        // check for NULL array
        if (array == NULL)
            throw HeapEx(HPX_NULLARRAY);

        // make sure array fits in Limit
        if (no > Limit)
```

```
        throw HeapEx(HPX_FULL);

    // copy elements
    Count = no;

    for (size_t n = 0; n < Count; ++n)
        Insert(array[n]);
    }
```

Assignment is similar to the copy constructor in that the function copies the elements of an existing heap.

```
// assignment operator
template <class D, size_t Levels>
    void Heap<D,Levels>::operator =
        (
        const Heap & h
        )
        {
        Count = h.Count;

        // copy elements
        for (size_t n = 0; n < Count; ++n)
            Data[n] = h.Data[n];
        }
```

The Heapify Function

The most important function is *Heapify*, which makes sure that a heap's elements conform to the heap property.

```
template <class D, size_t Levels>
    void Heap<D,Levels>::Heapify
        (
        size_t idx
        )
        {
        // set beginning indexes
```

```
size_t l = LessIdx(idx);
size_t m = MoreIdx(idx);
size_t largest;

// choose greater of "less" child or current
if ((l < Count) && (Data[l] > Data[idx]))
    largest = l;
else
    largest = idx;

// choose greater of "more" child and largest
if ((m < Count) && (Data[m] > Data[largest]))
    largest = m;

// if one of the children was greater, swap
if (largest != idx)
    {
    D temp = Data[idx];
    Data[idx] = Data[largest];
    Data[largest] = temp;

    // recurse to further adjust heap
    Heapify(largest);
    }
}
```

Heapify is a recursive function. Given an index, *Heapify* exchanges a smaller item with the largest of its children; if the element at idx is larger than both its children (empty children being considered infinitely small), no exchange takes place. If an exchange occurs, *Heapify* calls itself for the affected child node. *Heapify* thus sifts larger keys down in the array, maintaining the heap property.

Insertion

The *Insert* function adds a new element to the heap if there's room.

```
template <class D, size_t Levels>
    void Heap<D,Levels>::Insert
```

```
(
const D & item
)
{
// if heap is full, complain!
if (Count == Limit)
    throw HeapEx(HPX_FULL);

// increment count
++Count;

// insertion sort
size_t i = Count - 1;

while ((i > 0) && (Data[ParentIdx(i)] < item))
    {
    Data[i] = Data[ParentIdx(i)];
    i = ParentIdx(i);
    }

Data[i] = item;
}
```

Insert increments *Count,* adding one more active element (or *leaf,* in tree terms) to the array. Following the chain of parents down to the root, *Insert* searches for a node whose parent is greater than or equal to *item.* On each pass through the loop, elements smaller than *item* get shifted into higher indexes until the appropriate place for *item* is found.

Extraction

The *Maximum* function simply returns whatever is stored in element zero—the root—of the heap, without changing the heap.

```
template <class D, size_t Levels>
    inline D Heap<D,Levels>::Maximum()
        {
        // element 0 always has biggest item
```

```
return Data[0];
}
```

ExtractMax returns whatever was in the heap's root and then removes that item. *Heapify* reorganizes the heap.

```
template <class D, size_t Levels>
    D Heap<D,Levels>::ExtractMax()
        {
        // complain if heap is empty
        if (Count == 0)
            throw HeapEx(HPX_UNDERFLOW);

        // get largest item, and swap in last item in list
        D max   = Data[0];
        Data[0] = Data[Count - 1];
        —Count;

        // adjust heap
        Heapify(0);

        return max;
        }
```

Interrogation

The remaining two functions return the parameters of a heap.

```
template <class D, size_t Levels>
    inline size_t Heap<D,Levels>::GetCount()
        {
        return Count;
        }

template <class D, size_t Levels>
    inline size_t Heap<D,Levels>::GetLimit()
        {
        return Limit;
        }
```

APPLICATION

Chapter 12 uses priority queues in creating a table of code values for compressing data. I also use priority queues when working with fuzzy logic.

The *Heap* exception classes are located in the files **heapx.h** and **heapx.cpp**; you'll find the *Heap* class in **heap.h**. Look in **tbtree.cpp** for an example of using heaps.

CHAPTER 5

DICTIONARIES

Although trees and other structures allow programs to both sort and look up information, they involve considerable overhead. The task of searching a binary tree for a specific item can be time-consuming when you're working with large data sets. In many cases, a program doesn't need data to be sorted; the software is only required to find something based on a specific key. And that's when hashing comes into play.

HASH TABLE THEORY AND DESIGN

A *hash table* contains a fixed number of buckets. A *bucket* contains data associated with a key or is empty. To find the data for a key, a bucket number is calculated from the key value by a *hash function*. The hash function will always generate the same bucket number for a given key so that a key will always retrieve the same data from the same bucket.

To see how this works, let's examine simple hash tables. A 26-bucket hash table could contain data associated with each letter of the alphabet, using the ordinal value of the letter as a bucket index. The hash function would look like this:

```
int Hash(char ch)
    {
    // return ordinal value of character relative to 'A'
    return (int)ch - 'A';
    }
```

Single letters make simple keys, but they aren't very useful in identifying most real-world information. In many financial applications, information is identified by a number—such as an account number, Social Security number, or ZIP code.

It isn't practical to define a hash table for five-digit ZIP codes where there is a bucket for each code; such a table would have hundreds of thousands of entries. A table with 256 buckets would be manageable; in that case, a ZIP code could be converted to a bucket number with a hash function such as this one:

```
int Hash(unsigned long ZIP)
    {
    return (int)(ZIP & 0xFF); // return lowest 8 bits of ZIP
    }
```

Using this function, a ZIP of 80901 (Colorado Springs) would "hash" to bucket number 5. The ZIP 80901 in hexadecimal is 13C05, and the hash function returns the lowest 8 bits, which are 05. A ZIP of 10019 (in Manhattan) would hash to bucket 194.

When the number of buckets is smaller than the number of possible keys, two or more keys may hash to the same bucket value. This is known as a *collision*. For example, the ZIP codes 21509 and 80901 both hash to the number 5 bucket. When this happens, two choices present themselves: expanding buckets to hold more than one entry or disallowing multiple bucket entries.

Disallowing multiple bucket entries is not a good solution, because it would force us to make very large hash tables to avoid collisions. In most cases, collisions are best handled by allowing each bucket to hold a list of entries that hashed to that location.

The best solution is for each bucket to contain a simple linked list of entries; empty buckets have an empty list, and new entries are appended to the end of the list for their bucket. A simple linear search of the list will find specific keys.

A good hash algorithm distributes data evenly among the buckets, avoiding collisions and limiting the number of entries per bucket. The effectiveness of a hash algorithm is affected by the nature of data used as key values. For example, if all your numbers end in the same set of digits or if the data is restricted to a specific range, that hash algorithm must take that into account when distributing keys among buckets.

Where keys are evenly distributed numeric values, the best hashing algorithm is one of the simplest:

```
int Hash(unsigned long ZIP, int buckets)
    {
    return (int)(ZIP % buckets);
    }
```

The modulus operator returns the remainder of dividing one number by another. In the preceding function, the remainder of dividing the ZIP by the number of buckets generates an index of between 0 and *buckets* - 1. Choosing the number of buckets is important; because of the nature of math, a prime number will distribute remainders more uniformly than non-primes. The number of buckets should be chosen to fit the number of keys stored in the table. Eleven buckets would be too few for a table containing 10,000 keys, because the linked lists would grow very long. In general, use this rough formula to get a feeling for the number of buckets you want:

$$buckets = \frac{number\ of\ keys}{desired\ length\ of\ linked\ lists}$$

Much of the data manipulated by programs is identified by a string. Fortunately, like C, C++ treats characters as numeric values. Thus, our hashing algorithm could be modified to handle strings in a variety of ways:

```
int Hash(const char * key, int buckets)
    {
    unsigned long n = 0;

    for (char * ptr = key; *ptr; ++ptr)
        {
        n <<= 1;
        n += *ptr;
        }

    return (int)(n % buckets);
    }
```

This function sums the characters in the string, shifting itself left one bit before each character is added. The left shift helps distribute keys evenly by lessening the impact of common character sequences.

To wrap up, here's a summary of the features found in a hash table.

- ❖ A hash table contains a list of buckets.
- ❖ A hash function calculates the bucket for data based on a key.
- ❖ The hash function should be unique for each type of data.
- ❖ Each bucket contains zero or more key/data entries, stored in a linked list.

The template for the *Dictionary* class will specify the key type, data types, and number of buckets. *Dictionary* implements its buckets as an array of doubly linked lists. By using the *Dlist* template from Chapter 3, the implementation of *Dictionary* takes only a few pages of code. A joy of C++ is how it lets you layer code, using tested code as building blocks.

I defined a set of hashing functions for instrinsic C++ data types. These functions assume that their input is randomly distributed; if your data is relatively ordered, you might want to replace these functions, as per the previous discussion.

```
inline size_t DictHash
    (
    int x,
    size_t buckets
    )
    {
    return size_t(x % int(buckets));
    }

inline size_t DictHash
    (
    unsigned int x,
    size_t buckets
    )
    {
    return size_t(x % (unsigned int)(buckets));
    }

inline size_t DictHash
    (
    long x, size_t buckets
    )
    {
    return size_t(x % long(buckets));
    }

inline size_t DictHash
    (
    unsigned long x, size_t buckets
    )
    {
```

```
    return size_t(x % (unsigned long)(buckets));
    }

size_t DictHash
    (
    const char * x, size_t buckets
    )
    {
    // assume that character array is null terminated!
    unsigned long n = 0;
    const char * ch = x;

    while (*ch)
        {
        n <<= 1;
        n += size_t(*ch);
        ++ch;
        }

    return size_t(n % (unsigned long)buckets);
    }
```

If you create a *Dictionary* for a non-intrinsic type, you must define a corresponding *DictHash* function. Remember to test your *DictHash* function,
just to see how well it distributes keys. The efficiency of a *Dictionary* is inti-
mately related to the even distribution of data in the buckets.

BUCKETS AS DOUBLY-LINKED LISTS

I implement my dictionary hash table with linked lists of entries for each
bucket. Since a doubly-linked list is useful in other applications, I defined
such structures with the *DList* class described here. *DList* throws the same
types of exceptions as do the linked-list classes of Chapter Two.

Since a doubly-linked list has pointers to both its predecessor and its
successor, a pointer can move both forward and backward through the
list's elements. Deletion is also simplified by having pointers in both
directions: simply link the deleted node's predececessor to the successor.

Definition

The *DList* class template is longer than the definitions for the singly-linked list classes, due to the greater number of capabilities that I've implemented through the use of two pointers.

```
template <class T>
    class DList
        {
        public:
            // constructors
            DList
                (
                Boolean circ = BOOL_FALSE
                );

            // copy constructor
            DList
                (
                const DList<T> & dlst,
                Boolean shallow = BOOL_FALSE
                );

            // construct from array
            DList
                (
                const T * array,
                size_t no
                );

            // destructor
            ~DList();

            // assignment operator (deep copy)
            void operator =
                (
                const DList<T> & dlst
                );

            // conversion to array operator
            operator T * ();
```

```
// append new item
void Append
    (
    const T & item
    );

// append an array of new items
void Append
    (
    const T * array,
    size_t no
    );

void Append
    (
    const DList<T> & dlst
    );

// delete current item
void Delete();

// insert new item in current location
void InsertBefore
    (
    const T & item
    );

void InsertBefore
    (
    const T * array,
    size_t no
    );

void InsertBefore
    (
    const DList<T> & dlst
    );

void InsertAfter
    (
    const T & item
    );
```

```
void InsertAfter
    (
    const T * array,
    size_t no
    );

void InsertAfter
    (
    const DList<T> & dlst
    );

// remove all items from the list
void Erase();

// get current item
T Get();

// directly reference current item
T & operator * ();

// TRUE if current item is last item
Boolean AtHead();
Boolean AtTail();

// set current item to head of list
void ToHead();
void ToTail();

// move to next item in list
Boolean ToNext();
Boolean ToPrev();

// interrogate list
size_t  GetCount();
Boolean IsShallow();
Boolean IsCircular();

protected:
// type defining a node in the list
struct Node
    {
    T Data;
```

```
            Node * Next;
            Node * Prev;
            };

      size_t Count; // # of items in list
      Node * Head;  // first item
      Node * Tail;  // last item
      Node * Work;  // current item

      Boolean Shallow;  // Is this a shallow copy?
      Boolean Circular; // is this a circular list?

      // internal utility functions
      void DeepCopy
          (
          const DList<T> & dlst
          );

      void ShallowCopy
          (
          const DList<T> & dlst
          );

      void SetNull();
};
```

DList defines its elements with a private structure, *DListNode*. Each element contains the obligatory pair of forward and backward pointers, along with data of template type *T*. *Count* holds the number of elements. Head points to the beginning of the list, and *Tail* to its end. If *Work* is not *NULL*, it points to the currently-selected element of the list. If *Shallow* is true, the *DList* is a shallow copy of another *DList*. If the list is circular, with head and tail connected, *Circular* is true.

Utility Functions

As with my other container classes, I created a few utility functions to encapsulate common operations. I allow the creation of both shallow and deep copies of an existing *DList*. The *ShallowCopy* function simply copies the member variables of an existing *DList*, so that it points to the same elements in dynamic memory.

162

```
template <class T>
    void DList<T>::DeepCopy
        (
        const DList<T> & dlst
        )
        {
        if (dlst.Count == 0)
            return;

        Node * n = dlst.Head;

        do  {
            Append(n->Data);
            n = n->Next;
            }
        while (n != NULL);

        Work = Head;
        Shallow  = BOOL_FALSE;
        Circular = dlst.Circular;
        }
```

DeepCopy creates new elements that copy the contents of the source *DList*.

```
template <class T>
    inline void DList<T>::ShallowCopy
        (
        const DList<T> & dlst
        )
        {
        Head  = dlst.Head;
        Tail  = dlst.Tail;
        Work  = dlst.Work;
        Count = dlst.Count;
        Shallow  = BOOL_TRUE;
        Circular = dlst.Circular;
        }
```

Erase destroys all elements in a list; it is both an internal utility function and a public tool for clearing out a *DList*.

```
template <class T>
    void DList<T>::Erase()
```

```
        {
    if (!Shallow)
        {
        Work = Head;

        while (Work != NULL)
            {
            Head = Work->Next;
            delete Work;
            Work = Head;
            }
        }

    SetNull();
    Shallow = BOOL_FALSE;
    }
```

SetNull simply sets a *SList's* variables to zero or *NULL* values, usually after an *Erase* or before copy operation.

```
template <class T>
    inline void DList<T>::SetNull()
        {
        Head  = NULL;
        Tail  = NULL;
        Work  = NULL;
        Count = 0;
        }
```

Constructors and Destructors

The default contructor creates a new, empty *DList*.

```
template <class T>
    inline DList<T>::DList
        (
        Boolean circ
        )
        {
        SetNull();
```

```
Shallow  = BOOL_FALSE;
Circular = circ;
}
```

The copy constructor takes a second argument specifying the type of copy to be made; by default, the copy is deep.

```
template <class T>
    DList<T>::DList
        (
        const DList<T> & dlst,
        Boolean shallow
        )
        {
        if (shallow)
            ShallowCopy(dlst);
        else
            {
            SetNull();
            DeepCopy(dlst);
            }
        }
```

It's also possible to create a DList from an array of values, using this constructor:

```
template <class T>
    DList<T>::DList
        (
        const T * array,
        size_t no
        )
        {
        SetNull();
        Circular = BOOL_FALSE;
        Shallow  = BOOL_FALSE;

        if ((array == NULL) || (no == 0))
            throw ContainerEx(CX_NULLARRAY);

        const T * aptr = array;

        for (size_t n = 0; n < no; ++n)
```

```
        {
        Append(*aptr);
        ++aptr;
        }
    }
```

The destructor call *Erase* to delete all elements.

```
template <class T>
    inline DList<T>::~DList()
        {
        Erase();
        }
```

Assignment and Conversions

The assignment operator destroys the contents of an existing *DList* with a deep copy of another list.

```
template <class T>
    void DList<T>::operator =
        (
        const DList<T> & dlst
        )
        {
        Erase();
        DeepCopy(dlst);
        }
```

I supply a conversion to pointer function, which returns the address of a dynamically-allocated array holding copies of the elements in a *DList*. It is the calling routine's responsibility to delete the array pointer when it is no longer required.

```
template <class T>
    DList<T>::operator T * ()
        {
        if (Count == 0)
```

```
        return NULL;

    T * result = new T [Count];

    if (result == NULL)
        throw ContainerEx(CX_ARRAYALLOC);

    Node * temp = Head;
    T    * aptr = result;

    while (temp != NULL)
        {
        *aptr = temp->Data;
        ++aptr;
        temp = temp->Next;
        }

    // note: caller must delete this array!
    return result;
    }
```

Appending

DList, like *SList*, allows the addition of new elements to the tail of the list. An appended element becomes the new tail.

```
template <class T>
    void DList<T>::Append
        (
        const T & item
        )
        {
        Node * n = new Node;

        if (n == NULL)
            throw ContainerEx(CX_ALLOC);

        n->Data = item;
        n->Next = NULL;
        n->Prev = Tail;
```

```
    if (Count == 0)
        {
        Head = n;
        Tail = n;
        Work = n;
        }
    else
        {
        Tail->Next = n;
        Tail = n;
        }

    ++Count;
    }
```

I also defined an *Append* function to add an entire array of items to the tail of a *DList*. For each element in array, this append function calls the single-item *Append*.

```
template <class T>
    void DList<T>::Append
        (
        const T * array,
        size_t no
        )
        {
        if ((array == NULL) || (no == 0))
            throw ContainerEx(CX_NULLARRAY);

        const T * aptr = array;

        for (size_t n = 0; n < no; ++n)
            {
            Append(*aptr);
            ++aptr;
            }
        }
```

A complete *DList* can be appended with this function:

```
template <class T>
    void DList<T>::Append
```

```
(
const DList<T> & dlst
)
{
const Node * n = dlst.Head;

while (n != NULL)
    {
    Append(n->Data);
    n = n->Next;
    }
}
```

Deleting

Delete removes the element pointed to by *Work*; if *Work* is *NULL* or the list is empty, *Delete* throws an exception.

```
template <class T>
    void DList<T>::Delete()
        {
        if (Count == 0)
            throw ContainerEx(CX_NULL);

        if (Work == NULL)
            throw ContainerEx(CX_NOTREADY);

        if (Work == Head)
            {
            if (Work->Next == NULL)
                {
                delete Work;
                SetNull();
                }
            else
                {
                Head = Work->Next;
                Head->Prev = NULL;
                delete Work;
                Work = Head;
```

```
                }
            }
        else
            {
            if (Work == Tail)
                {
                if (Work->Prev == NULL)
                    {
                    delete Work;
                    SetNull();
                    }
                else
                    {
                    Tail = Work->Prev;
                    Tail->Next = NULL;
                    delete Work;
                    Work = Tail;
                    }
                }
            else
                {
                Node * n = Work->Next;
                Work->Prev->Next = Work->Next;
                Work->Next->Prev = Work->Prev;
                delete Work;
                Work = n;
                }
            }

        —Count;
        }
```

Delete must be careful to recognize when it is deleting the head or tail element and when it is destroying the only node in the list. After deletion, *Work* will be set to point to the node following the one that was removed.

Inserting

The insert functions create a new node or nodes based on the setting of *Work*; if *Work* is *NULL*, they throw an exception. *InsertBefore* places a new element before *Work*, while *InsertAfter* stores new information after *Work*.

```
template <class T>
    void DList<T>::InsertBefore
        (
        const T & item
        )
        {
        if (Count == 0)
            throw ContainerEx(CX_NULL);

        if (Work == NULL)
            throw ContainerEx(CX_NOTREADY);

        Node * newnode = new Node;

        if (newnode == NULL)
            throw ContainerEx(CX_ALLOC);

        newnode->Data = item;

        if (Work == Head)
            {
            newnode->Next = Head;
            newnode->Prev = NULL;
            Head->Prev    = newnode;
            Head          = newnode;
            }
        else
            {
            Work->Prev->Next = newnode;
            newnode->Prev    = Work->Prev;
            newnode->Next    = Work;
            Work->Prev       = newnode;
            }

        ++Count;
        }

template <class T>
    void DList<T>::InsertAfter
        (
        const T & item
        )
        {
```

```
if (Count == 0)
    throw ContainerEx(CX_NULL);

if (Work == NULL)
    throw ContainerEx(CX_NOTREADY);

Node * newnode = new Node;

if (newnode == NULL)
    throw ContainerEx(CX_ALLOC);

newnode->Data = item;

if (Work == Tail)
    {
    newnode->Next = NULL;
    newnode->Prev = Tail;
    Tail->Next    = newnode;
    Tail          = newnode;
    }
else
    {
    Work->Next->Prev = newnode;
    newnode->Next    = Work->Next;
    newnode->Prev    = Work;
    Work->Next       = newnode;
    }

++Count;
}
```

I also implemented versions of *InsertBefore* and *InsertAfter* for adding arrays of data to a *DList*.

```
template <class T>
    void DList<T>::InsertBefore
        (
        const T * array,
        size_t no
        )
        {
        for (size_t n = 0; n < no; ++n)
```

```
            InsertBefore(array[n]);
        }

template <class T>
    void DList<T>::InsertAfter
        (
        const T * array,
        size_t no
        )
        {
        // insert in reverse order, so they're stored in order
        for (size_t n = no; n > 0; -n)
            InsertAfter(array[n-1]);
        }
```

And these two functions insert one *DList* into another.

```
template <class T>
    void DList<T>::InsertBefore
        (
        const DList<T> & dlst
        )
        {
        const Node * n = dlst.Head;

        while (n != NULL)
            {
            InsertBefore(n->Data);
            n = n->Next;
            }
        }

template <class T>
    void DList<T>::InsertAfter
        (
        const DList<T> & dlst
        )
        {
        const Node * n = dlst.Tail;

        while (n != NULL)
            {
```

```
        InsertAfter(n->Data);
        n = n->Prev;
        }
    }
```

Retrieving Data

Work begins set to *NULL*; various member functions and manipulations of the list move or set *Work*'s value. All of these functions report an exception is Work is NULL of the list is empty.

Work can be set to either the head or tail of the list by the respective *ToHead* and *ToTail* functions.

```
template <class T>
    inline void DList<T>::ToHead()
        {
        Work = Head;
        }

template <class T>
    inline void DList<T>::ToTail()
        {
        Work = Tail;
        }
```

Once *Work* points to an element, it can be moved through the list, forward and backward, by the *ToNext* and *ToPrev* functions.

```
template <class T>
    Boolean DList<T>::ToNext()
        {
        if (Count == 0)
            throw ContainerEx(CX_NULL);

        if (Work == NULL)
            throw ContainerEx(CX_NOTREADY);

        if (Work == Tail)
```

```
            {
            if (Circular)
                Work = Head;
            else
                return BOOL_FALSE;
            }
        else
            Work = Work->Next;

        return BOOL_TRUE;
        }
```

AtHead and *AtTail* return a boolean value indicating if Work points to the specified end of the list.

```
template <class T>
    inline Boolean DList<T>::AtHead()
        {
        if (Work == Head)
            return BOOL_TRUE;
        else
            return BOOL_FALSE;
        }

template <class T>
    inline Boolean DList<T>::AtTail()
        {
        if (Work == Tail)
            return BOOL_TRUE;
        else
            return BOOL_FALSE;
        }
```

Two functions allow non-destructive retrieval of the value stored in the element pointed to by *Work*. Both *Get* and *operator* * have identical implementations; only their headers define their difference. *Get* returns a copy of an element's value, while *operator* * returns a reference to the data.

```
template <class T>
    T DList<T>::Get()
        {
```

```
        if (Count == 0)
            throw ContainerEx(CX_NULL);

        if (Work == NULL)
            throw ContainerEx(CX_NOTREADY);

        return Work->Data;
        }

// directly reference current item
template <class T>
    T & DList<T>::operator * ()
        {
        if (Count == 0)
            throw ContainerEx(CX_NULL);

        if (Work == NULL)
            throw ContainerEx(CX_NOTREADY);

        return Work->Data;
        }
```

Interrogation

Three functions retrieve various parameters of a *DList*:

```
template <class T>
    inline size_t DList<T>::GetCount()
        {
        return Count;
        }

template <class T>
    inline Boolean DList<T>::IsShallow()
        {
        return Shallow;
        }

template <class T>
    inline Boolean DList<T>::IsCircular()
```

```
    {
    return Circular;
    }
```

Exceptions

The *Dictionary* class can throw a couple of different exceptions, as
defined by these types.

```
enum DictError
    {
    DX_NULL,
    DX_NOTFOUND
    };

class DictEx : public ExceptionBase
    {
    public:
        DictEx
            (
            DictError err
            )
            {
            Error = err;
            }

        DictError WhatsWrong()
            {
            return Error;
            }

        void Explain
            (
            DiagOutput & out
            );

    private:
        DictError Error;
    };
```

Here is the implementation of the *Explain* function for *DictEx*.

```
void DictEx::Explain(DiagOutput & out)
    {
    switch (Error)
        {
        case DX_NULL:
            out.DisplayMsg("Attempt to use empty dictionary",
                        DIAG_WARNING);
            break;
        case DX_NOTFOUND:
            out.DisplayMsg("Dictionary record not found",
                        DIAG_WARNING);
            break;
        default:
            out.DisplayMsg("Unexpected dictionary exception",
                        DIAG_FATAL);
        }
    }
```

CLASS TEMPLATE DEFINITION

The template definition takes two type arguments and one parameter argument, defining, respectively, the key type (*K*), data type (*D*), and number of buckets (*NumBuck*) that make up the hash table.

```
template <class K, class D, size_t NumBuck>
    class Dictionary
        {
        public:
            Dictionary();

            Dictionary
                (
                const Dictionary<K,D,NumBuck> & ht
                );

            ~Dictionary();
```

```
    void operator =
        (
        const Dictionary<K,D,NumBuck> & ht
        );

    void Insert
        (
        const K & kx,
        const D & dx
        );

    Boolean Delete
        (
        const K & kx
        );

    Boolean Holds
        (
        const K & kx
        );

    D LookUp
        (
        const K & kx
        );

    void Traverse
        (
        void (* func)(const K & kx,const D & dx)
        );

    size_t GetCount();
    size_t GetNumBuck();

    void Erase();

protected:
    struct Entry
        {
        K Key;
        D Data;
        };
```

```
size_t      Count;
DList<Entry> Bucket[NumBuck];

void DeepCopy
    (
    const Dictionary<K,D,NumBuck> & ht
    );
};
```

Dictionary is not a terribly complicated class; it defines a few constructors and the required basic operations, relying on an array of *Dlist* objects to handle much of the work.

Data and Structure Elements

The most important data element is *Bucket*, an array of *Dlist<Entry>* objects. *Entry* is a simple structure that contains both a key and its associated information.

Because the number of buckets is known at compile time through the template argument *NumBuck*, the *Bucket* array is allocated statically rather than dynamically. *Dictionary* itself does not call *new* at any time; only the individual *Buckets* allocate dynamic memory, as they append new *Entry* objects to *Dlists*.

The only other data element is *Count*, which holds the number of entries stored in a *Dictionary*.

Utility Functions

As with most of my classes, *Dictionary* implements some common tasks as utility functions. The copy constructor and assignment operator call *DeepCopy* to duplicate an existing *Dictionary*, while the destructor and the assignment operator use *Erase* to eliminate all existing entries.

```
template <class K, class D, size_t NumBuck>
    void Dictionary<K,D,NumBuck>::DeepCopy
        (
```

```
        const Dictionary<K,D,NumBuck> & ht
        )
        {
        Count = ht.Count;

        for (size_t n = 0; n < NumBuck; ++n)
            Bucket[n] = ht.Bucket[n];
        }

template <class K, class D, size_t NumBuck>
    void Dictionary<K,D,NumBuck>::Erase()
        {
        Count = 0;

        for (size_t n = 0; n < NumBuck; ++n)
            Bucket[n].Erase();
        }
```

Constructors and Destructors

Constructing a *Dictionary* isn't very complicated; because the *Dlist* constructor is automatically called for each element in *Bucket*, the primary constructor's only explicit job is to set *Count* to *0*. The *copy* constructor, the assignment operator, and the destructor all rely on the utility functions to perform their tasks.

```
template <class K, class D, size_t NumBuck>
    inline Dictionary<K,D,NumBuck>::Dictionary()
        {
        Count = 0;
        }

template <class K, class D, size_t NumBuck>
    inline Dictionary<K,D,NumBuck>::Dictionary
        (
        const Dictionary<K,D,NumBuck> & dict
        )
        {
        DeepCopy(dict);
        }
```

```
template <class K, class D, size_t NumBuck>
    inline Dictionary<K,D,NumBuck>::~Dictionary()
        {
        Erase();
        }

template <class K, class D, size_t NumBuck>
    inline void Dictionary<K,D,NumBuck>::operator =
        (
        const Dictionary<K,D,NumBuck> & dict
        )
        {
        Erase();
        DeepCopy(dict);
        }
```

Operations

The simplest operation is inserting a new key/data pair into a *Dictionary* via the *Insert* function. It creates an *Entry* structure and then calls the *Append* function for a *Bucket Dlist*. The bucket is chosen by calling the *DictHash* function for the key.

```
template <class K, class D, size_t NumBuck>
    void Dictionary<K,D,NumBuck>::Insert
        (
        const K & kx,
        const D & dx
        )
        {
        Entry e;

        e.Key  = kx;
        e.Data = dx;

        Bucket[DictHash(kx,NumBuck)].Append(e);

        ++Count;
        }
```

The *Delete* function searches a hash-selected bucket for an entry matching the given key; a successful search results in the removal of the key and its data and a return value of *BOOL_TRUE*. If the key isn't found, *Delete* returns *BOOL_FALSE*.

```
template <class K, class D, size_t NumBuck>
    Boolean Dictionary<K,D,NumBuck>::Delete(const K & kx)
        {
        if (Count == 0)
            throw DictEx(DX_NULL);

        size_t bno = DictHash(kx,NumBuck);

        if (Bucket[bno].GetCount() != 0)
            {
            Bucket[bno].ToHead();

            do  {
                if (kx == (*Bucket[bno]).Key)
                    {
                    Bucket[bno].Delete();
                    —Count;
                    return BOOL_TRUE;
                    }
                }
                while (Bucket[bno].ToNext());
            }

        return BOOL_FALSE;
        }
```

Holds and *Lookup* both search for a key using the same technique as *Delete*. *Holds* simply returns a true/false value based on the presence of the key. *Lookup* retrieves the data associated with the search key or throws an exception if the key isn't found.

```
template <class K, class D, size_t NumBuck>
    Boolean Dictionary<K,D,NumBuck>::Holds(const K & kx)
        {
        if (Count != 0)
```

```
            {
            size_t bno = DictHash(kx,NumBuck);

            if (Bucket[bno].GetCount() != 0)
                {
                Bucket[bno].ToHead();

                do  {
                    if (kx == (*Bucket[bno]).Key)
                        return BOOL_TRUE;
                    }
                    while (Bucket[bno].ToNext());
                }
            }

        return BOOL_FALSE;
        }

template <class K, class D, size_t NumBuck>
    D Dictionary<K,D,NumBuck>::LookUp(const K & kx)
        {
        if (Count == 0)
            throw DictEx(DX_NULL);

        size_t bno = DictHash(kx,NumBuck);

        if (Bucket[bno].GetCount() != 0)
            {
            Bucket[bno].ToHead();

            do  {
                if (kx == (*Bucket[bno]).Key)
                    return (*Bucket[bno]).Data;
                }
                while (Bucket[bno].ToNext());
            }

        throw DictEx(DX_NOTFOUND);
        }
```

None of these functions worries about duplicate keys. If you insert a
duplicate key, it is appended to the appropriate bucket. When you search

for a key, the first key stored in a bucket is found; when you delete a key, the first key found is removed.

Miscellaneous Functions

Traverse calls a given function for each entry in the *Dictionary*.

```
template <class K, class D, size_t NumBuck>
    void Dictionary<K,D,NumBuck>::Traverse
        (
        void (* func)(const K & kx,const D & dx)
        )
        {
        if (Count == 0)
            throw DictEx(DX_NULL);

        for (size_t n = 0; n < NumBuck; ++n)
            {
            if (Bucket[n].GetCount() != 0)
                {
                Bucket[n].ToHead();

                do  {
                    func((*Bucket[n]).Key,(*Bucket[n]).Data);
                    }
                while (Bucket[n].ToNext());
                }
            }
        }
```

The interrogation functions *GetCount* and *GetNumBuck* return, respectively, the number of entries and the number of buckets in a *Dictionary*.

```
template <class K, class D, size_t NumBuck>
    inline size_t Dictionary<K,D,NumBuck>::GetCount()
        {
        return Count;
        }

template <class K, class D, size_t NumBuck>
```

```
inline size_t Dictionary<K,D,NumBuck>::GetNumBuck()
    {
    return NumBuck;
    }
```

APPLICATION

You'll find the *Dictionary* template and the definition of its exception types in the file **dict.h** and the implementation of its exception functions in **dict.cpp**. Look at the **tblist.cpp** module for code that exercises the *Dictionary*.

CONCLUSION

Dictionary is an excellent example of a general tool built with another general tool. And you'll see how useful *Dictionary* is when I present advanced algorithms later in this book.

I presented an implementation of hash tables in the second edition my book *C++ Components and Algorithms*. That version of hashing is focused on storing information in external files and is part of a complex library of file-management functions. *Dictionary* is very different from *HashTable*; the two designs are focused on efficient lookup of information in different environments.

CHAPTER 6

SETS

A *set* is a collection of distinguishable items; sets can be compared to see which members they share or what their differences are. Some programming languages, such as Pascal and Modula-2, provide built-in support for sets of integer values. This chapter shows how I've used templates to implement sets in C++.

Set Theory 101

Sometime during elementary or high school you probably encountered set theory. The definitions and rules for sets are relatively simple, as mathematical principles go. Within a set, each item is unique; an item may belong to any number of different sets, but no set holds two of the same element. To describe a set, list its members; if a set has no members, it is called an *empty set*. The number of elements in a set is its *cardinality*.

If all the members of set A are members of set B, you can refer to set A as a *subset* of B—and if B has more members than its subset A, A is termed a *proper subset* of B. Two sets without any common members are said to be *disjoint*. When two sets have exactly the same elements, they are equal, and each is a subset of the other. Other comparisons, such as greater than or less than, have no application for sets.

Operations on sets include union, intersection, and difference. The *union* of sets A and B is a new set containing all members of A and B. For example, if set A = {1, 2, 3, 4} and set B = {0, 2, 4, 6}, their union creates a set C = {0, 1, 2, 3, 4, 6}. The *intersection* of sets A and B includes elements that are members of both A and B: {2, 4}. The *difference* of A and B returns a set containing all members of A that are not members of B. Using sets A and B above, the difference set would be {1, 3}.

Implementation Considerations

In mathematics—and computers—sets hold numbers. It's possible to have sets of people or sets of silverware, but these sets are different from numeric sets. Computers act on numbers, and numeric sets are a natural programming device. In the next chapter, I'll talk about ways to implement nonnumeric sets using the templates I'll define.

In each set, an element is either present or not present. That's a binary decision, leading to a binary implementation. Modula-2 and Pascal implement their built-in set support in this fashion, using a binary string of bits to represent set members' status.

Here's how it works. Each bit represents the presence of an integer in the set; for example, if 4 is a member of a set, the fourth bit will be turned on. This 8-bit (one-byte) set contains the integers 1, 2, 4, and 7:

```
bit  7 6 5 4 3 2 1 0
- - - - - - - - - - - - - - - - - - -
set: 0 1 0 0 1 0 1 1
```

Most computers handle bits 16, 32, or 64 bits at a time. To make sets having more members, I'll be using an array of *unsigned int* values. In theory, a C++ compiler automatically defines an *int* to be the most efficient type for the environment. In 16-bit DOS and Windows, for example, an *int* is 16 bits; under 32-bit UNIX or Windows, an *int* contains 32 bits. By using *unsigned int*, I guarantee that my set class's bitwise operations will be as efficient as possible.

The size of the bit array depends on the number of bits in an *unsigned int* and on the range of the set's elements. For example, in a 16-bit environment, a set of *char* will generate a bit array of 16 *unsigned ints*, each containing 16 bits, for a total of 256 bits. For a 16-bit *unsigned short* set in a 32-bit *int* environment, the program will allocate a bit array with 2048 elements.

I seldom need sets for all 65,536 *unsigned short* values; I might, for example, be marking a set of years from 1950 through 2010, where only 61 bits will represent my set. With that in mind, I designed my set template to allow the specification of a range of values. I'll explain more about how this is done when we look at the function implementations.

Now that I've defined my internal representation of sets, I need to design operation functions. In a standard math text, set operations use a variety of operator symbols that C++ doesn't make available. The next task, then, is to decide on a correspondence between set operators and C++ operators or function names. Table 6.1 shows my choices.

TABLE 6.1 SET OPERATORS

OPERATION	STANDARD SYMBOL	C++ FUNCTION OR SYMBOL
is member	$\in$	[] (index operator)
is not member	$\notin$	[] (index operator)
union	$\cup$	& (bitwise AND)
intersection	$\cap$		(bitwise OR)
difference	$-$	- (substraction)
exclusive union	n/a	^ (exclusive OR)
proper subset	$\supseteq$ or $\subseteq$	SubsetOf
subset	$\supset$ or $\subset$	ProperSubsetOf
disjoint	$\not\subset$	Disjoint
equal	$=$	==
not equal	$\neq$	!=
cardinality	n/a	Cardinality
check for empty set	n/a	IsEmpty

In my implementation, an indexing ([]) operator function will return zero if a given value is not a member, and nonzero if it is. The union and intersection operations are equivalent to *bitwise AND* and *OR* operations, so I represent them with binary implementations of the C++ & and | operators. The difference operator is a binary - operator, and the equality operators naturally fit with C++'s == and != operators. For subset and disjoint operations, I created named functions because no C++ operators fit the bill.

The "exclusive union" operation is something I added, even though I haven't found it in any texts; it creates a new set containing members of A that are not in B and members of B that are not in A. This works like the *bitwise exclusive OR*, and by including it I provide a suite of set operations that correlate nicely with C++'s bitwise operations.

Other set operations include the ability to include and exclude operators, and various utility functions described later.

EXCEPTIONS

A *Set* class needs an exception type to be thrown when a set fails to allocate memory, when an attempt is made to compare incompatible sets, or when a program tries to include or exclude a member that is out of a specified range. Following the pattern set in earlier chapters, I derived the following enumerated type and exception class:

```
enum SetEx_Error
    {
    SX_ALLOC,
    SX_MISMATCH,
    SX_BOUNDS
    };

class SetEx : public ExceptionBase
    {
    public:
        SetEx
            (
            SetEx_Error err
            )
            {
            Error = err;
            }

        virtual void Explain(DiagOutput & diag);

    private:
        SetEx_Error Error;
    };

#endif
```

The implementation of the *Explain* function is as follows:

```
void SetEx::Explain(DiagOutput & diag)
    {
    switch (Error)
        {
        case SX_ALLOC:
            diag.DisplayMsg("Set: Memory allocation failure",
                            DIAG_ERROR);
            break;
        case SX_MISMATCH:
            diag.DisplayMsg("Set: Mismatched sets in operation",
                            DIAG_WARNING);
            break;
        case SX_BOUNDS:
            diag.DisplayMsg("Set: Out-of-bounds bit operation",
                            DIAG_WARNING);
        }
    }
```

THE SET CLASS TEMPLATE

The *Set* class template takes a single type parameter that declares the type of the set's integer elements. The template allows the creation of sets for *longs*, *ints*, *shorts*, *chars*, and their unsigned equivalents. Defining a *Set<float>* generates a compile-time error, because the *Set* template uses bitwise operators on the element type.

The basic class definition looks like this:

```
template <class T>
    class Set
        {
        public:
            // constructors
            Set();

            Set
                (
                T max,
```

```
    T min
    );

Set
    (
    const Set<T> & s
    );

Set
    (
    const T * array,
    size_t no
    );

// destructor
virtual ~Set();

// assignment operator
void operator =
    (
    const Set<T> & s
    );

// member status
unsigned int operator []
    (
    T x
    )
    const;

// include and exclude members
void Incl
    (
    T x
    );

void Incl
    (
    const T * array,
    size_t no
    );
```

```
void Excl
    (
    T x
    );

void Excl
    (
    const T * array,
    size_t no
    );

// turn all members on or off
void AllOn();
void AllOff();

// union operators
Set<T> operator |
    (
    const Set<T> & s
    )
    const;

void operator |=
    (
    const Set<T> & s
    );

// intersection operators
Set<T> operator &
    (
    const Set<T> & s
    )
    const;

void operator &=
    (
    const Set<T> & s
    );

// exclusive or operator
Set<T> operator ^
```

```
            (
            const Set<T> & s
            )
            const;

void operator ^=
            (
            const Set<T> & s
            );

// difference operator
Set<T> operator -
            (
            const Set<T> & s
            )
            const;

void operator -=
            (
            const Set<T> & s
            );

// complement operator
Set<T> operator ~ ();

// comparison operator
Boolean operator ==
            (
            const Set<T> & s
            )
            const;

Boolean operator !=
            (
            const Set<T> & s
            )
            const;

Boolean Disjoint
            (
            const Set<T> & s
```

```
        )
        const;

    Boolean SubsetOf
        (
        const Set<T> & s
        )
        const;

    Boolean ProperSubsetOf
        (
        const Set<T> & s
        )
        const;

    Boolean IsNull();

    size_t Cardinality();

    friend ostream & operator <<
        (
        ostream & os,
        const Set<T> & s
        );

private:
    Boolean Bounded;    // is this set bounded?
    T MinValue;         // minimum bit value
    T MaxValue;         // maximum bit value
    T Offset;           // offset first bit when bounded
    size_t Alloc;       // number of elements in Data
    size_t Bytes;       // number of bytes in Data
    size_t Count;       // number of elements in set
    unsigned int * Data;// array of set bits

    // internal utility functions
    void Calculate();

    void Allocate();

    void Copy
        (
```

```
            const Set<T> & s
            );

     void Destroy();

       static void CalcIdxOff
          (
          T x,
          size_t & idx,
          unsigned int & off
          );
     };
```

I'll break down *Set's* implementation by categories, beginning with the data elements.

Data Elements

The *Bounded* member is a Boolean flag. When *Bounded* is true, a *Set* knows that it has a high and low bounds on element values. *Offset* is the difference between *MinValue* and *MaxValue*, routines use this precalculated value when calculating bit offsets. Those bounds are defined by the *MinValue* and *MaxValue* data members. If *Bounded* is false, the *Set* ignores *MinValue*, *MaxValue*, and *Offset*. Most operations on a set will be faster if it isn't bounded; on the other hand, an unbounded set may use memory far in excess of a program's needs.

Alloc contains the size of the dynamically allocated *Data* array. *Data* is the bit array of member flags. *Bytes* holds the number of bytes in *Data*, which is useful primarily in the routines *AllOn* and *AllOff*, which include or exclude all elements. The last data member, *Count*, is the number of elements in the set.

Private Utility Functions

Calculate determines how many elements need to be allocated in the *Data* array. It sets values for *Bytes* and *Alloc* based on the number of bits in a byte (*CHAR_BIT*), the number of bits in the element types *T*, and the number of bytes in an *unsigned int.* Also, if the *Set* is *Bounded, Calculate* subtracts the minimum and maximum values to obtain *Offset.*

```
template <class T>
    inline void Set<T>::Calculate()
        {
        unsigned long bits;

        if (Bounded)
            {
            Offset = MinValue;
            bits = MaxValue - MinValue + CHAR_BIT;
            }
        else
            {
            bits = 1ul << (sizeof(T) * CHAR_BIT);
            }

        Bytes = (size_t)(bits  / (unsigned long)CHAR_BIT);

        if (Bytes <= sizeof(unsigned int))
            Alloc = 1;
        else
            Alloc = Bytes / sizeof(unsigned int);
        }
```

Allocate calls *new* to create the *Data* array and then sets all bits to zero via *AllOff.* Thus, every new *Set* is empty. If the call to *new* fails, *Allocate* throws an exception.

```
template <class T>
    inline void Set<T>::Allocate()
        {
        Data = new unsigned int [Alloc];

        if (Data == NULL)
            throw SetEx(SX_ALLOC);

        AllOff();
        }
```

The destructor and assignment operator use *Destroy* to free the *Data* array.

```
template <class T>
    inline void Set<T>::Destroy()
        {
        delete [] Data;
        Count = 0;
        }
```

Both the copy constructor and the assignment operator call *Copy* to do the bulk of their work. *Copy* assumes that *Destroy* has been called to delete any memory allocated to *Data*.

```
template <class T>
    void Set<T>::Copy
        (
        const Set<T> & s
        )
        {
        Bounded  = s.Bounded;
        MinValue = s.MinValue;
        MaxValue = s.MaxValue;
        Offset   = s.Offset;
        Bytes    = s.Bytes;
        Alloc    = s.Alloc;

        Allocate();

        Count    = s.Count;

        for (size_t n = 0; n < Alloc; ++n)
            Data[n] = s.Data[n];
        }
```

The last private function is *CalcIdxOff*, a static function that calculates the *Data* array index and a mask for the bit representing a given element. The [] operator, *Incl*, and *Excl* functions call *CalcIdxOff*.

```
template <class T>
    inline void Set<T>::CalcIdxOff
        (
        T x,
        size_t & idx,
        unsigned int & off
        )
        {
        idx = x / T(sizeof(unsigned int) * CHAR_BIT);

        off = 1u << (unsigned int)((x - (idx *
                        sizeof(unsigned int) * CHAR_BIT)));
        }
```

The calculations in *CalcIdxOff* aren't quite as messy as they look. The numerous casts complicate the syntax, but they prevent the nasty promotion problems that I've encountered with some compilers. When in doubt, always explicitly cast values, even if you don't think it's necessary.

Constructors and Destructors

The preceding utility functions do most of the common work, so the constructors, the destructor, and the assignment operator are simple to implement.

```
template <class T>
    inline Set<T>::Set()
        {
        Bounded  = BOOL_FALSE;

        Calculate();
        Allocate();
        }

template <class T>
    Set<T>::Set
        (
        T max,
        T min
        )
```

```
        {
        // swap min and max, if necessary
        if (max < min)
            {
            T temp = max;
            max = min;
            min = temp;
            }

        Bounded  = BOOL_TRUE;
        MinValue = min;
        MaxValue = max;

        Calculate();
        Allocate();
        }

template <class T>
    inline Set<T>::Set
        (
        const Set<T> & s
        )
        {
        Copy(s);
        }

template <class T>
    inline Set<T>::Set
        (
        const T * array,
        size_t no
        )
        {
        Bounded  = BOOL_FALSE;

        Calculate();
        Allocate();
        Incl(array,no);
        }

template <class T>
    Set<T>::~Set()
        {
```

```
        Destroy();
        }

template <class T>
    inline void Set<T>::operator =
        (
        const Set<T> & s
        )
        {
        Destroy();
        Copy(s);
        }
```

The default constructor creates an empty, unbounded array. By providing a minimum and maximum value, you define a bounded set using the second constructor. The third constructor creates an unbounded set that contains initial members defined by the array parameter. The copy constructor, destructor, and assignment operator should be self-explanatory.

Member Operations

I overloaded the [] operator to determine whether a given value is a member of a set. This function is very similar to the *Excl(T x)* and *Incl(T x)* functions, because they basically do the same thing: find the the appropriate bit in *Data*, and do something with it.

```
template <class T>
    unsigned int Set<T>::operator []
        (
        T x
        )
        const
        {
        if (Bounded)
            {
            if ((x <= MaxValue) && (x >= MinValue))
                x = (T)(x - Offset);
            else
                throw SetEx(SX_BOUNDS);
```

```
            }

        size_t idx;
        unsigned int off;

        CalcIdxOff(x,idx,off);

        return Data[idx] & off;
        }

template <class T>
    void Set<T>::Incl
        (
        T x
        )
        {
        if (Bounded)
            {
            if ((x <= MaxValue) && (x >= MinValue))
                x = (T)(x - Offset);
            else
                throw SetEx(SX_BOUNDS);
            }

        size_t idx;
        unsigned int off;

        CalcIdxOff(x,idx,off);

        if (!(Data[idx] & off))
            {
            ++Count;
            Data[idx] |= off;
            }
        }

template <class T>
    void Set<T>::Excl
        (
        T x
        )
        {
        if (Bounded)
```

```
        {
        if ((x <= MaxValue) && (x >= MinValue))
            x = (T)(x - Offset);
        else
            throw SetEx(SX_BOUNDS);
        }

    size_t idx;
    unsigned int off;

    CalcIdxOff(x,idx,off);

    if (Data[idx] & off)
        {
        —Count;
        Data[idx] &= ~off;
        }
    }
```

The *operator []* function simply returns the appropriate *unsigned int* in *Data* or'd with a bitmask (*off*) created by *CalcIdxOff*. The return value will be nonzero if the requested element is included, and zero if it is not included. Note that the nonzero value will be an *unsigned int* with any of its bits set; don't assume that it returns 1 when the value is an element!

I also allow arrays of values to be included and excluded in a *Set* via these overloads of *Incl* and *Excl*:

```
template <class T>
    void Set<T>::Incl
        (
        const T * array,
        size_t no
        )
        {
        for (size_t i = 0; i < no; ++i)
            Incl(array[i]);
        }

template <class T>
    void Set<T>::Excl
```

```
(
const T * array,
size_t no
)
{
for (size_t i = 0; i < no; ++i)
    Excl(array[i]);
}
```

As with the array-based constructor, these functions simply loop through the array, calling the single-item versions of *Incl* and *Excl* as appropriate.

It's sometimes handy to remove all elements from a set; in some circumstances, I've wanted to start with a set that contains all possible elements. To do that, I created the *AllOn* and *AllOff* functions, which use *memset* to turn off or on all the bits in the *Data* array.

```
template <class T>
    inline void Set<T>::AllOn()
        {
        memset(Data,'\xff',Bytes);

        if (Bounded)
            Count = size_t(MaxValue - MinValue + 1);
        else
            Count = size_t((1ul << (sizeof(T) * CHAR_BIT)) - 1);
        }

template <class T>
    inline void Set<T>::AllOff()
        {
        memset(Data,0,Bytes);

        Count = 0;
        }
```

Although *AllOff* can simply set *Count* to zero, *AllOn* must do a bit more work to find the total number of set elements. For a bounded set, *Count* is simply the *Offset* value plus one. For complete sets, *AllOn* calculates *Count* based on the number of bits in the element type *T*.

Set Operations

As explained previously, I use the C++ | operator for generating the union of two sets.

```
template <class T>
    Set<T> Set<T>::operator |
        (
        const Set<T> & s
        )
        const
        {
        if (Alloc != s.Alloc)
            throw SetEx(SX_MISMATCH);

        Set<T> result(*this);

        for (size_t n = 0; n < Alloc; ++n)
            result.Data[n] |= s.Data[n];

        return result;
        }
```

The shorthand |= operator is slightly simpler.

```
template <class T>
    void Set<T>::operator |=
        (
        const Set<T> & s
        )
        {
        if (Alloc != s.Alloc)
            throw SetEx(SX_MISMATCH);

        for (size_t n = 0; n < Alloc; ++n)
                Data[n] |= s.Data[n];
        }
```

The operators for intersection (& and &=), difference (- and -=), and exclusive union (-and -=) look nearly the same as the union implementations; the only change is in the operation performed in the *for* loop.

```
template <class T>
    Set<T> Set<T>::operator &
        (
        const Set<T> & s
        )
        const
        {
        if (Alloc != s.Alloc)
            throw SetEx(SX_MISMATCH);

        Set<T> result(*this);

        for (size_t n = 0; n < Alloc; ++n)
            result.Data[n] &= s.Data[n];

        return result;
        }

template <class T>
    void Set<T>::operator &=
        (
        const Set<T> & s
        )
        {
        if (Alloc != s.Alloc)
            throw SetEx(SX_MISMATCH);

        for (size_t n = 0; n < Alloc; ++n)
            Data[n] &= s.Data[n];
        }

template <class T>
    Set<T> Set<T>::operator ^
        (
        const Set<T> & s
        )
        const
        {
        if (Alloc != s.Alloc)
            throw SetEx(SX_MISMATCH);

        Set<T> result(*this);

        for (size_t n = 0; n < Alloc; ++n)
```

```
            result.Data[n] ^= s.Data[n];

        return result;
        }

template <class T>
    void Set<T>::operator ^=
        (
        const Set<T> & s
        )
        {
        if (Alloc != s.Alloc)
            throw SetEx(SX_MISMATCH);

        for (size_t n = 0; n < Alloc; ++n)
            Data[n] ^= s.Data[n];
        }

template <class T>
    Set<T> Set<T>::operator -
        (
        const Set<T> & s
        )
        const
        {
        if (Alloc != s.Alloc)
            throw SetEx(SX_MISMATCH);

        Set<T> result(*this);

        for (size_t n = 0; n < Alloc; ++n)
            result.Data[n] &= ~s.Data[n];

        return result;
        }

template <class T>
    void Set<T>::operator -=
        (
        const Set<T> & s
        )
        {
        if (Alloc != s.Alloc)
```

```
        throw SetEx(SX_MISMATCH);

    for (size_t n = 0; n < Alloc; ++n)
        Data[n] &= ~s.Data[n];
    }
```

One frustration I have with C++ is monotonous functions such as these. Unfortunately, the language doesn't provide any way of creating a template function in which you can provide tokens other than data types or values. The Set class would have better integrity if I could provide an "operator" token to a single function template.

On the other hand, C++ is criticized in some circles for having too many features. I expect that power programmers will never be satisfied, while compiler writers will scowl about too much complexity in the language.

But I digress. One last operator remains to be presented: complement. The ~ operator returns the opposite of a set; every element in the original set is excluded, and any missing elements are included. This is similar to the function of the *bitwise* ~ operator.

```
template <class T>
    Set<T> Set<T>::operator ~ ()
        {
        Set<T> result(*this);

        for (size_t n = 0; n < Alloc; ++n)
            result.Data[n] = ~result.Data[n];

        return result;
        }
```

Comparisons and Subsets

Determining set equality and inequality involves looping through the *Data* array and comparing elements until the appropriate condition is met.

```
template <class T>
    Boolean Set<T>::operator ==
        (
        const Set<T> & s
        )
        const
        {
        if (Alloc != s.Alloc)
            throw SetEx(SX_MISMATCH);

        for (size_t n = 0; n < Alloc; ++n)
            {
            if (Data[n] != s.Data[n])
                return BOOL_FALSE;
            }

        return BOOL_TRUE;
        }

template <class T>
    Boolean Set<T>::operator !=
        (
        const Set<T> & s
        )
        const
        {
        if (Alloc != s.Alloc)
            throw SetEx(SX_MISMATCH);

        for (size_t n = 0; n < Alloc; ++n)
            {
            if (Data[n] != s.Data[n])
                return BOOL_TRUE;
            }

        return BOOL_FALSE;
        }
```

Unfortunately, these functions may do a lot of looping before determining the relationship of the sets. I've experimented with more efficient techniques of comparing sets and haven't found one yet.

The *Disjoint, SubsetOf,* and *ProperSubsetOf* functions are similar, although the subset function can include an early escape clause for comparisons of sets with different cardinalities. For example, *SubsetOf* knows that a set with nine elements can't be a subset of a set containing five elements.

```
template <class T>
    Boolean Set<T>::Disjoint
        (
        const Set<T> & s
        )
        const
        {
        if (Alloc != s.Alloc)
            throw SetEx(SX_MISMATCH);

        for (size_t n = 0; n < Alloc; ++n)
            {
            if (Data[n] & s.Data[n])
                return BOOL_FALSE;
            }

        return BOOL_TRUE;
        }

template <class T>
    Boolean Set<T>::SubsetOf
        (
        const Set<T> & s
        )
        const
        {
        if (Alloc != s.Alloc)
            throw SetEx(SX_MISMATCH);

        if (Count > s.Count)
            return BOOL_FALSE;

        for (size_t n = 0; n < Alloc; ++n)
            {
            if (Data[n] != (Data[n] & s.Data[n]))
```

```
                    return BOOL_FALSE;
        }

    return BOOL_TRUE;
    }

template <class T>
    Boolean Set<T>::ProperSubsetOf
        (
        const Set<T> & s
        )
        const
        {
        if (Alloc != s.Alloc)
            throw SetEx(SX_MISMATCH);

        if (s.Count <= Count)
            return BOOL_FALSE;

        for (size_t n = 0; n < Alloc; ++n)
            {
            if (Data[n] != (Data[n] & s.Data[n]))
                return BOOL_FALSE;
            }

        return BOOL_TRUE;
        }
```

Miscellaneous Functions

The *IsEmpty* function identifies an empty set.

```
template <class T>
    Boolean Set<T>::IsNull()
        {
        if (Count == 0)
            return BOOL_TRUE;
        else
            return BOOL_FALSE;
        }
```

Cardinality returns *Count.*

```
template <class T>
    inline size_t Set<T>::Cardinality()
        {
        return Count;
        }
```

I created a stream output function to display a set as a string of binary digits. The leftmost one is the status of the lowest possible element value, usually zero. As we move right, the element values increase.

```
template <class T>
    ostream & operator <<
        (
        ostream & os,
        const Set<T> & s
        )
        {
        size_t bits = sizeof(unsigned int) * CHAR_BIT;

        for (size_t i = 0; i < s.Alloc; ++i)
            {
            for (size_t n = 0; n < bits; ++n)
                os << ((s.Data[i] & (1 << n)) ? '1' : '0');

            os << ' ';
            }

        return os;
        }
```

APPLICATION

On the source disk, look for the *Set* template code in the header file *set.h*; the files *setx.h* and *setx.cpp* contain the exception types. In the TestBed application, look for the *tbset.cpp* module. Therein you'll find code that exercises the set class thoroughly.

CHARACTER SETS

When I first began creating set classes, I had a goal in mind: the ability to define sets of characters. The character set is an incredibly useful tool I employed in Pascal and Modula-2. When accepting input or parsing information, I use character sets to determine valid groups of characters—for example, when parsing a number, I often compare input characters against a set containing the 10 digits and a decimal point. You'll see this technique in Chapter 9.

Class Definition

My character set class enhances the capabilities it inherits from a *Set<char>*.

```
class CharSet : public Set<char>
    {
    public:
        CharSet();

        CharSet
            (
            const CharSet & cs
            );

        CharSet
            (
            const Set<char> & s
            );

        CharSet
            (
            const char * array,
            size_t no = UCHAR_MAX + 1
            );

        void operator =
            (
            const CharSet & cs
```

```
            );

    friend ostream & operator <<
        (
        ostream & os,
        const CharSet & s
        );
};
```

You might wonder why I didn't simply declare *CharSet* like this:

```
typedef Set<char> CharSet;
```

In my original design, I went the *typedef* route. Then I discovered a problem: *typedef*s are synonyms, not true types. When I tried defining a stream output function specifically for *CharSet*, the compiler complained, because *CharSet* wasn't a recognizable type for the purposes of function overloading. So I define *CharSet* as a wrapper class. A bit more code, yes—but now *CharSet* is a real type, not a pseudonym for *Set<char>*.

Functions

Because *CharSet* is a derived class, it must define its own constructors and assignment operator.

```
inline CharSet::CharSet()
    : Set<char>()
    {
    // inline call to base class constructor
    }

inline CharSet::CharSet
    (
    const CharSet & cs
    )
    : Set<char>(cs)
    {
    // inline call to base class constructor
    }
```

```
inline CharSet::CharSet
    (
    const Set<char> & s
    )
    : Set<char>(s)
    {
    // inline call to base class constructor
    }

inline CharSet::CharSet
    (
    const char * array,
    size_t no
    )
    : Set<char>
        (
        array,
        (no > UCHAR_MAX ? strlen(array) : no)
        )
    {
    // inline call to base class constructor
    }

inline void CharSet::operator =
    (
    const CharSet & cs
    )
    {
    // inline call base class operator
    Set<char>::operator = (cs);
    }
```

The only interesting note in the preceding code is the implementation of the base class call in the array-based constructor. Because character strings are generally NULL terminated, I defined a default value for the *no* parameter so that the standard library function *strlen* determines the number of characters in the array if no length is specified.

The output function supersedes the standard *Set* function. Rather than displaying a *charset* as a string of ones and zeros, the *Charset* << operator shows the actual characters in the set.

```
ostream & operator <<
    (
    ostream & os,
    const CharSet & s
    )
    {
    for (size_t n = 0; n < UCHAR_MAX; ++n)
        {
        if (s[char(n)])
            os << char(n);
        }

    return os;
    }
```

Predefined Character Classes

I created several static *CharSet* objects, reflecting sets of characters I use in my work.

```
const CharSet CS_Uppercase("ABCDEFGHIJKLMNOPQRSTUVWXYZ");
const CharSet CS_Lowercase("abcdefghijklmnopqrstuvwxyz");
const CharSet CS_Letters = CS_Uppercase | CS_Lowercase;
const CharSet CS_Numbers("0123456789");
const CharSet CS_AlphaNumeric = CS_Letters | CS_Numbers;
const CharSet CS_Punctuation(",.;:?!");
const CharSet CS_Symbol("~`@#$%^&*()_-+=|\\{}[]\"'/");
const CharSet CS_Whitespace(" \t");
const CharSet CS_Words = CS_AlphaNumeric | CS_Whitespace;
const CharSet CS_Operators("+-/*^");
const CharSet CS_Printable = CS_AlphaNumeric | CS_Punctuation
                                 | CS_Symbol | CS_Whitespace;
```

APPLICATION

Look for the *CharSet* definition and implementation in the files **charset.h** and **charset.cpp**. The **tbset.cpp** module does some rudimentary tests on *CharSets*.

CONCLUSION

As an alternative to a bit-based set, it is possible to create sets using dictionaries or binary trees. Using such tools allows a set to contain something other than numeric data—assuming that your sets don't get too big. If you store people's names, for instance, in a set, you'll need to use the dictionary or tree search operations when making comparisons, checking for intersection, or looking for subsets. Linked list searches, even the most efficient ones, take much longer than bit operations.

Sets containing numbers aren't as limited as you might think. Many numeric identifiers can be used to relate set members to more complex objects. In one application, I used integer employee IDs to assign various workers to different sets that represented responsibilities and clearances. Throughout my applications, I've found integer sets to be quite useful.

CHAPTER 7

OBJECT SETS AND FUZZY LOGIC

Any attempt at explaining fuzzy logic runs up against the term itself. *Fuzzy* invites thoughts of teddy bears and absent-minded professors; rarely is it associated with something as precise as a computer. If something is fuzzy, how can it be logical, too? This chapter tries to dispel some of that confusion with an example of fuzzy logic.

SOME BASIC THOUGHTS

In computer terms, *fuzzy* refers to the ability of a computer to mimic the way in which people make precise determinations based on incomplete information. For example, the following piece of text would be incomprehensible to most grammar-checking or spell-checking software:

```
Eye dnt unnurstand wat this sehs.
```

Encountering this text, a typical empirical algorithm will emit errors, seeing only spelling errors, deeming the text indecipherable. A person, however, can look at the same text and figure out that it says, "I don't understand what this says."

Here's another example. The statement "You should slow down and drive more carefully when it is dark and the road is busy" contains four ambiguities. "Slow down," "more carefully," "dark," and "busy" do not have exact numerical equivalents; human beings can easily interpret the sentence based on experience, but computers have considerable difficulty in making sense of such sentences.

Enter fuzzy logic, which works with gradations of meaning. In traditional—also known as "crisp"—logic, something either is or is not; all concepts have an absolute true (one) or false (zero) determination. Fuzzy logic allows "truth" values in a range between one and zero, representing a degree of certainty. For example, the term *dark* might be defined by a set of values representing levels of illumination, and *busy* could be counted in terms of the number of visible vehicles on the road.

A commonplace inexact human concept is "few." Exactly how many is a few? Is five a few, or is it "many"? The definitions of "many" and "few" often depend on who is making the determination about what. A few stars might be a dozen; a few coins might be three. In a fuzzy logic system, it's necessary to define what is called "the universe of discourse," which in turn defines the several fuzzy sets defining specific concepts. The universe of discourse defines the parameters of the environment and experience from which a program can draw conclusions.

A fuzzy set contains members that are associated with a level of membership, and a membership function maps a given value with the elements of a fuzzy set to retrieve its grade of membership. In the fuzzy set FEW, the value of 5 might be assigned a membership value of 0.7, indicating that 5 is usually—but not always—considered representative of the concept "few." If an element of a fuzzy set has a "grade of membership" equal to zero, it is never considered part of the set; if an element's membership grade is one, it is always considered part of the fuzzy concept.

Many fuzzy-based expert system define fuzzy sets as ordered lists of elements, with each element associated with a specific grade of membership. The universe of discourse is a collection of fuzzy sets from which conclusions can be drawn by analyzing a given set of inputs against their membership in various fuzzy sets.

For example, we could take the number of cars present and the level of illumination as inputs to a universe of discourse that contains the fuzzy sets BUSY and DARK. Based on the grade of membership returned from BUSY and DARK, a program could determine whether a vehicle was moving too fast or too slow for the conditions.

In a recent application, I needed to apply some basic principles of fuzzy logic. The simplest approach was to build on my existing types; for example, I defined a fuzzy set in terms of a *BinaryTree* object that contains text associated with a grade of membership. That was easily accomplished by creating a type definition as follows:

```
typedef BinaryTree<StringID,float> Concept;
```

I then defined an "object set" type from *Dictionary*, in which I store several concepts that define a universe of discourse. I'll begin by looking at how these classes are constructed, and then I'll detail how I put these classes together to implement basic fuzzy-logic techniques.

STRING IDs

In general, fuzzy concepts come from language so that we're looking up a human word or phrase in a fuzzy set. I created a standard "string" type, named *StringID*, for naming concepts and their elements. The *StringID* class is relatively simple: a fixed-length array of characters with a specific set of operations. I've defined operators that allow *StringID*s to work as keys for various container types.

```
const size_t IDMAX = 32;

class StringID
    {
    public:
        StringID
            (
            const char * si = NULL
            );

        StringID
            (
            const StringID & si
            );

        void operator =
            (
            const StringID & si
            );

        void operator =
            (
            const char * s
            );

        int operator ==
            (
            const StringID & si
            ) const;

        int operator ==
```

```
        (
        const char * s
        ) const;

    int operator !=
        (
        const StringID & si
        ) const;

    int operator !=
        (
        const char * s
        ) const;

    int operator <
        (
        const StringID & si
        ) const;

    int operator <
        (
        const char * s
        ) const;

    int operator <=
        (
        const StringID & si
        ) const;

    int operator <=
        (
        const char * s
        ) const;

    int operator >
        (
        const StringID & si
        ) const;

    int operator >
        (
        const char * s
```

```
            ) const;

        int operator >=
            (
            const StringID & si
            ) const;

        int operator >=
            (
            const char * s
            ) const;

        operator const char * ();

    private:
        char Text[IDMAX];
    };
```

The *StringID* class does not allocate memory, and it doesn't throw any exceptions. I defined the *StringID* functions inline, making the class an efficient and regularized tool for handling short pieces of text.

```
inline StringID::StringID
    (
    const char * s
    )
    {
    if ((s == NULL) || (s[0] == 0))
        Text[0] = 0;
    else
        strncpy(Text,s,IDMAX);
    }

inline StringID::StringID
    (
    const StringID & si
    )
    {
    strncpy(Text,si.Text,IDMAX);
    }

inline void StringID::operator =
```

```
    (
    const StringID & si
    )
    {
    strncpy(Text,si.Text,IDMAX);
    }

inline void StringID::operator =
    (
    const char * s
    )
    {
    if ((s == NULL) || (s[0] == 0))
        Text[0] = 0;
    else
        strncpy(Text,s,IDMAX);
    }

inline int StringID::operator ==
    (
    const StringID & si
    ) const
    {
    return (0 == strcmpi(Text, si.Text));
    }

inline int StringID::operator ==
    (
    const char * s
    ) const
    {
    return (0 == strcmpi(Text, s));
    }

inline int StringID::operator !=
    (
    const StringID & si
    ) const
    {
    return (0 != strcmpi(Text, si.Text));
    }

inline int StringID::operator !=
```

```
    (
    const char * s
    ) const
    {
    return (0 != strcmpi(Text, s));
    }

inline int StringID::operator <
    (
    const StringID & si
    ) const
    {
    return (strcmpi(Text, si.Text) < 0);
    }

inline int StringID::operator <
    (
    const char * s
    ) const
    {
    return (strcmpi(Text, s) < 0);
    }

inline int StringID::operator <=
    (
    const StringID & si
    ) const
    {
    return (strcmpi(Text, si.Text) <= 0);
    }

inline int StringID::operator <=
    (
    const char * s
    ) const
    {
    return (strcmpi(Text, s) <= 0);
    }

inline int StringID::operator >
    (
    const StringID & si
    ) const
```

```
    {
    return (strcmpi(Text, si.Text) > 0);
    }

inline int StringID::operator >
    (
    const char * s
    ) const
    {
    return (strcmpi(Text, s) > 0);
    }

inline int StringID::operator >=
    (
    const StringID & si
    ) const
    {
    return (strcmpi(Text, si.Text) >= 0);
    }

inline int StringID::operator >=
    (
    const char * s
    ) const
    {
    return (strcmpi(Text, s) >= 0);
    }

inline StringID::operator const char * ()
    {
    return (const char *)(Text);
    }
```

All comparisons between *StringID*s take place without regard to case; this prevents "few" and "Few" from representing different pieces of information.

OBJECT SETS

I defined the ObjectSet template as follows:

```
template <class K, class D>
    class ObjectSet
        {
        friend
            class ObjSetIterator<K,D>;

        public:
            // constructors
            ObjectSet();

            ObjectSet
                (
                const ObjectSet<K,D> & s
                );

            // assignment operator
            void operator =
                (
                const ObjectSet<K,D> & s
                );

            // member status
            D operator []
                (
                K key
                )
                const;

            // does this set hold a certain key?
            Boolean Holds
                (
                K key
                )
                const;

            // include and exclude members
            void Incl
                (
                K key,
                D data
                );

            void Excl
```

```
        (
        K key
        );

// remove all members
void Erase();

// union operators
ObjectSet<K,D> operator |
        (
        const ObjectSet<K,D> & s
        ) const;

void operator |=
        (
        const ObjectSet<K,D> & s
        );

// intersection operators
ObjectSet<K,D> operator &
        (
        const ObjectSet<K,D> & s
        ) const;

void operator &=
        (
        const ObjectSet<K,D> & s
        );

// exclusive or operator
ObjectSet<K,D> operator ^
        (
        const ObjectSet<K,D> & s
        ) const;

void operator ^=
        (
        const ObjectSet<K,D> & s
        );

// difference operator
ObjectSet<K,D> operator -
        (
```

```
            const ObjectSet<K,D> & s
            ) const;

        void operator -=
            (
            const ObjectSet<K,D> & s
            );

        // comparison operator
        Boolean operator ==
            (
            const ObjectSet<K,D> & s
            ) const;

        Boolean operator !=
            (
            const ObjectSet<K,D> & s
            ) const;

        Boolean Disjoint
            (
            const ObjectSet<K,D> & s
            ) const;

        Boolean SubsetOf
            (
            const ObjectSet<K,D> & s
            ) const;

        Boolean ProperSubsetOf
            (
            const ObjectSet<K,D> & s
            ) const;

        Boolean IsNull() const;

        size_t Cardinality() const;

private:
    Dictionary<K,D> Elements;
};
```

An *ObjectSet* contains only one data member: a *Dictionary* that contains the set's members.

Constructors and Assignment Operator

The *ObjectSet* constructors have the limited purpose of creating or copying the *Elements Dictionary*.

```
template <class K, class D>
    inline ObjectSet<K,D>::ObjectSet()
        {
        // place holder
        }

template <class K, class D>
    inline ObjectSet<K,D>::ObjectSet
        (
        const ObjectSet<K,D> & s
        )
        : Elements(s.Elements)
        {
        // placeholder
        }

// assignment operator
template <class K, class D>
    inline void ObjectSet<K,D>::operator =
        (
        const ObjectSet<K,D> & s
        )
        {
        Elements = s.Elements;
        }
```

ObjectSet does not require an explicit constructor, because the compiler will generate an automatic destructor call to destroy the *Dictionary* and its component objects.

Element Manipulation

The *Holds* function returns true or false based on the membership of an element key.

```
template <class K, class D>
    inline Boolean ObjectSet<K,D>::Holds
        (
        K key
        )
        const
        {
        return Elements.Holds(key);
        }
```

To add a new item to an *ObjectSet*, call the *Incl* function with a key (probably a *StringID*) and an associated object.

```
template <class K, class D>
    inline void ObjectSet<K,D>::Incl
        (
        K key,
        D data
        )
        {
        Elements.Insert(key,data);
        }
```

Removing an element requires passing a key value in a call to the *Excl* function.

```
template <class K, class D>
    inline void ObjectSet<K,D>::Excl
        (
        K key
        )
        {
        Elements.Delete(key);
        }
```

Passing a key to the *operator []* function will retrieve the value of a specific *ObjectSet* element.

```
template <class K, class D>
    inline D ObjectSet<K,D>::operator []
        (
        K key
        )
        const
        {
        return Elements.LookUp(key);
        }
```

Operations

The most important difference between a *Dictionary* and an *ObjectSet* is that the *ObjectSet* defines a collection of set-oriented operations. In Chapter 6, I showed how intersection, union, and difference could be implemented for sets based on bit masks; in the case of the Set template, those operations involved manipulation of bits representing numeric values. For an *ObjectSet*, an operation must scan the sets involved to determine the existence (or nonexistence) of members identified by a key.

For example, the | operator functions implement the union operation by copying one operand and then adding the elements of the second operand. Note the use of *Dictionary* iterators to scan through the *Elements* of a set.

```
template <class K, class D>
    ObjectSet<K,D> ObjectSet<K,D>::operator |
        (
        const ObjectSet<K,D> & s
        ) const
        {
        ObjectSet<K,D> sunion(*this);

        DictIterator<K,D> * iter =
            new DictIterator<K,D>(s.Elements);
```

```
        do {
             if (!sunion.Holds(iter->GetKey()))
                 sunion.Incl(iter->GetKey(),iter->GetData());
             }
        while (++(*iter));

        delete iter;

        return sunion;
        }

template <class K, class D>
    void ObjectSet<K,D>::operator |=
        (
        const ObjectSet<K,D> & s
        )
        {
        DictIterator<K,D> iter(s.Elements);

        do {
            Incl(iter.GetKey(),iter.GetData());
            }
        while (++iter);
        }
```

The intersection operators—& and &=—accomplish their task by searching each *ObjectSet* for the members of the other set.

```
template <class K, class D>
    ObjectSet<K,D> ObjectSet<K,D>::operator &
        (
        const ObjectSet<K,D> & s
        ) const
        {
        ObjectSet<K,D> intersect;

        DictIterator<K,D> * iter =
            new DictIterator<K,D>(s.Elements);

        do {
            K skey = iter->GetKey();
            D sdat = iter->GetData();
```

```
        if (this->Holds(skey))
            intersect.Incl(skey,sdat);
        }
    while (++(*iter));

    delete iter;

    return intersect;
    }

template <class K, class D>
    void ObjectSet<K,D>::operator &=
        (
        const ObjectSet<K,D> & s
        )
        {
        (*this) = (*this) & s;
        }
```

I defined the exclusive-or operators ^ and ^= to make a pass through each operand, including only those elements in the result that do not occur in both operands.

```
template <class K, class D>
    ObjectSet<K,D> ObjectSet<K,D>::operator ^
        (
        const ObjectSet<K,D> & s
        ) const
        {
        K skey;
        D sdat;
        ObjectSet<K,D> xor;

        DictIterator<K,D> * iter1 =
            new DictIterator<K,D>(Elements);

        // scan this
        do  {
            skey = iter1->GetKey();
            sdat = iter1->GetData();

            if (!(s.Holds(skey)))
```

```
            xor.Incl(skey,sdat);
        }
    while (++(*iter1));

    delete iter1;

    // scan s
    DictIterator<K,D> * iter2 =
        new DictIterator<K,D>(s.Elements);

    do  {
        skey = iter2->GetKey();
        sdat = iter2->GetData();

        if (!(this->Holds(skey)))
            xor.Incl(skey,sdat);
        }
    while (++(*iter2));

    delete iter2;

    return xor;
    }

template <class K, class D>
    void ObjectSet<K,D>::operator ^=
        (
        const ObjectSet<K,D> & s
        )
        {
        (*this) = (*this) ^ s;
        }
```

The difference operation copies one *ObjectSet* and then removes any elements found in the second set.

```
template <class K, class D>
    ObjectSet<K,D> ObjectSet<K,D>::operator -
        (
        const ObjectSet<K,D> & s
        ) const
        {
```

```
        ObjectSet<K,D> diff(*this);

        DictIterator<K,D> * iter =
            new DictIterator<K,D>(s.Elements);

        do {
            diff.Excl(iter->GetKey());
            }
        while (++(*iter));

        delete iter;

        return diff;
        }

template <class K, class D>
    void ObjectSet<K,D>::operator -=
        (
        const ObjectSet<K,D> & s
        )
        {
        DictIterator<K,D> iter(s.Elements);

        do {
            Excl(iter.GetKey());
            }
        while (++iter);
        }
```

Comparisons

Comparing two *ObjectSets* involves comparing their *Elements* members. I accomplish this through direct calls to comparison functions defined by *Dictionary*.

```
template <class K, class D>
    Boolean ObjectSet<K,D>::operator ==
        (
        const ObjectSet<K,D> & s
        ) const
```

```
            {
        DictIterator<K,D> * iter =
            new DictIterator<K,D>(s.Elements);

        if (Elements.GetCount() != s.Elements.GetCount())
            return BOOL_FALSE;

        do  {
            if (!Holds(iter->GetKey()))
                return BOOL_FALSE;
            }
        while (++(*iter));

        return BOOL_TRUE;
        }

template <class K, class D>
    inline Boolean ObjectSet<K,D>::operator !=
        (
        const ObjectSet<K,D> & s
        ) const
        {
        if ((*this).operator == (s))
            return BOOL_FALSE;
        else
            return BOOL_TRUE;
        }
```

Special Set Types

Following the *Set* template, the *ObjectSet* template declares functions that
determine the relationships of two sets. The *Disjoint* function returns a
Boolean value based on whether the target sets have any elements in
common.

```
template <class K, class D>
    Boolean ObjectSet<K,D>::Disjoint
        (
        const ObjectSet<K,D> & s
        ) const
```

```
    {
    DictIterator<K,D> iter1(Elements);

    do  {
        if (s.Holds(iter1.GetKey()))
            return BOOL_FALSE;
        }
    while (++iter1);

    DictIterator<K,D> iter2(s.Elements);

    do  {
        if (this->Holds(iter2.GetKey()))
            return BOOL_FALSE;
        }
    while (++iter2);

    return BOOL_TRUE;
    }
```

If all members of the target *ObjectSet* are also resident in the parameter set, the *SubsetOf* function returns a Boolean true.

```
template <class K, class D>
    Boolean ObjectSet<K,D>::SubsetOf
        (
        const ObjectSet<K,D> & s
        ) const
        {
        DictIterator<K,D> iter(Elements);

        do  {
            if (!(s.Holds(iter.GetKey())))
                return BOOL_FALSE;
            }
        while (++iter);

        return BOOL_TRUE;
        }
```

The *IsNull* function returns true if an *ObjectSet* is empty, or false if it contains any elements.

```
template <class K, class D>
    inline Boolean ObjectSet<K,D>::IsNull() const
        {
        if (Elements.GetCount())
            return BOOL_FALSE;
        else
            return BOOL_TRUE;
        }
```

Cardinality returns the number of elements in an *ObjectSet*.

```
template <class K, class D>
    inline size_t ObjectSet<K,D>::Cardinality() const
        {
        return Elements.GetCount();
        }
```

ITERATORS

In developing my *ObjectSet* template, I encountered the need to scan through all elements in a *Dictionary*. To do that, I added an iterator for *Dictionary* template types.

Dictionary Iterators

The *DictIterator* type relies on the ability to scan the component *DList* objects in a *Dictionary*. Its definition looks like this:

```
template <class K, class D, size_t NumBuck = 43>
    class DictIterator
        {
        public:
            // constructors
            DictIterator
                (
                const Dictionary<K,D,NumBuck> & d
```

```
            );

        DictIterator
            (
            const DictIterator<K,D,NumBuck> & iter
            );

        // destructors
        ~DictIterator();

        // assignment
        void operator =
            (
            const DictIterator<K,D,NumBuck> & iter
            );

        Boolean operator ++ ();

        void Reset();

        D GetData();
        K GetKey();
    protected:
        Dictionary<K,D,NumBuck> * Dict;
        size_t Bno;
    };
```

Dict contains a pointer to the *Dictionary* being iterated, and the *Bno* member keeps track of the currently addressed bin in *Dict*'s *Bucket* array. Note that a *DictIterator* does not return values in any useful sorted order; it simply moves through the array of *DLists*, iterating through their members in whatever order items were stored.

The constructor creates a *DictIterator* that points to the first element in the first bucket that contains anything. It also increments the *Dictionary*'s lock count to prevent the iterated data from changing.

```
template <class K, class D, size_t NumBuck>
    DictIterator<K,D,NumBuck>::DictIterator
        (
```

```
const Dictionary<K,D,NumBuck> & d
)
{
if (d.LockCount == UINT_MAX)
    throw DictEx(DX_LOCKMAX);

if (d.Count == 0)
    throw DictEx(DX_NULL);

Dict = const_cast< Dictionary<K,D,NumBuck> * >(&d);

++(Dict->LockCount);
Reset();
}
```

When a *DictIterator* is destroyed, the *Dictionary*'s lock count is decremented.

```
template <class K, class D, size_t NumBuck>
    DictIterator<K,D,NumBuck>::~DictIterator()
        {
        if (Dict->LockCount == 0)
            throw DictEx(DX_LOCKZERO);

        -(Dict->LockCount);
        }
```

The copy constructor and assignment operator create duplicates of existing *DictIterator*s.

```
template <class K, class D, size_t NumBuck>
    DictIterator<K,D,NumBuck>::DictIterator
        (
        const DictIterator<K,D,NumBuck> & iter
        )
        {
        Dict = iter.Dict;

        if (Dict->LockCount == UINT_MAX)
            throw DictEx(DX_LOCKMAX);

        ++(Dict->LockCount);
```

```
        Bno = iter.Bno;
        }


// assignment
template <class K, class D, size_t NumBuck>
    void DictIterator<K,D,NumBuck>::operator =
        (
        const DictIterator<K,D,NumBuck> & iter
        )
        {
        Dict = iter.Dict;
        Bno  = iter.Bno;
        }
```

The operator ++ function "increments" the *DictIterator* by moving to
the next item in the currently selected *Bucket*. If the end of the bucket is reached, *Bno* is incremented to the next bucket that contains
data.

```
template <class K, class D, size_t NumBuck>
    Boolean DictIterator<K,D,NumBuck>::operator ++ ()
        {
        if (Bno == NumBuck)
            return BOOL_FALSE;

        if (!Dict->Bucket[Bno].ToNext())
            {
            ++Bno;

            if (Bno == NumBuck)
                return BOOL_FALSE;

            while (Dict->Bucket[Bno].GetCount() == 0)
                {
                ++Bno;

                if (Bno == NumBuck)
                    return BOOL_FALSE;
                }
```

```
            Dict->Bucket[Bno].ToHead();
            }

        return BOOL_TRUE;
        }
```

The *Reset* function returns the *DictIterator* to the first item in the first *Bucket* that contains data.

```
template <class K, class D, size_t NumBuck>
    void DictIterator<K,D,NumBuck>::Reset()
        {
        Bno = 0;

        while (Dict->Bucket[Bno].GetCount() == 0)
            ++Bno;

        Dict->Bucket[Bno].ToHead();
        }
```

Finally, the *GetData* and *GetKey* functions return, respectively, the data and the key stored in the currently selected element of the *Dictionary*.

```
template <class K, class D, size_t NumBuck>
    D DictIterator<K,D,NumBuck>::GetData()
        {
        return (*(Dict->Bucket[Bno])).Data;
        }

template <class K, class D, size_t NumBuck>
    K DictIterator<K,D,NumBuck>::GetKey()
        {
        return (*(Dict->Bucket[Bno])).Key;
        }
```

ObjectSet Iterators

I defined an *ObjectSet* iterator that essentially acts as a shell for the *DictIterator* type.

```
template <class K, class D>
    class ObjSetIterator : public DictIterator<K,D>
        {
        public:
            ObjSetIterator
                (
                const ObjectSet<K,D> & set
                );

            ObjSetIterator
                (
                const ObjSetIterator<K,D> & osi
                );

            void operator =
                (
                const ObjSetIterator<K,D> & osi
                );
        };

template <class K, class D>
    ObjSetIterator<K,D>::ObjSetIterator
        (
        const ObjectSet<K,D> & set
        )
        : DictIterator<K,D>(set.Elements)
        {
        }

template <class K, class D>
    inline ObjSetIterator<K,D>::ObjSetIterator
        (
        const ObjSetIterator<K,D> & osi
        )
        : DictIterator<K,D>(osi)
        {
        }

template <class K, class D>
    inline void ObjSetIterator<K,D>::operator =
        (
        const ObjSetIterator<K,D> & osi
        )
```

```
{
DictIterator<K,D>::operator = (osi);
}
```

APPLICATION

Look in the file **objset.h** for the object set class, and in **tbfuzzy.cpp** for examples of using *ObjectSet*s and *Concept*s in basic fuzzy logic problems.

CHAPTER 8

SPARSE MATRICES

The container types covered so far organize information based on comparisons of data items. For many applications, data should be stored in a matrix, which locates data based on its position within a two-dimensional grid. This chapter looks at sparse matrices, which store only those elements containing data. Chapter 9 will discuss mathematical matrices that provide a basis for powerful calculations.

WHY USE SPARSE MATRICES?

Many programs use a two-dimensional matrix to store data items. The simplest way of representing a matrix is to use a two-dimensional array:

```
int imatrix[100][100];
```

This array uses 20,000 bytes of memory to hold a 100 by 100 matrix of *ints*. Accessing the contents of *imatrix* is quick and simple, and no special programming needs to be done. But what happens if you want a matrix of the same size that holds complex objects?

```
complex cmatrix[100][100];
```

A *complex* object—usually based on two *doubles*—contains 16 bytes of data; the 10,000 complex objects in *carray* will use 160,000 bytes of memory!

Two-dimensional arrays are particularly inefficient when used to represent partially filled matrices. If only 1,000 *complex* objects are stored at various coordinates within *cmatrix*, the space allocated for the 9,000 empty array elements would waste 154,000 bytes of memory! In scientific or mathematical work, the vast majority of elements in a matrix will contain a constant value (such as 0). Considering the problems, we must either give up having large matrices or find an alternative to the two-dimensional array.

A problem with a two-dimensional array is that all of its elements are allocated when the array is created. Even if you don't use an element, space has still been allocated. The best solution would be to somehow have a matrix adjust the amount of memory it needs at run time. A data structure known as a *sparse matrix* can do just that.

Space for data is dynamically allocated by a sparse matrix for those elements that actually contain data. This saves memory by allocating space for the matrix only as needed. The major disadvantage of a sparse matrix is that it is slower to use than an equivalent two-dimensional array. That's why a sparse matrix is best used for grid-indexed data storage;

when you're performing calculations, such as matrix multiplication, a different matrix type is called for. Chapter 9 implements a mathematical matrix class template.

The sparse matrix template implemented here uses a dynamically allocated array of red-black trees to represent a matrix. When a sparse matrix is created, the number of rows it contains is specified, and an array of *RebBlackTree* objects is allocated. When a new element is added, it is inserted into the tree in the appropriate row. The trees automatically keep the elements in sorted, columnwise order.

EXCEPTION HANDLING

I created a single set of exception types for both sparse and complete matrices (see Chapter 9.) An enumerated type defines the type of exceptions:

```
enum MatrixError
    {
    MTX_ALLOC,
    MTX_INCOMPAT,
    MTX_INVINDEX,
    MTX_SINGULAR,
    MTX_TOOBIG,
    MTX_ZERODIM
    };
```

Creating a *MatrixEx* object requires a *MatrixError* value to identify the problem.

```
class MatrixEx : public ExceptionBase
    {
    public:
        MatrixEx
            (
            MatrixError err
            )
```

```
        {
        Error = err;
        }

    MatrixError WhatsWrong()
        {
        return Error;
        }

    virtual void Explain
        (
        DiagOutput & out
        );

private:
    MatrixError Error;
    };
```

The *Explain* function displays an appropriate error message for a given exception.

```
void MatrixEx::Explain(DiagOutput & out)
    {
    switch (Error)
        {
        case MTX_ALLOC:
            out.DisplayMsg("Can't allocate memory for matrix",
                        DIAG_ERROR);
            break;
        case MTX_INCOMPAT:
            out.DisplayMsg("Operation w/ incompatible matrices",
                        DIAG_WARNING);
            break;
        case MTX_INVINDEX:
            out.DisplayMsg("Out-of-range index for matrix",
                        DIAG_ERROR);
            break;
        case MTX_SINGULAR:
            out.DisplayMsg("Can't invert singular matrix",
                        DIAG_WARNING);
            break;
        case MTX_TOOBIG:
```

```
        out.DisplayMsg("Requested matrix too big",
                       DIAG_ERROR);
        break;
    case MTX_ZERODIM:
        out.DisplayMsg("Matrix row and column must be > 0",
                       DIAG_ERROR);
        break;
    default:
        out.DisplayMsg("Unknown matrix exception",
                       DIAG_FATAL);
    }
}
```

AUXILIARY STRUCTURES

To store both a column and a data item in an element, I created *SMData*,
an auxiliary structure template.

```
template <class D>
    struct SMData
        {
        size_t Col;
        D       Data;

        SMData()
            : Data()
            {
            Col = 0;
            }

        SMData
            (
            size_t c,
            D       x
            )
            : Data(x)
            {
            Col  = c;
            Data = x;
```

```
        }

int operator ==
    (
    const SMData & d
    )
    const
    {
    return (Col == d.Col);
    }

int operator !=
    (
    const SMData & d
    )
    const
    {
    return (Col != d.Col);
    }

int operator <
    (
    const SMData & d
    )
    const
    {
    return (Col < d.Col);
    }

int operator >
    (
    const SMData & d
    )
    const
    {
    return (Col > d.Col);
    }
};
```

I define a minimal set of functions for *SMData*, including comparison functions required for storage in a tree object. The red-black column trees contain *SMData<D>* objects, which are keyed by column number. Thus, the trees store elements in column order.

DEFINING A SPARSE MATRIX

The use of templates vastly simplified my sparse matrix class, which is one of the oldest in my library. The original class relied on a clumsy arrangement of *void* pointers and type-specific shell classes.

The *SparseMatrix* class, implemented with templates, looks like this:

```
template <class D>
    class SparseMatrix
        {
        public:
            // constructor
            SparseMatrix
                (
                size_t rows,
                size_t cols,
                D       def
                );

            // copy constructor
            SparseMatrix
                (
                const SparseMatrix<D> & sm
                );

            // destructor
            ~SparseMatrix();

            // assignment operator
            void operator =
                (
                const SparseMatrix & sm
                );

            // store an item
            void Store
                (
                D item,
                size_t row,
                size_t col
```

```
        );

    // does an element exist?
    Boolean Exists
        (
        size_t row,
        size_t col
        )
        const;

    // retrieve an item
    D Get
        (
        size_t row,
        size_t col
        )
        const;

    D & operator ()
        (
        size_t row,
        size_t col
        );

    // remove an item at a location
    Boolean Delete
        (
        size_t row,
        size_t col
        );

    // delete all items from matrix (USE WITH CAUTION!)
    void Erase();

    // interrogate for # of items
    size_t GetCount();

protected:
    size_t R;
    size_t C;
    size_t Count;
    D Default;
```

```
RedBlackTree< SMData<D> > * Rows;

// utility method to copy matrix
void DeepCopy
    (
    const SparseMatrix & sm
    );
};
```

A *SparseMatrix* contains an array, *Rows*, of *RedBlackTree< SMData<D> >* pointers, each of which points to the first element in a linked list of entries. *Row* is dynamically allocated when the *SparseMatrix* is constructed. *R* retains the number of rows, and *C* the number of columns, in the matrix. *Count* keeps track of how many elements are stored in the matrix.

The only private utility function is *DeepCopy*, which is responsible for duplicating an existing *SparseMatrix* object.

```
template <class D>
    void SparseMatrix<D>::DeepCopy
        (
        const SparseMatrix<D> & sm
        )
        {
        R = sm.R;
        C = sm.C;
        Default = sm.Default;
        Count   = sm.Count;

        Rows = new RedBlackTree< SMData<D> > [R];

        if (Rows == NULL)
            throw MatrixEx(MTX_ALLOC);

        for (size_t n = 0; n < R; ++n)
            Rows[n] = sm.Rows[n];
        }
```

Erase is a utility function that deletes all the enrties in the matrix.

```
template <class D>
    void SparseMatrix<D>::Erase()
        {
        for (size_t n = 0; n < R; ++n)
            Rows[n].Erase();

        Count = 0;
        }
```

Constructors

I defined two constructors for a *SparseMatrix*. The first constructor accepts values specifying the number of rows and columns for the new *SparseMatrix*. The constructor then allocates the *Row* array. The *def* parameter specifies the *Default* value to be returned when a nonexistent element is requested.

```
template <class D>
    SparseMatrix<D>::SparseMatrix
        (
        size_t rows,
        size_t cols,
        D      def
        )
        {
        if ((rows == 0) || (cols == 0))
            throw MatrixEx(MTX_ZERODIM);

        R = rows;
        C = cols;
        Default = def;
        Count   = 0;

        Rows = new RedBlackTree< SMData<D> > [R];

        if (Rows == NULL)
            throw MatrixEx(MTX_ALLOC);
        }
```

The copy constructor creates a new *SparseMatrix* that is a duplicate of an existing one. The assignment operator first *Erases* the content of a matrix before copying the contents of the source matrix.

```
template <class D>
    SparseMatrix<D>::SparseMatrix
        (
        const SparseMatrix<D> & sm
        )
        {
        DeepCopy(sm);
        }

// assignment operator
template <class D>
    void SparseMatrix<D>::operator =
        (
        const SparseMatrix<D> & sm
        )
        {
        Erase();
        DeepCopy(sm);
        }
```

The destructor simply calls *Erase* to destroy the array of column trees.

```
// destructor
template <class D>
    SparseMatrix<D>::~SparseMatrix()
        {
        Erase();
        delete [] Rows;
        }
```

Working with Elements

The *Store* function inserts data into a *SparseMatrix* at a given coordinate in the matrix.

```
template <class D>
    void SparseMatrix<D>::Store
        (
        D item,
        size_t row,
        size_t col
        )
        {
        if ((row >= R) || (col >= C))
            throw MatrixEx(MTX_INVINDEX);

        Rows[row].Insert(SMData<D>(col,item));
        }
```

The tree automatically replaces any item already stored in a column position.

The *Exists* function searches a column tree to see whether an element already exists.

```
template <class D>
    Boolean SparseMatrix<D>::Exists
        (
        size_t row,
        size_t col
        )
        const
        {
        if ((row >= R) || (col >= C))
            throw MatrixEx(MTX_INVINDEX);

        RBTreeIterator< SMData<D> > i(Rows[row]);

        while ((*i).Col != col)
            {
            try
                {
                ++i;
                }
            catch (TreeEx & ex)
                {
                if (ex.WhatsWrong() == BTX_NOTFOUND)
```

```
                return BOOL_FALSE;
            else
                throw;
            }
        }

    return BOOL_TRUE;
    }
```

For a constant matrix, *Get* first checks that the row requested in parameter *row* is within the range specified by *R*. Get then begins searching for the requested column in the tree in *row*th element of *Row*. If the item is found, the data element of the *SMData* item is returned; otherwise, *Get* returns *Default*.

```
template <class D>
    D SparseMatrix<D>::Get
        (
        size_t row,
        size_t col
        )
        const
        {
        if ((row >= R) || (col >= C))
            throw MatrixEx(MTX_INVINDEX);

        RBTreeIterator< SMData<D> > i(Rows[row]);

        while ((*i).Col != col)
            {
            try
                {
                ++i;
                }
            catch (TreeEx & ex)
                {
                if (ex.WhatsWrong() == BTX_NOTFOUND)
                    return Default;
                else
                    throw;
                }
```

```
        }

    return (*i).Data;
    }
```

The *operator ()* function returns a reference to an element in a noncon-
stant *SparseMatrix*. An exception is thrown if the requested element
doesn't exist, because there is no way to provide a reference to a data
item that doesn't exist.

```
template <class D>
    D & SparseMatrix<D>::operator ()
        (
        size_t row,
        size_t col
        )
        {
        if ((row >= R) || (col >= C))
            throw MatrixEx(MTX_INVINDEX);

        RBTreeIterator< SMData<D> > i(Rows[row]);

        while ((*i).Col != col)
            {
            try
                {
                ++i;
                }
            catch (TreeEx & ex)
                {
                if (ex.WhatsWrong() == BTX_NOTFOUND)
                    throw MatrixEx(MTX_INVINDEX);
                else
                    throw;
                }
            }

        return (*i).Data;
        }
```

Delete is works like *Get; Delete* searches the *SparseMatrix* for an element at a
specified row/column coordinate. If the element is empty, *Delete* does

nothing further and returns *BOOL_FALSE*. Otherwise, the element in that row and column is deleted.

```
// remove an item at a location
template <class D>
    Boolean SparseMatrix<D>::Delete
        (
        size_t row,
        size_t col
        )
        {
        return Rows[row].Delete(SMData<D>(col,Default));
        }
```

The final function, *GetCount,* returns the number of elements currently stored in a *SparseMatrix*:

```
template <class D>
    inline size_t SparseMatrix<D>::GetCount()
        {
        return Count;
        }
```

APPLICATION

One common use of sparse matrices is in spreadsheet programs. A spreadsheet program can be viewed as a sparse matrix manager, where each cell in the worksheet represents an element in a sparse matrix. The sparse matrix allows a spreadsheet to store only those cells that are currently holding data.

Look for the matrix exception classes in **matrixx.h** and **matrixx.cpp**. The *SparseMatrix* class is completely implemented in the file **spmatrix.h**, and you'll find examples of its use in the module **tbmatrix.h**.

CHAPTER 9

MATRICES AND LINEAR ALGEBRA

A sparse matrix works well for large, highly distributed grids of data. For mathematical operations, however, a faster matrix implementation is in order. A template can create a powerful matrix shell around a standard C++ array, providing a powerful mathematical programming tool.

MATRIX THEORY

There are many college courses and textbooks devoted to matrix theory, so I won't try to provide an in-depth look at the topic. This chapter gives you a crash course in matrix theory, covering the basics implemented by my *Matrix* template.

A *matrix* is a two-dimensional array that can be perceived as a rectangle containing rows and columns of numeric values. A 3 by 4 matrix, for example, has 12 elements arranged in three rows and four columns. This is a 2-row by 3-column (2–by–3) matrix of integers:

$$A = \begin{pmatrix} 0 & 1 & 2 \\ 3 & 0 & 6 \end{pmatrix}$$

The *transpose* of a matrix is created by exchanging rows and columns. The transpose of matrix A, for example, is:

$$A^T = \begin{pmatrix} 0 & 3 \\ 1 & 0 \\ 2 & 6 \end{pmatrix}$$

If the transpose of a matrix is identical to the original matrix, the matrix is said to be symmetrical.

A *square matrix* has an equal number of rows and columns. A vector, a one-dimensional array of numbers, is equivalent to a row or column of a two-dimensional array. Each column and row in an array can be considered a vector.

Grid CLASS

The term *matrix* usually assumes that elements are numbers—but the preceding definitions also apply to nonnumeric data types. So I created a template defining a two-dimensional "grid" of any data type.

Definition

The *Grid* class is defined as follows:

```
template <class D>
    class Grid
        {
        public:
            // constructors
            Grid();

            Grid
                (
                size_t rows,
                size_t cols
                );

            Grid
                (
                const Grid<D> & m
                );

            // destructors
            ~Grid();

            // assignment operator
            void operator =
                (
                const Grid<D> & m
                );

            void operator =
                (
                const D * array
                );

            // interrogation
            size_t GetRows() const;
            size_t GetCols() const;

            Boolean IsVector() const;
```

```
Boolean IsRowVector() const;
Boolean IsColVector() const;
Boolean IsSquare() const;

// retrieve elements
D Get
    (
    size_t row,
    size_t col
    ) const;

D & operator ()
    (
    size_t row,
    size_t col
    );

// internal function w/o exception check!
D & Elem
    (

D * Data;
protected:
    size_t R;
    size_t C;
    size_t N;

size_t Index
    size_t (
        size_t row,
        size_t col
        )
    const size_t row,
    size_t col
    const;

// apply a function to each element
void Apply
    (
    D (* func)(const D & n)
    );

friend Grid<D> Apply
```

```
        (
        const Grid<D> & m,
        D (* func)(const D & n)
        );

    // fill matrix with specific value
    void Fill
        (
        const D & x
        );

    // create a row matrix
    Grid<D> VectorRow
        (
        size_t row
        );

    // create a column vector
    Grid<D> VectorCol
        (
        size_t col
        )
        const;
    };
```

R and *C* contain, respectively, the numbers of rows and columns in a *Grid*; *N* is *R* times *C*, the total number of elements. A *Grid* stores its elements in the dynamically allocated array pointed to by *Data*.

Element Access

A C-style two-dimensional array stores its elements as a one-dimensional array, with the compiler performing automatic math to select elements. Rows are stored consecutively. For example, the array *A* (see preceding section) would be stored in memory as:

0 1 2 3 0 6

The statement *A[1][2]* needs to access the number "5"; to do that, the compiler finds the requested element by multiplying the row index against the number of columns and adding the column index. *A* has three columns and two rows; therefore, for element *A[1][2]*, the compiler multiplies 1 by 3 and adds 2, creating a zero-based array index of 5—which points to the requested element, "6th."

A *Grid* allocates its *Data* array with *new*, and dyanmic arrays can have only one dimension. Therefore, I created an inline function, *Index*, to generate the same calculation that the compiler provides for a two-dimensional array.

```
template <class D>
    inline size_t Grid<D>::Index
        (
        size_t row,
        size_t col
        )
        const
        {               // transpose a matrix
        Grid<D> Transpose();

        // change size (destroying contents)
        void Resize
        (
        size_t rows,
        size_t cols
        );

        return (row * C + col);
        }
```

I also created a set of three functions for retrieving a *Grid*'s elements. The *Get* function works with *const Grids*, returning a copy of the element.

```
template <class D>
    D Grid<D>::Get
        (
        size_t row,
        size_t col
        ) const
        {
        if ((row >= R) || (col >= C))
```

```
        throw MatrixEx(MTX_INVINDEX);

    return Data[Index(row,col)];
        }
```

The [] operator, normally used for indexing arrays, cannot be over-loaded with more than one parameter. In its place, I've implemented the () operator to return a reference to an element.

```
template <class D>
    inline D & Grid<D>::operator ()
        (
        size_t row,
        size_t col
        )
        {
        if ((row >= R) || (col >= C))
            throw MatrixEx(MTX_INVINDEX);

   return Data[Index(row,col)];
        }
```

Returning a reference allows code that looks like this:

```
Grid<int> A(2,3);

A(0,1) = 2;
int x = A(1,2);
```

Both *operator()* and *Get* contain code that throws an exception when the specified coordinates are invalid—something that arrays don't do. However, that check is inefficient when we know we're working within *Grid*'s boundaries—and for that purpose, I created the *Elem* function.

```
template <class D>
    inline D & Grid<D>::Elem
        (
        size_t row,
        size_t col
        )
```

```
const
{
return Data[row * C + col];
}
```

Constructors and Destructor

The default constructor creates a one-element (1-by-1) *Grid*.

```
template <class D>
    Grid<D>::Grid()
        {
        R = 1;
        C = 1;
        N = 1;

        Data = new D [N];

        if (Data == NULL)
            throw MatrixEx(MTX_ALLOC);
        }
```

In most cases, you'll want to create a new *Grid* by providing the number of rows and columns. The corresponding constructor copies these values into the new object's data elements, makes some validity checks, and allocates the *Data* array.

```
template <class D>
    Grid<D>::Grid
        (
        size_t rows,
        size_t cols
        )
        {
        R = rows;
        C = cols;
        N = rows * cols;

        if ((R == 0) || (C == 0))
```

```
        throw MatrixEx(MTX_ZERODIM);

if ((N < R) || (N < C))
    throw MatrixEx(MTX_TOOBIG);

Data = new D [N];

if (Data == NULL)
    throw MatrixEx(MTX_ALLOC);
}
```

The copy constructor copies the values from an existing *Grid*.

```
template <class D>
    Grid<D>::Grid
        (
        const Grid<D> & m
        )
        {
        R = m.R;
        C = m.C;
        N = m.N;

        Data = new D [N];

        if (Data == NULL)
            throw MatrixEx(MTX_ALLOC);

        for (size_t i = 0; i < N; ++i)
            Data[i] = m.Data[i];
        }
```

The *Resize* function changes the dimensions of any *Grid*, destroying the existing contents in the process.

```
template <class D>
    void Grid<D>::Resize
        (
        size_t rows,
        size_t cols
        )
```

```
        {
        delete [] Data;

        R = rows;
        C = cols;
        N = rows * cols;

        if ((R == 0) || (C == 0))
            throw MatrixEx(MTX_ZERODIM);

        if ((N < R) || (N < C))
            throw MatrixEx(MTX_TOOBIG);

        Data = new D [N];

        if (Data == NULL)
            throw MatrixEx(MTX_ALLOC);
        }
```

The destructor cleans up by deleting the *Data* array.

```
template <class D>
    Grid<D>::~Grid()
        {
        delete [] Data;
        }
```

Assignment

The assignment operator destroys a *Grid*'s current *Data* array before copying the source *Grid*.

```
template <class D>
    void Grid<D>::operator =
        (
        const Grid<D> & m
        )
        {
        R = m.R;
```

```
      C = m.C;
      N = m.N;

      delete [] Data;

      Data = new D [N];

      if (Data == NULL)
          throw MatrixEx(MTX_ALLOC);

      for (size_t i = 0; i < N; ++i)
          Data[i] = m.Data[i];
      }
```

I also created an assignment-from-array operator, which assumes that the source array has the same number of elements as the *Matrix* has.

```
template <class D>
    void Grid<D>::operator =
        (
        const D * array
        )
        {
        // note: must assume that array has N members
        const D * aptr = array;
            D * mptr = Data;

        for (size_t i = 0; i < N; ++i)
            {
            (*mptr) = (*aptr);
            ++aptr;
            ++mptr;
            }
        }
```

Interrogators

The dimensions of a *Matrix* can be retrieved by using the *GetRows* and *GetCols* functions:

```
template <class D>
    inline size_t Grid<D>::GetRows() const
        {
        return R;
        }

template <class D>
    inline size_t Grid<D>::GetCols() const
        {
        return C;
        }
```

If a *Matrix* has the same number of rows as columns, *IsSquare* returns *true*.

```
template <class D>
    inline Boolean Grid<D>::IsSquare() const
        {
        if (R == C)
            return BOOL_TRUE;
        else
            return BOOL_FALSE;
        }
```

Applying a Function

To call a function for every element in a matrix, creating a new matrix, use this of the version *Apply* function:

```
template <class D>
    void Grid<D>::Apply
        (
        D (* func)(const D & n)
        )
        {
        for (size_t i = 0; i < N; ++i)
            Data[i] = func(Data[i]);
        }
```

A function can alter the elements of an array in place with this version of *Apply*:

```
template <class D>
    Grid<D> Apply
        (
        const Grid<D> & m,
        D (* func)(const D & n)
        )
        {
        Grid<D> result(m);

        for (size_t i = 0; i < m.N; ++i)
            result.Data[i] = func(result.Data[i]);

        return result;
        }
```

Filling a Grid

The *Fill* function sets all elements to a specific value:

```
template <class D>
    void Grid<D>::Fill
        (
        const D & x
        )
        {
        for (size_t i = 0; i < N; ++i)
            Data[i] = x;
        }
```

Vectors

Any column or row in a matrix can be extracted as a vector using these functions:

```
template <class D>
    Grid<D> Grid<D>::VectorRow
        (
        size_t row
        )
        {
        if (row >= R)
            throw MatrixEx(MTX_INVINDEX);

        Grid<D> vector(C,1);

        for (size_t i = 0; i < C; ++i)
            vector(i,0) = Data[Index(row,i)];

        return vector;
    {

// create a column vector
template <class D>
    Grid<D> Grid<D>::VectorCol
        (
        size_t col
        )
        {
        if (col >= C)
            throw MatrixEx(MTX_INVINDEX);

        Grid<D> vector(1,R);

        for (size_t i = 0; i < R; ++i)
            vector(0,i) = Data[Index(i,col)];

        return vector;
        }
```

These interrogation functions determine whether a *Matrix* is also a vector.

```
template <class D>
    inline Boolean Grid<D>::IsVector() const
        {
        if ((R == 1) || (C == 1))
            return BOOL_TRUE;
```

```
        else
            return BOOL_FALSE;
        }

template <class D>
    inline Boolean Grid<D>::IsRowVector() const
        {
        if (C == 1)
            return BOOL_TRUE;
        else
            return BOOL_FALSE;
        }

template <class D>
    inline Boolean Grid<D>::IsColVector() const
        {
        if (R == 1)
            return BOOL_TRUE;
        else
            return BOOL_FALSE;
        }
```

Transposition

The *Transpose* function creates a new *Matrix* that is the transpose of the original:

```
template <class D>
    Grid<D> Grid<D>::Transpose()
        {
        Grid<D> result(C,R);

        const D * tptr = Data;
        D * rptr;

        for (size_t i = 0; i < R; ++i)
            {
            rptr = result.Data + i;

            for (size_t j = 0; j < C; ++j)
```

```
          {
          (*rptr) = (*tptr);
          ++tptr;
          rptr += R;
          }
      }

   return result;
   }
```

NUMERIC MATRICES

However useful a *Grid* might be, a mathematical matrix requires something more. From *Grid*, I derived a *Matrix* template that assumes its elements are numbers. *Matrix* adds a number of new features, based on the following definitions

In a *zero* matrix, every element is zero. In a *diagonal* matrix, all elements are zero except those in which the row index equals the column index; if all nonzero values in a diagonal matrix are 1, it is called an *identity* matrix.

Two matrices can be added only if they have exactly the same number of rows and columns. The result of adding two matrices is a new matrix of the same dimensions; each element in the result equals the sum of the corresponding elements in the source matrices. Here's an example:

$$\begin{pmatrix} 7 & 7 & 4 \\ 4 & 4 & 8 \end{pmatrix} = \begin{pmatrix} 0 & 1 & 2 \\ 3 & 4 & 5 \end{pmatrix} + \begin{pmatrix} 7 & 6 & 2 \\ 1 & 0 & 3 \end{pmatrix}$$

A matrix subtraction follows a similar algorithm.

Scalar operations apply a single operation to every member of a matrix. Here is an example of a scalar multiply:

$$2 \cdot \begin{pmatrix} 1 & 2 \\ 3 & 4 \end{pmatrix} = \begin{pmatrix} 2 & 4 \\ 6 & 8 \end{pmatrix}$$

Matrix multiplication requires two compatible matrices: The number of columns in matrix A must be equal to the number of rows in column B. If A is an m by n matrix and if B is an n by p matrix, then the result by multiplication, matrix C, will be a an m by p matrix. Each element of C is calculated according to the following formula:

$$C_{ik} = \sum_{j=1}^{n} A_{ij} B_{jk}$$

for $i = 1$ to m and $k = 1$ to p. For example:

$$\begin{pmatrix} 1 & 0 & 2 \\ 1 & 3 & 2 \end{pmatrix} \cdot \begin{pmatrix} 1 & 4 \\ 2 & 5 \\ 3 & 6 \end{pmatrix} + \begin{pmatrix} 7 & 16 \\ 13 & 31 \end{pmatrix}$$

In general, the rules of algebra apply to matrix operations. For example, multiplying any matrix by a zero matrix results in a zero matrix. Multiplication is associative and distributive over addition; however, the multiplication is not commutative. Multiplying a column and row matrix generates a single number known as the *inner product*.

The *outer product* of two matrices works like matrix addition, where two like-dimensioned matrices generate a matrix of the same size whose elements are the result of multiplying corresponding source elements.

Chapter 10, which covers linear algebra, will delve into advanced matrix operations such as solutions to line equations and the calculation of matrix inverses. For now, let's look at implementing the preceding theory in a basic matrix class.

MATRIX CLASS

I've implemented a few extensions in my *Matrix* class. For example, I created a series of functions to compare matrices, producing an *int* matrix that shows the relationship of corresponding elements; my template also defines a set of scalar operations both for constants and for pairs of matrices.

```
template <class D>
    class Matrix : public Grid<D>
        {
        public:
            // constructors
            Matrix();

            Matrix
                (
                size_t rows,
                size_t cols,
                const D & init = (D)0
                );

            Matrix
                (
                const Matrix<D> & m
                );

            Matrix
                (
                const Grid<D> & m
                );

            // assignment operator
            void operator =
                (
                const Matrix<D> & m
                );

            void operator =
                (
                const Grid<D> & m
                );

            void operator =
                (
                const D * array
                );

            // interrogation
            Boolean IsZero() const;
```

```
Boolean IsDiagonal() const;
Boolean IsIdentity() const;
Boolean IsTridiagonal() const;
Boolean IsUpperTriangular() const;
Boolean IsLowerTriangular() const;
Boolean IsPermutation() const;
Boolean IsSingular() const;

// scalar addition
Matrix<D> operator +
    (
    const Matrix<D> & m
    );

void operator +=
    (
    const Matrix<D> & m
    );

Matrix<D> operator +
    (
    const D & x
    );

void operator +=
    (
    const D & x
    );

// scalar subtraction
Matrix<D> operator -
    (
    const Matrix<D> & m
    );

void operator -=
    (
    const Matrix<D> & m
    );

Matrix<D> operator -
    (
```

```
        const D & x
        );

void operator -=
        (
        const D & x
        );

// scalar multiplication
Matrix<D> operator *
        (
        const Matrix<D> & m
        );

void operator *=
        (
        const Matrix<D> & m
        );

Matrix<D> operator *
        (
        const D & x
        );

void operator *=
        (
            const D & x

                );
 // scalar division
Matrix<D> operator /
        (
        const Matrix<D> & m
        );

void operator /=
        (
        const Matrix<D> & m
        );

Matrix<D> operator /
        (
        const D & x
```

```
        );

void operator /=
    (
    const D & x
    );

// matrix multiplication
Matrix<D> operator %
    (
    const Matrix<D> & m
    );

// comparison operators
Boolean Equals
    (
    const Matrix<D> & m
    );

Matrix<int> operator ==
    (
    const Matrix<D> & m
    );

Matrix<int> operator !=
    (
    const Matrix<D> & m
    );

Matrix<int> operator <
    (
    const Matrix<D> & m
    );

Matrix<int> operator <=
    (
    const Matrix<D> & m
    );

Matrix<int> operator >
    (
    const Matrix<D> & m
    );
```

```
Matrix<int> operator >=
    (
    const Matrix<D> & m
    );

// negate a matrix
Matrix<D> operator - ();

// change size (destroying contents)
void Resize
    (
    size_t rows,
    size_t cols,
    const D & init = D(0)
    );

// inner and outer products
D InnerProduct
    (
    const Matrix<D> & m
    );

// calculation euclidean norm
double Norm();

// calculate determinant value
D Determinant();

// create a minor matrix
Matrix<D> Minor
    (
    size_t rdel,
    size_t cdel
    );

// solve system of linear equations
Matrix<D> LinSolve();

// LUP decomposition
Grid<size_t> LUPDecompose();

// LUP decomposition (call w/ result of LUPDecomp)
Matrix<D> LUPSolve
```

```
            (
            const Grid<size_t> & perm,
            const Matrix<D> & b
            );

        // LUP inversion (call w/ result of LUPDecomp)
        Matrix<D> LUPInvert
            (
            const Grid<size_t> & perm
            );

protected:
        // internal recursive function for determinant
        D DetRecursive();
    };
```

Constructors and Destructor

For the most part, *Matrix*'s constructors and assignment operators are nothing more than inline shells that call corresponding functions inherited from *Grid*. Only the primary and default constructors differ, in assigning an initial value to all elements.

```
template <class D>
    inline Matrix<D>::Matrix()
        : Grid<D>()
        {
        *Data = D(0);
        }

template <class D>
    Matrix<D>::Matrix
        (
        size_t rows,
        size_t cols,
        D init
        )
        : Grid<D>(rows,cols)
        {
        for (size_t i = 0; i < N; ++i)
```

```
            Data[i] = init;
        }

template <class D>
    inline Matrix<D>::Matrix
        (
        const Matrix<D> & m
        )
        : Grid<D>(m)
        {
        // place holder
        }

template <class D>
    inline Matrix<D>::Matrix
        (
        const Grid<D> & m
        )
        : Grid<D>(m)
        {
        // place holder
        }

// assignment operator
template <class D>
    inline void Matrix<D>::operator =
        (
        const Matrix<D> & m
        )
        {
        Grid<D>::operator = (m);
        }

template <class D>
    inline void Matrix<D>::operator =
        (
        const Grid<D> & m
        )
        {
        Grid<D>::operator = (m);
        }

template <class D>
```

```
inline void Matrix<D>::operator =
    (
    const D * array
    )
    {
    Grid<D>::operator = (array);
    }
```

The Matrix class does not define a destructor, because Grid's destructor handles object cleanup.

Interrogators

To determine whether a matrix belongs to a special category, I provide a set of *Is???* functions.

```
template <class D>
    Boolean Matrix<D>::IsZero() const
        {
        const D * ptr = Data;

        for (size_t i = 0; i < N; ++i)
            {
            if ((*ptr) != (D)0)
                return BOOL_FALSE;

            ++ptr;
            }

        return BOOL_TRUE;
        }

template <class D>
    Boolean Matrix<D>::IsDiagonal() const
        {
        if (C != R)
            return BOOL_FALSE;

        const D * ptr = Data;

        for (size_t ir = 0; ir < R; ++ir)
```

```
            {
            for (size_t ic = 0; ic < C; ++ic)
                {
                if (ir == ic)
                    {
                    if ((*ptr) == (D)0)
                        return BOOL_FALSE;
                    }
                else
                    {
                    if ((*ptr) != (D)0)
                        return BOOL_FALSE;
                     }

                ++ptr;
                }
            }

        return BOOL_TRUE;
        }

template <class D>
    Boolean Matrix<D>::IsIdentity() const
        {
        if (C != R)
            return BOOL_FALSE;

        const D * ptr = Data;

        for (size_t ir = 0; ir < R; ++ir)
            {
            for (size_t ic = 0; ic < C; ++ic)
                {
                if (ir == ic)
                    {
                    if ((*ptr) != (D)1)
                        return BOOL_FALSE;
                    }
                else
                    {
                    if ((*ptr) != (D)0)
                        return BOOL_FALSE;
```

```
                }

            ++ptr;
            }
        }

    return BOOL_TRUE;
    }

template <class D>
    Boolean Matrix<D>::IsTridiagonal() const
        {
        if ((C != R) || (C < 3))
            return BOOL_FALSE;

        const D * ptr = Data;

        for (size_t ir = 0; ir < R; ++ir)
            {
            for (size_t ic = 0; ic < C; ++ic)
                {
                if (ir != ic)
                    {
                    if (ir > ic)
                        {
                        if ((ir - ic) > 1)
                            {
                            if ((*ptr) != (D)0)
                                return BOOL_FALSE;
                            }
                        }
                    else
                        {
                        if ((ic - ir) > 1)
                            {
                            if ((*ptr) != (D)0)
                                return BOOL_FALSE;
                            }
                        }
                    }

                ++ptr;
```

```
                }
            }

        return BOOL_TRUE;
        }

template <class D>
    Boolean Matrix<D>::IsUpperTriangular() const
        {
        if ((C != R) || (C < 2))
            return BOOL_FALSE;

        size_t steps = 1;
        const D * ptr = Data + C;

        for (size_t ir = 1; ir < R; ++ir)
            {
            for (size_t s = 0; s < steps; ++s)
                {
                if (ptr[s] != (D)0)
                    return BOOL_FALSE;
                }

            ++steps;
            ptr += C;
            }

        return BOOL_TRUE;
        }

template <class D>
    Boolean Matrix<D>::IsLowerTriangular() const
        {
        if ((C != R) || (C < 2))
            return BOOL_FALSE;

        size_t steps = C - 1;
        const D * ptr = Data;

        for (size_t ir = 1; ir < R; ++ir)
            {
            for (size_t s = steps; s > 0; --s)
                {
```

```
                    if (ptr[s] != (D)0)
                        return BOOL_FALSE;
                    }

                -steps;
                ptr += C + 1;
                }

        return BOOL_TRUE;
        }

template <class D>
    Boolean Matrix<D>::IsPermutation() const
        {
        if (C != R)
            return BOOL_FALSE;

        char * ctags = new char[C];

        if (ctags == NULL)
            throw MatrixEx(MTX_ALLOC);

        char * rtags = new char[R];

        if (rtags == NULL)
            throw MatrixEx(MTX_ALLOC);

        memset(ctags,0,C);
        memset(rtags,0,R);

        Boolean result = BOOL_TRUE;

        const D * ptr = Data;

        for (size_t ri = 0; ri < R; ++ri)
            {
            for (size_t ci = 0; ci < C; ++ci)
                {
                if ((*ptr))
                    {
                    if (((*ptr) > 1)
                    ||  (rtags[ri] == 1)
                    ||  (ctags[ci] == 1))
```

```
                              {
                              result = BOOL_FALSE;
                              goto finished;
                              }

                        rtags[ri] = 1;
                        ctags[ci] = 1;
                        }

                ++ptr;
                }
          }

      // a goto label!
      finished:

      delete [] ctags;
      delete [] rtags;
      return result;
      }

template <class D>
    Boolean Matrix<D>::IsSingular() const
        {
        if (C != R)
            return BOOL_FALSE;

        Matrix<D> csum(1,C), rsum(R,1);
        const D * ptr = Data;

        for (size_t ri = 0; ri < R; ++ri)
            {
            for (size_t ci = 0; ci < C; ++ci)
                {
                csum(0,ci) += *ptr;
                rsum(ri,0) += *ptr;
                ++ptr;
                }
            }

        for (size_t i = 0; i < R; ++i)
            {
            if ((csum(0,i) == 0) || (rsum(i,0) == 0))
```

```
            return BOOL_TRUE;
        }

    return BOOL_FALSE;
    }
```

Of course, you can use any of *Grid*'s interrogation functions with a *Matrix*.

Scalar Operations

A scalar operation applies a single operation to every element of a matrix. I define two broad classes of scalar operations for binary and shorthand addition, substraction, multiplication, and division operators.

When a scalar operation involves two matrices, corresponding elements are combined using the appropriate operation. The binary operators create new matrices; the shorthand operators alter the target object.

```
template <class D>
    Matrix<D> Matrix<D>::operator +
        (
        const Matrix<D> & m
        )
        {
        if ((R != m.R) || (C != m.C))
            throw MatrixEx(MTX_INCOMPAT);

        Matrix<D> result(m);

        for (size_t i = 0; i < N; ++i)
            result.Data[i] += Data[i];

        return result;
        }

template <class D>
    void Matrix<D>::operator +=
        (
        const Matrix<D> & m
        )
```

```
    {
if ((R != m.R) || (C != m.C))
    throw MatrixEx(MTX_INCOMPAT);

for (size_t i = 0; i < N; ++i)
    Data[i] += m.Data[i];
    }
```

I've shown only the functions for addition; 12 nearly identical functions provide for subtraction, multiplication, and division. Note that the multiplication functions create an outer product; true matrix multiplication is provided by the % operator, discussed next.

Matrix Multiplication

After ensuring that two matrices are compatible, the % operator creates a new matrix and calculates its elements according to the formula defined previously.

```
template <class D>
    Matrix<D> Matrix<D>::operator %
        (
        const Matrix<D> & m
        )
        {
        if (C != m.R)
            throw MatrixEx(MTX_INCOMPAT);

        Matrix<D> result(R,m.C);

        D * rptr = result.Data;
        const D * tptr, * mptr;

        for (size_t i = 0; i < R; ++i)
            {
            for (size_t j = 0; j < m.C; ++j)
                {
                tptr =    Data + (i * R);
                mptr = m.Data +   j;
```

```
            for (size_t k = 0; k < C; ++k)
                {
                (*rptr) += (*tptr) * (*mptr);

                ++tptr;
                mptr += m.C;
                }

            ++rptr;
            }
        }

    return result;
    }
```

A shorthand %= operator cannot be defined, because the dimensions of the resulting Matrix differ from those of both source matrices, preventing assignment of new values to either *this or m.

Comparisons

The *Equals* function compares elements of two matrices, returning *BOOL_TRUE* if all elements are equal, and *BOOL_FALSE* if they are not equal.

```
template <class D>
    Boolean Matrix<D>::Equals
        (
        const Matrix<D> & m
        )
        {
        if ((R != m.R) || (C != m.C))
            throw MatrixEx(MTX_INCOMPAT);

        for (size_t ri = 0; ri < R; ++ri)
            {
            for (size_t ci = 0; ci < C; ++ci)
                {
                if (Data[Index(ri,ci)] != m.Data[Index(ri,ci)])
```

```
            return BOOL_FALSE;
        }
    }

    return BOOL_TRUE;
    }
```

I define a set of scalar comparison functions that create a new *Matrix<int>*, reflecting a comparison of corresponding elements.

```
template <class D>
    Matrix<int> Matrix<D>::operator ==
        (
        const Matrix<D> & m
        )
        {
        if ((R != m.R) || (C != m.C))
            throw MatrixEx(MTX_INCOMPAT);

        Matrix<int> result(R,C);

        for (size_t ri = 0; ri < R; ++ri)
            {
            for (size_t ci = 0; ci < C; ++ci)
                {
                result(ri,ci) =
                    (Data[Index(ri,ci)] == m.Data[Index(ri,ci)]);
                }
            }

        return result;
        }

template <class D>
    Matrix<int> Matrix<D>::operator !=
        (
        const Matrix<D> & m
        )
        {
        if ((R != m.R) || (C != m.C))
            throw MatrixEx(MTX_INCOMPAT);
```

```
        Matrix<int> result(R,C);

        for (size_t ri = 0; ri < R; ++ri)
            {
            for (size_t ci = 0; ci < C; ++ci)
                {
                result(ri,ci) =
                    (Data[Index(ri,ci)] != m.Data[Index(ri,ci)]);
                }
            }

        return result;
        }

template <class D>
    Matrix<int> Matrix<D>::operator <
        (
        const Matrix<D> & m
        )
        {
        if ((R != m.R) || (C != m.C))
            throw MatrixEx(MTX_INCOMPAT);

        Matrix<int> result(R,C);

        for (size_t ri = 0; ri < R; ++ri)
            {
            for (size_t ci = 0; ci < C; ++ci)
                {
                result(ri,ci) =
                    (Data[Index(ri,ci)] < m.Data[Index(ri,ci)]);
                }
            }

        return result;
        }

template <class D>
    Matrix<int> Matrix<D>::operator <=
        (
        const Matrix<D> & m
        )
```

```
        {
        if ((R != m.R) || (C != m.C))
            throw MatrixEx(MTX_INCOMPAT);

        Matrix<int> result(R,C);

        for (size_t ri = 0; ri < R; ++ri)
            {
            for (size_t ci = 0; ci < C; ++ci)
                {
                result(ri,ci) =
                    (Data[Index(ri,ci)] <= m.Data[Index(ri,ci)]);
                }
            }

        return result;
        }

template <class D>
    Matrix<int> Matrix<D>::operator >
        (
        const Matrix<D> & m
        )
        {
        if ((R != m.R) || (C != m.C))
            throw MatrixEx(MTX_INCOMPAT);

        Matrix<int> result(R,C);

        for (size_t ri = 0; ri < R; ++ri)
            {
            for (size_t ci = 0; ci < C; ++ci)
                {
                result(ri,ci) =
                    (Data[Index(ri,ci)] > m.Data[Index(ri,ci)]);
                }
            }

        return result;
        }

template <class D>
```

```
Matrix<int> Matrix<D>::operator >=
    (
    const Matrix<D> & m
    )
    {
    if ((R != m.R) || (C != m.C))
        throw MatrixEx(MTX_INCOMPAT);

    Matrix<int> result(R,C);

    for (size_t ri = 0; ri < R; ++ri)
        {
        for (size_t ci = 0; ci < C; ++ci)
            {
            result(ri,ci) =
                (Data[Index(ri,ci)] >= m.Data[Index(ri,ci)]);
            }
        }

    return result;
    }
```

Similar functions implement the operations for not equal, greater than, greater than or equal, less than, and less than or equal.

Here's an example of a scalar matrix comparison:

$$\begin{pmatrix} 1 & 0 \\ 2 & 1 \\ 4 & 3 \end{pmatrix} > \begin{pmatrix} 0 & 1 \\ 3 & 0 \\ 4 & 1 \end{pmatrix} = \begin{pmatrix} 1 & 0 \\ 0 & 1 \\ 0 & 1 \end{pmatrix}$$

Inner Product

An inner product is the summation of the products of corresponding elements in a row and column vector, as defined by this formula:

$$Inner(x,y) = \sum_{i=1}^{n} x_i \, y_i$$

I've implemented an *InnerProduct* function with by this function:

```
template <class D>
    D Matrix<D>::InnerProduct
        (
        const Matrix<D> & m
        )
        {
        D result = (D)0;

        if (((R == 1) && (m.C == 1) && (C == m.R))
        || ((C == 1) && (m.R == 1) && (R == m.C)))
            {
            const D * ptr1 = Data;
            const D * ptr2 = m.Data;

            size_t end = (C == 1 ? R : C);

            for (size_t n = 0; n < end; ++n)
                {
                result += (*ptr1) * (*ptr2);
                ++ptr1;
                ++ptr2;
                }
            }
        else
            throw MatrixEx(MTX_INCOMPAT);

        return result;
        }
```

InnerProduct generates an exception when called for two incompatible matrices.

Minors

A *minor* is formed by removing a specific row and column from a matrix; its best known use is in recursively calculating the determinant of a *Matrix*. For example, for this matrix

$$A = \begin{pmatrix} 2 & 1 & 4 & 7 \\ 3 & 0 & 9 & 7 \\ 8 & 0 & 1 & 3 \\ 1 & 2 & 6 & 5 \end{pmatrix}$$

the minor created by removing row 1, column 2 is:

$$A_{[12]} = \begin{pmatrix} 3 & 9 & 7 \\ 8 & 1 & 3 \\ 1 & 6 & 5 \end{pmatrix}$$

The *Matrix Minor* function creates a new matrix with the appropriate row and column removed:

```
template <class D>
    Matrix<D> Matrix<D>::Minor
        (
        size_t rdel,
        size_t cdel
        )
        {
        if ((R != C) || (R < 2))
            throw MatrixEx(MTX_INCOMPAT);

        Matrix<D> result(R-1,C-1);

        const D * psrc = Data;
        D * pdest = result.Data;

        for (size_t rsrc = 0; rsrc < R; ++rsrc)
            {
            if (rsrc != rdel)
                {
                for (size_t csrc = 0; csrc < C; ++csrc)
                    {
                    if (csrc != cdel)
                        {
                        *pdest = *psrc;
                        ++pdest;
```

```
                    }

               ++psrc;
               }
          }
      else
          psrc += C;
      }

   return result;
   }
```

You can calculate the determinant of an n-by-n matrix from its minors by following this formula:

$$\det(A)=\begin{cases} a_{11} & n=1 \\ a_{11}\det(A_{[11]})-a_{12}\det(A_{[12]})+\cdots+(-1)^{n+1}a_{1n}\det(A_{[1n]}) & n>1 \end{cases}$$

Using the preceding rules, I created a recursive *Determinant* function, as follows:

```
template <class D>
    D Matrix<D>::Determinant()
        {
        if (R != C)
            throw MatrixEx(MTX_INCOMPAT);

        if (C == 1)
            return (*Data);

        if (IsSingular())
            return (D)0;

        return DetRecursive();
        }

template <class D>
    D Matrix<D>::DetRecursive()
        {
        if (C == 2)
```

```
    {
    return   (     (*Data)    * (*(Data + 3)) )
           - ( (*(Data + 1)) * (*(Data + 2)) );
    }

D result      = (D)0;
const D * ptr = Data;

for (size_t x = 0; x < C; ++x)
    {
    if (x & 1) // if on an even column
        result -= (*ptr) * (Minor(0,x)).DetRecursive();
    else
        result += (*ptr) * (Minor(0,x)).DetRecursive();

    ++ptr;
    }

return result;
}
```

Linear Equations and Gaussian Elimination

Scientific calculations often involve the search for solutions to systems of linear equations. Such solutions can be found from a square matrix in which the number of unknown values is equal to the number of equations. For example, the simultaneous equations

$$x_1 + 3x_2 - 4x_3 = 8$$
$$x_1 + x_2 - 2x_3 = 2$$
$$-x_1 - 2x_2 + 5x_3 = -1$$

can be conveniently rewritten as this matrix-vector equation:

$$\begin{pmatrix} 1 & 3 & -4 \\ 1 & 1 & -2 \\ -1 & 2 & 5 \end{pmatrix} \cdot \begin{pmatrix} x_1 \\ x_2 \\ x_3 \end{pmatrix} = \begin{pmatrix} 8 \\ 2 \\ -1 \end{pmatrix}$$

One method of solving linear equations is to use a 150-year-old technique known as *Gaussian elimination*. Based on the properties of matrices, certain manipulations can be performed without altering the solution. The order of the equations does not affect the outcome, and we can, with impunity, multiply the equations by a constant. Also, any equation can be replaced by summing it with another equation.

For example, the second equation can be replaced by its difference with the first equation:

$$\begin{pmatrix} 1 & 3 & -4 \\ 0 & 2 & -2 \\ -1 & 2 & 5 \end{pmatrix} \cdot \begin{pmatrix} x_1 \\ x_2 \\ x_3 \end{pmatrix} = \begin{pmatrix} 8 \\ 6 \\ -1 \end{pmatrix}$$

That eliminates x_1 from the second equation. The same technique can be used to eliminate x_1 from the third equation by summing the first and third equations:

$$\begin{pmatrix} 1 & 3 & -4 \\ 0 & 2 & -2 \\ 0 & 1 & 1 \end{pmatrix} \cdot \begin{pmatrix} x_1 \\ x_2 \\ x_3 \end{pmatrix} = \begin{pmatrix} 8 \\ 6 \\ 7 \end{pmatrix}$$

This operation can be performed over and over, until the original system of equations has been transformed into a triangular matrix that can easily be solved:

$$\begin{pmatrix} 1 & 3 & -4 \\ 0 & 2 & -2 \\ 0 & 0 & -4 \end{pmatrix} \cdot \begin{pmatrix} x_1 \\ x_2 \\ x_3 \end{pmatrix} = \begin{pmatrix} 8 \\ 6 \\ -8 \end{pmatrix}$$

The third equation has been reduced to a point where we can calculate x_3 as 2. If we substitute x_3 into the second equation, it is simple to compute x_2 as 5. Substituting both x_3 and x_2 into the first equation solves for the third unknown, x_1, which equals 1.

Forward substitution is the first phase of reducing the equations; after reducing the coefficient matrix to a triangular form, we employ *backward substitution* to calculate the values of each unknown in x.

To make the procedure simpler, I designed my Gaussian elimination function to work with an $n * n+1$ matrix, where the $n+1$st column holds the solution vector b.

```
template <class D>
    Matrix<D> Matrix<D>::LinSolve()
        {
        if (((C - R) != 1) || (IsSingular()))
            throw MatrixEx(MTX_INCOMPAT);

        size_t i, j, k, max;
        D temp;

        // forward elimination
        for (i = 0; i < R; ++i)
            {
            max = i;

            for (j = i + 1; j < R; ++j)
                {
                if (AbsVal(Elem(j,i)) > AbsVal(Elem(max,i)))
                    max = j;
                }

            for (k = i; k < C; ++k)
                {
                temp = Elem(i,k);
                    Elem(i,k) = Elem(max,k);
                        Elem(max,k) = temp;
                }

            for (j = i + 1; j < R; ++j)
                {
                for (k = R; k >= i; --k)
                    {
                    Elem(j,k) -=    Elem(i,k)
                                * Elem(j,i)
                                / Elem(i,i);

                    if (k == 0)
                        break;
                    }
```

```
            }
        }

    // backward substitution
    Matrix<D> X(R,1); // results

    for (j = R - 1; ; —j)
        {
        temp = (D)0;

        for (k = j + 1; k < R; ++k)
            temp += Elem(j,k) * X.Elem(k,0);

        X.Elem(j,0) = (Elem(j,R) - temp) / Elem(j,j);

        if (j == 0)
            break;
        }

    return X;
    }
```

To avoid the chance of division by zero, *LinSolve* includes code to exchange rows. If called for a singular matrix, division by zero cannot be avoided, and *LinSolve* throws an exception.

LinSolve destroys the original matrix in its calculation; I could have created a copy of the input matrix (*this*), but for large matrices, creating the copy would use considerable memory. If you want to preserve the original matrix, simply create an explicit copy for use in *LinSolve*.

LUP Decomposition

Gaussian elimination is a common tool for solving equations, but it isn't the only technique available. LUP decomposition, for instance, offers interesting capabilities.

Begin by decomposing matrix *A* into a pair of matrices *L* and *U* so that:

$$L \cdot U = A$$

The process of creating L and U is called *decomposition*. L is a lower-triangular matrix, and U is an upper-triangular matrix. According to matrix math, a linear equation can be rewritten as:

$$A \cdot x = (1 \cdot U) \cdot x = L \cdot (U \cdot x) = b$$

In turn, *forward substitution* can solve:

$$L \cdot y = b$$

allowing backward substitution to find a solution to:

$$U \cdot x = y$$

At first, it might not seem that L and U can provide a solution that is superior to Gaussian elimination. However, once we have L and U, we can solve the set of equations for any b. Also, the decomposition into L and U allows for the simple calculation of the inverse of a matrix. And, in most cases, decomposition is faster than Gaussian elimination.

Where does the P come from in *LUP*? While we're solving for the two triangular components, rows may (and probably will) be swapped—and a permutation matrix P is maintained to track these exchanges.

It's possible to create a single composite matrix of L and U. Known as *Crout's algorithm*, this technique copies the combined triangular matrices into the source matrix. This is accomplished by the following formulas:

```
for (j = 0; j < n; ++j)
    {
    for (i = 0; i < j; ++i)
```

$$\beta_{ij} = \alpha_{ij} - \sum_{k=0}^{i-1} \alpha_{ik} \beta_{kj}$$

```
    for (i = j; i < n; ++n)
```

$$\alpha_{ij} = \frac{1}{\beta_{jj}} \left(\alpha_{ij} - \sum_{k=0}^{j-1} \alpha_{ik} \beta_{kj} \right)$$

```
}
```

This process results in a combined *LU* matrix that looks like this:

$$\begin{pmatrix} \beta_{00} & \beta_{01} & \beta_{02} & \beta_{03} \\ \alpha_{10} & \beta_{11} & \beta_{12} & \beta_{13} \\ \alpha_{20} & \alpha_{21} & \beta_{22} & \beta_{23} \\ \alpha_{30} & \alpha_{31} & \alpha_{32} & \beta_{33} \end{pmatrix}$$

Swapping rows to avoid division by zero creates a permutation of the preceding matrix; furthermore, the algorithm makes the best selection for the fraction $1/\beta_{jj}$ by exchanging rows so as to make an optimal (largest) choice for β_{jj}.

```cpp
template <class D>
    Grid<size_t> Matrix<D>::LUPDecompose()
        {
        // make sure its square
        if ((R != C) || (R < 2))
            throw MatrixEx(MTX_INCOMPAT);

        // LU decomposition
        size_t i, j, k, k2, t;
        D p, temp;
        Grid<size_t> perm(R,1); // permutation matrix

        // initialize permutation
        for (i = 0; i < R; ++i)
            perm(i,0) = i;

        for (k = 0; k < (R - 1); ++k)
            {
            p = D(0);

            for (i = k; i < R; ++i)
                {
                temp = AbsVal(Elem(i,k));
```

```
            if (temp > p)
                {
                p  = temp;
                k2 = i;
                }
        }

    if (p == D(0))
        throw MatrixEx(MTX_SINGULAR);

    // exchange rows
    t = perm(k,0);
    perm(k,0)  = perm(k2,0);
    perm(k2,0) = t;

    for (i = 0; i < R; ++i)
        {
        temp = Elem(k,i);
        Elem(k,i) = Elem(k2,i);
        Elem(k2,i) = temp;
        }

    for (i = k + 1; i < R; ++i)
        {
        Elem(i,k) /= Elem(k,k);

        for (j = k + 1; j < R; ++j)
            Elem(i,j) -= Elem(i,k) * Elem(k,j);
        }
    }

// return values
return perm;
}
```

The *LUPDecompose* function returns the permutation matrix representing the row exchanges performed. Then it replaces the original matrix with its *LU* decomposition.

To solve for a given solution matrix *b*, call *LUPSolve* with a matrix processed by *LUPDecompose*. *LUPSolve* perfroms forward substitution to calculate *y* from *L* and *b*; then the routine uses backward substitution to compute *x* from *U* and *y*.

```cpp
template <class D>
    Matrix<D> Matrix<D>::LUPSolve
        (
        const Grid<size_t> & perm,
        const Matrix<D> & b
        )
        {
        if ((R != b.R) || (R != perm.GetRows()))
            throw MatrixEx(MTX_INCOMPAT);

        size_t i, j, j2;
        D sum, u;
        Matrix<D> y(R,1), x(R,1);

        for (i = 0; i < R; ++i)
            {
            sum = D(0);
            j2  = 0;

            for (j = 1; j <= i; ++j)
                {
                sum += Elem(i,j2) * y.Elem(j2,0);
                ++j2;
                }

            y.Elem(i,0) = b.Elem(perm.Elem(i,0),0) - sum;
            }

        i = R - 1;

        while (1)
            {
            sum = D(0);
            u   = Elem(i,i);

            for (j = i + 1; j < R; ++j)
                sum += Elem(i,j) * x.Elem(j,0);

            x.Elem(i,0) = (y.Elem(i,0) - sum) / u;
```

```
        if (i == 0)
            break;

        --i;
        }

    return x;
    }
```

Don't change the permutation or decomposition returned by
LUPDecompose, because doing so would result in bogus output from
LUPSolve.

Inversion

Once a matrix is decomposed, its inverse can be calculated by using a
permutation matrix to systematically compute an inverse for each row.

```
template <class D>
    Matrix<D> Matrix<D>::LUPInvert
        (
        const Grid<size_t> & perm
        )
        {
        size_t i, j;
        Matrix<D> p(R,1);
        Matrix<D> result(R,R);

        for (j = 0; j < R; ++j)
            {
            for (i = 0; i < R; ++i)
                p.Elem(i,0) = D(0);

            p.Elem(j,0) = D(1);

            p = LUPSolve(perm,p);

            for (i = 0; i < R; ++i)
                result.Elem(i,j) = p.Elem(i,0);
            }
```

```
        return result;
    }
```

APPLICATION

The matrix exception types can be found in the files **matrixx.h** and **matrixx.cpp**. The *Matrix* and *Grid* class templates are located in the file **matrix.h**. Look in the module **tbmatrix.cpp** for example code.

CHAPTER 10

POLYNOMIALS

Polynomials are often used in common computation tasks. This chapter introduces a basic polynomial class that supports efficient addition, subtraction, and multiplication.

POLYNOMIAL BASICS

A *polynomial* is a function that sums the products of corresponding coefficients and powers of a variable, as in:

$$7x^5 - 2x^4 + x^2 + 3x - 9$$

A computer needs to keep track of a polynomial's coefficients only for each power. For example, the preceding polynomial could be (and is, in my implementation) stored as the following array:

$$\{-9, 3, 1, 0, -2, 7\}$$

Notice that the order of the coefficients is "backwards." This is because the zero element of an array is the leftmost element, and I store coefficients so that their index corresponds to the power of x. Thus, –2 is placed at index location 4 in the coefficient array.

Adding two polynomials is easy; simply add the corresponding coefficients. For example, adding the following two polynomials

$$f(x) = -3x^3 + x^2 - 6$$
$$g(x) = 5x^3 + x + 1;$$

results in the new polynomial

$$g(x) + f(x) = 2x^3 + x^2 + x - 5$$

Subtracting polynomials follows the same algorithm, in which corresponding coefficients are subtracted. Here's an example:

$$f(x) - g(x) = -8x^3 + x^2 - x - 7$$

As you might expect, multiplying two polynomials is a bit more complicated. In algebraic terms, every coefficient in $f(x)$ is multiplied by every coefficient in $g(x)$, producing a new polynomial that potentially has twice as many coefficients as the largest of its multiplicands. In the case of $f(x)$ and $g(x)$,

$$h(x) = f(x)g(x) = -15x^6 + 5x^5 - 3x^4 - 32x^3 + x^2 - 6x - 6$$

Any polynomial class will need to allow the function to be evaluated for a given value of x. The fastest way to evaluate a polynomial involves a looping technique known as *Horner's rule*, which alternates addition and multiplication. For example, to evaluate *h(x)* using Horner's rule, I would implement this formula:

$$f(x) = (x(x(x(x(x(x(-15) + 5) - 3) - 32) + 1) - 6) - 6)$$

POLYNOMIAL CLASS

I created a simple class template to implement the polynomial properties just discussed.

```
template <class D>
    class Polynomial
        {
        public:
            // constructor
            Polynomial
                (
                size_t terms,
                const D * array = NULL
                );

            // copy constructor
            Polynomial
                (
                const Polynomial<D> & poly
                );

            // destructor
            ~Polynomial();
```

```
// assignment operator
void operator =
    (
    const Polynomial<D> & poly
    );

void operator =
    (
    const D * array
    );

// conversion to array
operator D * () const;

// increase degree
Polynomial<D> Stretch
    (
    size_t newN
    ) const;

// interrogation
size_t Degree() const;

// get coefficients
D Get
    (
    size_t term
    ) const;

D & operator []
    (
    size_t term
    );

// evaluate a polynomial for given value
D operator ()
    (
    D x
    ) const;

// operations
Polynomial<D> operator - () const;
```

```
Polynomial<D> operator + () const;

Polynomial<D> operator +
    (
    const Polynomial<D> & poly
    ) const;

void operator +=
    (
    const Polynomial<D> & poly
    );

Polynomial<D> operator -
    (
    const Polynomial<D> & poly
    ) const;

void operator -=
    (
    const Polynomial<D> & poly
    );

Polynomial<D> operator *
    (
    const Polynomial<D> & poly
    ) const;

protected:
    D * Coeff;
    size_t N;
};
```

Each *Polynomial* object contains a dynamically allocated array pointed to by *Coeff*. *N* holds the number of coefficients stored, and *N-1* is the largest exponent of *x*.

Constructors and Destructor

The primary constructor requires that the degree of the polynomial be supplied. An optional second parameter may point to an array of values for initializing the *Coeff* values. If *array* is NULL (its default value), the constructor fills *Coeff* with zeros.

```cpp
template <class D>
    Polynomial<D>::Polynomial
        (
        size_t terms,
        const D * array = NULL
        )
        {
        if (terms < 2)
            throw PolyEx(PX_TOOSMALL);

        N = terms;

        Coeff = new D [N];

        if (Coeff == NULL)
            throw PolyEx(PX_ALLOC);

        if (array == NULL)
            {
            for (size_t i = 0; i < N; ++i)
                Coeff[i] = (D)0;
            }
        else
            {
            for (size_t i = 0; i < N; ++i)
                Coeff[i] = array[i];
            }
        }
```

The copy constructor performs a deep copy by duplicating the coefficients of an existing polynomial.

```cpp
template <class D>
    Polynomial<D>::Polynomial
        (
        const Polynomial<D> & poly
        )
        {
```

```
N      = poly.N;
Coeff = new D [N];

if (Coeff == NULL)
    throw PolyEx(PX_ALLOC);

for (size_t i = 0; i < N; ++i)
    Coeff[i] = poly.Coeff[i];
}
```

The destructor simply deletes the *Coeff* array.

```
template <class D>
    Polynomial<D>::~Polynomial()
        {
        delete [] Coeff;
        }
```

Assignment

This function assigns one *Polynomial* to another. The destination copies the source coefficients if both *Polynomial*s have the same degree. If the degrees differ, the destination *Polynomial* deletes the *Coeff* array and creates a new one of the appropriate size.

```
template <class D>
    void Polynomial<D>::operator =
        (
        const Polynomial<D> & poly
        )
        {
        if (N != poly.N)
            {
            delete [] Coeff;

            N = poly.N;

            Coeff = new D [N];
```

```
            if (Coeff == NULL)
                throw PolyEx(PX_ALLOC);
        }

    for (size_t i = 0; i < N; ++i)
        Coeff[i] = poly.Coeff[i];
    }
```

The array assignment operator assumes that *array* has *N* elements, an asumption that your program will need to ensure.

```
template <class D>
    void Polynomial<D>::operator =
        (
        const D * array
        )
        {
        if (array == NULL)
            return;

        for (size_t i = 0; i < N; ++i)
            Coeff[i] = array[i];
        }
```

Examining Coefficients

The *Get* function returns a copy of a coefficient, and you can use it with constant *Polynomials*.

```
template <class D>
    D Polynomial<D>::Get
        (
        size_t term
        )
        const
        {
        if (term >= N)
            throw PolyEx(PX_RANGE);
```

```
return Coeff[term];
}
```

The brackets operator returns a reference to a coefficient, allowing it to be both read and changed. It cannot be used with constant *Polynomials*.

```
template <class D>
    D & Polynomial<D>::operator []
        (
        size_t term
        )
        {
        if (term >= N)
            throw PolyEx(PX_RANGE);

        return Coeff[term];
        }
```

Interrogators and Utilities

The inline *Degree* function returns *N*.

```
template <class D>
    inline size_t Polynomial<D>::Degree() const
        {
        return N;
        }
```

To obtain a constant pointer to the coefficient array, use the *const D ** operator.

```
template <class D>
    Polynomial<D>::operator const D * () const
        {
        return (const D *)Coeff;
        }
```

The *Stretch* function allows the addition of new, higher-degree coefficients to an existing *Polynomial.*

```cpp
template <class D>
    Polynomial<D> Polynomial<D>::Stretch
        (
        size_t newN
        )
        const
        {
        if (newN <= N)
            return (*this);

        Polynomial<D> result(newN);

        for (size_t i = 0; i < N; ++i)
            result.Coeff[i] = Coeff[i];

        return result;
        }
```

The function initializes all new coefficients to zero.

I've implemented both unary plus and minus. The plus returns the target *Polynomial* unchanged, whereas the minus creates a new *Polynomial* in which it has negated the coefficients copied from the source.

```cpp
template <class D>
    Polynomial<D> Polynomial<D>::operator - () const
        {
        Polynomial<D> result(N);

        for (size_t i = 0; i < N; ++ i)
            result.Coeff[i] = -Coeff[i];

        return result;
        }

template <class D>
    inline Polynomial<D> Polynomial<D>::operator + () const
        {
        return *this;
        }
```

Addition and Subtraction

Adding two polynomials requires accounting for differing degrees of the polynomials. The operator + function duplicates the longest of the two *Polynomial*s and then adds the corresponding coefficients. The shorthand operator is an inline call to the binary + function.

```
template <class D>
    Polynomial<D> Polynomial<D>::operator +
        (
        const Polynomial<D> & poly
        )
        const
        {
        if (N > poly.N)
            {
            Polynomial<D> res1(*this);

            for (size_t i = 0; i < poly.N; ++i)
                res1.Coeff[i] += poly.Coeff[i];

            return res1;
            }
        else
            {
            Polynomial<D> res2(poly);

            for (size_t i = 0; i < N; ++i)
                res2.Coeff[i] += Coeff[i];

            return res2;
            }
        }

template <class D>
    inline void Polynomial<D>::operator +=
        (
        const Polynomial<D> & poly
        )
```

```
            {
            *this = (*this) + poly;
            }
```

Subtraction requires a slightly different approach. If the degree of the left-hand *Polynomial* is greater than or equal to the degree of the right-hand operand, *operator* - works like *operator* +. If, however, the left-hand polynomial has the higher degree, I create a negative copy of it and add the coefficients of the shorter polynomial.

```
template <class D>
    Polynomial<D> Polynomial<D>::operator -
        (
        const Polynomial<D> & poly
        )
        const
        {
        if (N > poly.N)
            {
            Polynomial<D> res1(*this);

            for (size_t i = 0; i < poly.N; ++i)
                res1.Coeff[i] -= poly.Coeff[i];

            return res1;
            }
        else
            {
            Polynomial<D> res2(-poly);

            for (size_t i = 0; i < N; ++i)
                res2.Coeff[i] += Coeff[i];

            return res2;
            }
        }

template <class D>
    inline void Polynomial<D>::operator -=
        (
        const Polynomial<D> & poly
        )
```

```
    {
    *this = (*this) - poly;
    }
```

As with addition, the shorthand subtraction operator is an inline call to its binary cousin.

Multiplication

Multiplying *Polynomials* requires the creation of a new polynomial to hold the expanded number of coefficients. This routine can multiply polynomials only of the same degree; nothing, however, prevents you from extending a polynomial with "zero" coefficients for higher-degree terms.

```
template <class D>
    Polynomial<D> Polynomial<D>::operator *
        (
        const Polynomial<D> & poly
        )
        const
        {
        if (N != poly.N)
            throw PolyEx(PX_INCOMPAT);

        Polynomial<D> result(2 * N - 1);

        for (size_t i = 0; i < N; ++i)
            {
            for (size_t j = 0; j < N; ++j)
                result[i + j] += Coeff[i] * poly.Coeff[j];
            }

        return result;
        }
```

I've seen a few "quick" polynomial multiplication functions and have generally rejected them. Most of them use more code than the prececing routine, and they often require time-consuming, on-the-fly, dynamic array creation. I've found that the reduction in multiplication is accompanied by an increase in other performance costs, so I stick with the straightforward routine.

Evaluation

The parenthesis function implements Horner's rule to evaluate a polynomial for a given value:

```
template <class D>
    D Polynomial<D>::operator ()
        (
        D x
        )
        const
        {
        D y = Coeff[N - 1];
        size_t i = N - 2;

        while(1)
            {
            y = x * y + Coeff[i];

            if (i == 0)
                break;

            --i;
            }

        return y;
        }
```

FAST FOURIER TRANSFORM

The Fast Fourier Transform (FFT) may be the most efficacious algorithm ever discovered, for its applicability is incredibly broad. From signal processing and data compression to geology and image enhancement, the FFT provides a powerful tool by converting information between domains. Much has been written about the FFT; for this book, I'll show how the FFT can improve the performance of polynomial multiplication.

So far, I've presented polynomials in coefficient form; some applications, however, work best with a polynomial represented in *point-value* form. Any polynomial of degree n can be represented by n pairs of points and values, where *value* is the polynomial evaluated at a given *point*. Many mathematical applications rely on the Fast Fourier Transform, which implements an efficient conversion between point-value and coefficients.

To quickly multiply two polynomials, A and B, follow this procedure:

1. Use a single set of values in converting both A and B from coefficient to point-value forms pA and pB.

2. Multiply the corresponding point-values of pA and pB, creating pC.

3. Interpolate pC to obtain the coefficient polynomial C, which equals A multiplied by B.

On the surface, the above technique appears no more efficient—and is more complicated—than the direct multiplication scheme I used for *operator **. However, a clever selection of evaluation values can make point-value multiplication very fast.

The mathematics underlying the selection of points is outside the scope of this book. The Discrete Fourier Transform (DFT), and its inverse, are the salient equations that map N coefficient values to and from point-value form at specific data values. The DFT converts coefficients to point values using this summation

$$H_n = \sum_{k=0}^{N-1} h_k e^{2\pi i k n/N}$$

while the inverse DFT (designated DFT-1) implements this summation to convert point-values to coefficients:

$$h_k = \frac{1}{N} \sum_{n=0}^{N-1} H_n e^{-2\pi i k n/N}$$

Notice the simple differences between the DFT and its inverse. If a DFT can be effectively implemented, its inverse can be constructed simply by reversing the sign of the exponent and by dividing each element of the result by N.

The Fast Fourier Transform takes advantage of the properties of the DFT summations. In algorithmic terms, the *operator ** function requires $O(N^2)$ operations to multiply two polynomials; the same multiplication can be accomplished by the FFT in only $O(N \log_2 N)$ operations. The larger the polynomials involved, the better the FFT performs in comparison to the *operator ** technique.

Here's how the FFT works. In both the DFT and DFT^{-1}, a constant can be extracted:

$$W \equiv e^{2\pi i/N}$$

Allowing the DFT, for example, to be rewritten as

$$H_n = \sum_{k=0}^{N-1} h_k W^{kn}$$

and the DFT-1 to be expressed as

$$H_n = \frac{1}{N} \sum_{k=0}^{N-1} \frac{h_k}{W^{kn}}$$

In the 1960s, the FFT emerged as a divide-and-conquer approach to calculating DFTs. The FFT is based on the ability to rewrite a DFT of length N as the sum of two DFT's of length $N/2$. From that fact, the most obvious implementation of an FFT would involve recursion, successively processive halves-of-halves to calculate a DFT. Recursion, however, has high overhead from nested function calls; an iterative version of the FFT is required to obtain full speed.

The iterative FFT works by rearranging the input values to match their order of processing under the recursive algorithm. This can be accomplished by bit-reversing the indexes of the input values. For example, in an order-16 polynomial, the values would be rearranged as follows:

INDEX	BINARY	NEW INDEX
0	0000	0000
1	0001	1000
2	0010	0100
3	0011	1100
4	0100	0010
5	0101	1010
6	0110	0110
7	0111	1110
8	1000	0001
9	1001	1001
10	1010	0101
11	1011	1101
12	1100	0011
13	1101	1011
14	1110	0111
15	1111	1111

The following function returns the reversed low-order b bits of k.

```
static size_t FlipBits
    (
    size_t k,
    size_t b
```

```
)
{
size_t lm = 1 << (b - 1);
size_t rm = 1;
size_t  r = 0;

while (lm)
    {
    if (k & rm)
        r |= (lm);

    lm >>= 1;
    rm <<= 1;
    }

return r;
}
```

Using *FlipBits, BitRevCopy* copies elements from a source polynomial to a destination polynomial:

```
static CPoly BitRevCopy
    (
    const DPoly & p
    )
{
size_t n = p.Degree();
size_t b = log2(n);
CPoly a(n);

for (size_t k = 0; k < n; ++k)
    a[FlipBits(k,b)] = p.Get(k);

return a;
}
```

The utility function *log2* returns the base-2 logarithm of a *size_t* integer.

```
static size_t log2
    (
    size_t n
```

```
)
{
// returns 1 if n == 0!
size_t x = 1, c = 0;

for (;;)
    {
    if (x >= n)
        break;

    ++c;
    x <<= 1;

    if (x == 0)
        break;
    }

return c;
}
```

The FFT relies on N being a power of two; this doesn't present much of a problem, since we can simply extend the length of any polynomial by adding coefficients with a value of zero. That's the purpose of the *FFTStretch* function:

```
template <class T>
    static size_t FFTStretch
        (
        Polynomial<T> & p
        )
        {
        size_t n = 1;
        size_t d = p.Degree();

        while (1)
            {
            if (d <= n)
                break;

            n <<= 1;
```

```
            if (n == 0)
                throw PolyEx(PX_OVERFLOW);
            }

    n <<= 1;

    p = p.Stretch(n);

    return n;
    }
```

The *FFTMultiply* function takes a pair of *DPoly* objects as parameters, returning another *DPoly* containg the coefficients of their multiplication:

```
DPoly FFTMultiply
    (
    const DPoly & p1,
    const DPoly & p2
    )
    {
    size_t n2, k;

    // duplicate p1 and p2 to preserve originals
    DPoly a1(p1);
    DPoly a2(p2);

    // expand polynomials to next-largest power of two
    if (a1.Degree() > a2.Degree())
        {
        n2 = FFTStretch(a1);
        a2 = a2.Stretch(n2);
        }
    else
        {
        n2 = FFTStretch(a2);
        a1 = a1.Stretch(n2);
        }

    // FFT polynomials
    CPoly dft1 = PolyFFT(a1);
    CPoly dft2 = PolyFFT(a2);
```

```
// multiply coefficients
for (k = 0; k < n2; ++k)
    dft1[k] *= dft2[k];

// inverse DFT to obtain result
dft2 = PolyInvFFT(dft1);

// convert back to DPoly
DPoly result(n2 - 1);

for (k = 0; k < n2 - 1; ++k)
    result[k] = real(dft2[k]);

// return result
return result;
}
```

FFTMultiply begins by calling *FFTStretch* to expand copies of both *DPoly* parameters. The extended *DPolys* then become parameters in separate calls to *PolyFFT*, which returns a *CPoly*.

```
static CPoly PolyFFT
    (
    const DPoly & p
    )
    {
    size_t n  = p.Degree();
    size_t nl = log2(n);
    size_t j, k, m, m2, s;
    complex wm, w, t, u;
    CPoly a = BitRevCopy(p);

    m  = 2;
    m2 = 1;

    for (s = 0; s < nl; ++s)
        {
        wm = exp(PI2I / double(m));
        w  = 1.0;

        for (j = 0; j <= (m2 - 1); ++j)
```

```
            {
            for (k = j; k <= n - 1; k += m)
                {
                t = w * a[k + m2];
                u = a[k];
                a[k] = u + t;
                a[k + m2] = u - t;
                }

        w *= wm;
            }

    m   <<= 1;
    m2 <<= 1;
    }

return a;
}
```

FFTMultiply then multiplies the corresponding values in the two *CPoly* DFTs, and calls *PolyInvFFT* to convert the result to coefficient form.

```
static CPoly PolyInvFFT
    (
    const CPoly & p
    )
    {
    size_t n  = p.Degree();
    size_t nl = log2(n);
    size_t j, k, m, m2, s;
    complex wm, w, t, u;
    CPoly a = BitRevCopy(p);

    m  = 2;
    m2 = 1;

    for (s = 0; s < nl; ++s)
        {
        wm = exp(-PI2I / double(m));
        w  = 1.0;

        for (j = 0; j <= (m2 - 1); ++j)
```

```
        {
        for (k = j; k <= n - 1; k += m)
            {
            t = w * a[k + m2];
            u = a[k];
            a[k] = u + t;
            a[k + m2] = u - t;
            }

        w *= wm;
        }

    m  <<= 1;
    m2 <<= 1;
    }

for (j = 0; j < n; ++j)
    a[j] /= double(n);

return a;
}
```

The only remaining act for *FFTMultiply* is to return a *DPoly* array containing the calculated coefficients.

EXCEPTIONS

Following the pattern I've set in other chapters, I create an enumerated type and an *ExceptionBase* class for handling exceptions raised by *Polynomial*s.

```
enum PolyError
    {
    PX_ALLOC,
    PX_TOOSMALL,
    PX_RANGE,
    PX_INCOMPAT
    };

class PolyEx : public ExceptionBase
```

```
    {
    public:
        PolyEx
            (
            PolyError err
            )
            {
            Error = err;
            }

        PolyError WhatsWrong()
            {
            return Error;
            }

        virtual void Explain
            (
            DiagOutput & out
            );

    private:
        PolyError Error;
    };

void PolyEx::Explain
    (
    DiagOutput & out
    )
    {
    switch (Error)
        {
        case PX_ALLOC:
            out.DisplayMsg("Can't allocate polynomial memory ",
                        DIAG_ERROR);
            break;
        case PX_TOOSMALL:
            out.DisplayMsg("Polynomial must have > 2 terms",
                        DIAG_WARNING);
            break;
        case PX_RANGE:
            out.DisplayMsg("Term out of range in polynomial",
                        DIAG_ERROR);
            break;
```

```
case PX_INCOMPAT:
    out.DisplayMsg("Op w/incompatible polynomials",
                    DIAG_ERROR);
    break;
default:
    out.DisplayMsg("Unknown polynomial exception",
                    DIAG_FATAL);
    }
}
```

APPLICATION

The polynomial exception types are defined in the files **polyx.h** and **polyx.cpp**. Look for the *Polynomial* class in **poly.h**, and for test code in the module **tbpoly.cpp**.

CHAPTER 11

PARSING

Most C++ classes define a new data type; in fact, many object-oriented programming adherents will refer to a class as the definition of an abstract data type. I've found that classes can also be easily used to define a process or action performed in a program. A class, encapsulating both data definitions and functions, can be viewed as a miniature "program" that is used by your applications. I've built a top-down formula parser that allows my programs to process arithmetic statements.

BUILDING A CALCULATOR

Over the years, I've run into a number of applications that need to calculate the value of formulas such as these:

```
(2 + 2) * 8
3.4 / 5.6 + 7.1
A + 3 * B
```

The solution is to create a "calculator" that provides the solution to equations stored in strings. The calculator must understand the precedence of operators—for example, all multiplications and divisions are performed before any additions and subtractions, except where parentheses are used. In essence, the calculator should calculate the value of a formula in the same way a mathematician would.

Extracting "meaning" from a string requires a parser. A *parser* breaks a piece of text into its component parts according to a set of specified rules; as it extracts each piece, the parser determines its meaning in context. This is what your compiler does, and it's a component of any program that tries to interpret text you've typed in.

The first step in creating a parser is to define a grammar describing the format of a formula. In general, a *grammar* defines replacement rules that determine how various pieces of text—tokens—relate to one another. An expression is evaluated by breaking it down into numeric values separated by operators and organized into subexpressions with parentheses. Subexpressions can be treated as expressions in their own right, and they can be recursively evaluated. For example, the expression

```
2 * (3 + 4)
```

requires the parser to evaluate the subexpression (3 + 4) before performing the multiplication. This is accomplished by feeding (3 + 4) into the parser as an expression and then multiplying the result by 2; the parser is now finished, and it should return a value.

Based on these thoughts, I define the following partial grammar:

```
   <exp> ::= <term> | <term> + <exp> | <term> - <exp>
  <term> ::= <factor> | <factor>* <term> | <factor> / <term>
<factor> ::= <value> | <value> ^ <value>
 <value> ::= ( <expression> ) | <number> | <ident>
<number> ::= <digits> | .<digits> | <digits>.
                                   | <digits>.digits>
 <ident> ::= <letters>
```

I could go on to define digits and letters, but I think you get the idea. The preceding grammar defines a hierarchy of replacements, declaring the order of evaluation in a formula string. This is the way people work on math problems, and the calculator will need to analyze a formula in a human fashion by breaking it into component parts that are calculated in the correct order based on operator precedence and the placement of parentheses. The preceding grammar defines operator precedence as shown in Table 11.1

TABLE 11.1 OPERATOR PRECEDENCE

PRECEDENCE	OPERATOR	DESCRIPTION
5	(...)	parenthetical expression
4	+	unary plus
	-	unary minus
3	^	exponentiation (power)
2	*	multiplication
	/	division
1	+	addition
	-	subtraction

Each component of an expression is called a *token*, and each token has a type: number, operator, or delimiter (parenthesis). A variable is another form of number; when I encounter a variable name, I look up its value in a table and replace the variable name text with a numeric value.

A formula consists of a series of tokens that are organized as terms separated by operators. A term is either number, a variable name, an operator, or an expression bracketed by parentheses. The grammar defines pieces of a formula in terms of other pieces—and that makes a recursive approach quite natural. The code in my evaluator literally follows the grammar's recursive description of a formula.

Note that expressions in parentheses can be thought of as miniature formulas in their own right. This means that a formula is a recursive structure; it can contain other formulas in the form of expressions in parentheses. This is where the "recursive" part of the evaluator comes from.

A few more rules will finialize the theory behind my parser. The parser will need to contain a function that extracts tokens from the expression string. Spaces and tabs will be skipped when parsing an expression, and an unrecognized character immediately ends the parsing process.

VARIABLE NAMES

My function evaluator supports named variables having as many as 32 characters. Each variable will be stored in a *Dictionary*, where it can be looked up quickly by hashing on its name. That technique required me to create a simple string type for holding variable names.

```
struct VarName
    {
    char Text[TOKEN_MAX + 1];

    VarName
        (
        const char * vname = NULL
        );

    VarName
        (
```

```
        const VarName & vn
        );

    void operator =
        (
        const VarName & vn
        );

    int operator ==
        (
        const VarName & vn
        ) const;
    };
```

VarName's functions reflect its simple purpose. To begin, I define *VarName* as a structure to allow direct access to its *Text* buffer. The functions I've created are either for convenience or to provide functionality required of types stored in *Dictionaries*.

The constructors and assignment operator use C++'s built-in string functions to copy values into a *VarName*'s *Text* buffer.

```
inline VarName::VarName
    (
    const char * vname
    )
    {
    if ((vname == NULL) || (vname[0] == 0))
        Text[0] = 0;
    else
        strncpy(Text,vname,TOKEN_MAX);
    }

inline VarName::VarName
    (
    const VarName & vn
    )
    {
    strncpy(Text,vn.Text,TOKEN_MAX);
    }

inline void VarName::operator =
```

```
(
const VarName & vn
)
{
strncpy(Text,vn.Text,TOKEN_MAX);
}
```

The comparison operator simply returns the result of a call to *strcmp*.

```
inline int VarName::operator ==
    (
    const VarName & vn
    )
    const
    {
    return (0 == strcmp(Text,vn.Text));
    }
```

EVALUATOR CLASS

My *Evaluator* class uses a set of private functions to extract tokens and recursively descend through a given formula's text.

```
class Evaluator
    {
    public:
        // default constructor
        Evaluator();

        // copy constructor
        Evaluator
            (
            const Evaluator & eval
            );

        // assignment operator
        void operator =
            (
```

```
        const Evaluator & eval
        );

    void SetVar
        (
        const char * vname,
        double vval
        );

    double Compute
        (
        const char * formula
        );

private:
    // types
    enum TokenType
        TT_NUMBER,
        {
        TT_VARIABLE,
        TT_DELIM,
        TT_UNKNOWN
        };

    // constants
    static const CharSet Delimiters;
    static const CharSet Numbers;

    // variables
    const char * Eq;           // current byte being parsed
    char  Token[TOKEN_MAX];    // current token text
    TokenType  Type;           // current token type

    // stored variables
    Dictionary<VarName,double,23> Vars;

    // copy next token into Token array
    void GetToken();

    // internal functions
    double AddSub();
    double MultDiv();
    double Power();
```

```
        double Sign();
        double Paren();
    };
```

Unlike most classes, *Evaluator* defines more private members than it does public ones. This approach encapsulates the private functions and types involved in formula evaluation. In essence, *Evaluator* is a black box into which your programs feed formula strings and variable assignments.

Evaluator uses the standard *CharSets CS_Whitespace* and *CS_Letters*; it also defines two character sets of its own, one containing the 10 digits and decimal point (period), and the other containing a list of operators that delimit an equation.

```
const CharSet Evaluator::Delimiters("+-*/^()");
const CharSet Evaluator::Numbers("0123456789.");
```

Each *Evaluator* also contains a *Dictionary* object that holds double values indexed by *VarNames*.

The *Eq* pointer addresses the current character position within the string being parsed. *Token* holds the text of the current token, and *Type* is a *TokenType* value that identifies the last token extracted by the *GetToken* function.

Constructors and Assignment

The default constructor creates a new *Evaluator* object with an empty variable dictionary. The constructor doesn't do anything explicitly; its only purpose is to provide a syntactic tool for initializing the *Vars Dictionary*.

```
Evaluator::Evaluator()
    {
    // placeholder
    }
```

The copy constructor creates a new *Evaluator* that has copies of the variable from an existing *Evaluator*.

```
Evaluator::Evaluator
    (
    const Evaluator & eval
    )
    : Vars(eval.Vars)
    {
    // placeholder
    }
```

The assignment operator just assigns the existing *Vars* dictionary to the new one.

```
void Evaluator::operator =
    (
    const Evaluator & eval
    )
    {
    Vars = eval.Vars;
    }
```

Storing Variable

SetVar accepts a variable name and its value for storage in *Vars*. If a variable of the same name already exists, the *Dictionary* will replace it with the new value. Variable names are case-sensitive, so "something", "Something", and "SOMETHING" all refer to different variables.

```
void Evaluator::SetVar
    (
    const char * vname,
    double vval
    )
    {
    VarName n(vname);
    Vars.Insert(n,vval);
    }
```

To assign the value of a calculation to a variable name, simply call *SetVar* with an invocation of the parenthesis operator with the text of the equation:

```
eval.SetVar("X", eval.Compute("2+2")); // x will be assigned 4
```

Evaluating Formulas

The *Compute* function evaluates an equation string based on a hierarchy of calls to recursive functions.

```
double Evaluator::Compute
    (
    const char * formula
    )
    {
    if ((formula == NULL) || ((*formula) == 0))
        throw EvalEx(EVX_NULLDATA);

    // start at beginning of formula
    Eq = formula;

    // get first token
    GetToken();

    // begin evaluating
    return AddSub();
    }
```

After ensuring that it is working with a non-NULL string, *Compute* extracts the first token and calls the *AddSub* function to begin the parsing cycle.

GetToken extracts tokens from the input text, storing them in *Token* and using *Eq* to work through the input string until a NULL character is encountered.

```
void Evaluator::GetToken()
    {
    size_t count;
    char * ptr = Token;
    Type = TT_UNKNOWN;

    while (CS_Whitespace[(*Eq)])
```

```
     ++Eq;

if (Delimiters[*Eq])
    {
    Type = TT_DELIM;
    (*ptr) = (*Eq);
    ++ptr;
    ++Eq;
    }
else
    {
    if (Numbers[(*Eq)])
        {
        int decimal = 0;
        count = 0;
        Type  = TT_NUMBER;

        while ((*Eq) && (Numbers[(*Eq)]))
            {
            (*ptr) = (*Eq);

            ++count;

            if (count == TOKEN_MAX)
                throw EvalEx(EVX_OVERFLOW);

            if ((*Eq) == '.')
                {
                if (decimal)
                    throw EvalEx(EVX_DECIMAL);
                else
                    decimal = 1;
                }

            ++ptr;
            ++Eq;
            }
        }
    else
        {
        if (CS_Letters[(*Eq)])
            {
            count = 0;
```

```
            Type  = TT_VARIABLE;

            while (CS_Letters[(*Eq)])
                {
                (*ptr) = (*Eq);

                ++count;

                if (count == TOKEN_MAX)
                    throw EvalEx(EVX_OVERFLOW);

                ++ptr;
                ++Eq;
                }
            }
        else
            {
            if (*Eq)
                throw EvalEx(EVX_INVCHAR);
            }
        }
    }

    *ptr = 0;
    }
```

GetToken begins by skipping over spaces and tab characters. If it finds a delimiter, it stores the character in *Token*.

If the character is a number, *GetToken* extracts the digits, throwing an exception if it finds more than one decimal point. Once a non-number is found, *GetToken* stops extracting characters.

If the token isn't a number or a delimiter, *GetToken* sees whether it can extract an alphabetic variable name. Characters that don't fit any of the preceding categories will cause a *GetToken* to raise an exception.

AddSub, the first function called in the hierarchy, represents the lowest order of precedence: addition and subtraction.

```
double Evaluator::AddSub()
    {
    // check next level
```

```
    double result = MultDiv();

char oper = Token[0];

while ((oper == '+') || (oper == '-'))
    {
    GetToken();

    double x = MultDiv();

    if (oper == '+')
        result += x;
    else
            result -= x;

    oper = Token[0];
    }

return result;
    }
```

Before it actually adds or subtracts numbers, *AddSub* calls the function *MultDiv*, which processes the next order of precedence.

```
double Evaluator::MultDiv()
    {
    // check next level
    double result = Power();

char oper = Token[0];

while ((oper == '*') || (oper == '/'))
    {
    GetToken();

    double x = Power();

    if (oper == '*')
        result *= x;
    else
        result /= x;

    oper = Token[0];
```

```
        }

    return result;
    }
```

MultDiv begins by calling *Power* to handle any exponential operations.

```
double Evaluator::Power()
    {
    double result = Sign();

    if (Token[0] == '^')
        {
        // get power
        GetToken();

        double value = Power();

        result = pow(result,value);
        }

    return result;
    }
```

Power's first act is to pass control up the precedence chain to *Sign*, which handles unary operators.

```
double Evaluator::Sign()
    {
    char oper = 0;

    if (Type == TT_DELIM)
        {
        oper = Token[0];

        if ((oper == '+') || (oper == '-'))
            GetToken();
        }

    double result = Paren();

    if (oper == '-')
```

```
        return -result;
    else
        return result;
    }
```

Sign checks to see whether *Token* is a plus or minus character; if it is, *sign* keeps track of the operator and calls *GetToken* to retrieve the next *Token*. Whether or not *Sign* finds an operator, it calls *Paren* before acting further.

```
double Evaluator::Paren()
    {
    double result;

    if ((Type == TT_DELIM) && (Token[0] == '('))
        {
        GetToken();

        result = AddSub();

        if (Token[0] != ')')
            throw EvalEx(EVX_PARENTHESIS);
        }
    else
        {
        switch (Type)
            {
            case TT_NUMBER:
                result = atof(Token);
                break;

            case TT_VARIABLE:
                {
                VarName vname(Token);

                try {
                    result = Vars.LookUp(vname);
                    }
                catch (DictEx & dex)
                    {
                    if (dex.WhatsWrong() == DX_NOTFOUND)
                        throw EvalEx(EVX_NOVAR);
                    else
```

```
                throw;
          }

        break;
        }

    default:
      throw EvalEx(EVX_SYNTAX);
      }
    }

  GetToken();

  return result;
  }
```

Paren is at the top of the hierarchy, and it is responsible for handling the highest levels of precedence. If *Paren* finds itself with a parenthesis character, it gets the next token before begining the cycle again with a call to *AddSub*.

Paren also ends the recursive cycle when it encounters a number or a variable name. If the token is a number, *Paren* returns its value. If *Paren* finds a variable name, it looks for the name in *Vars*, returning the associated *double* value therein. *Paren* throws an exception if the variable name is not found.

In essence, each recursive function waits for a higher-precedence function to generate a value before doing its own work. This technique creates the same sense of order that people see in equations.

Adding new features to *Evaluator* is a matter of defining new steps in the grammar hierarchy. To add built-in functions, such as square root or amortization, you'd need to define a syntax whereby a function name could be distinguished from a variable.

Many spreadsheet programs use the @ symbol to introduce a function name; when *GetToken* encounters an @ character, it could extract text until it found a parenthesis, at which point evaluation would begin with *Paren*. The possibilities are as endless as your ability to define a hierarchical grammar.

EXCEPTIONS

An *Evaluator* will generate an exception when it finds errors in a formula. The *EvalEx* class and *EvalError* type define these exceptions.

```
// error codes
enum EvalError
    {
    EVX_SYNTAX,
    EVX_PARENTHESIS,
    EVX_DECIMAL,
    EVX_INVCHAR,
    EVX_NULLDATA,
    EVX_NOVAR,
    EVX_OVERFLOW
    };

// exception objects
class EvalEx : public ExceptionBase
    {
    public:
        EvalEx
            (
            EvalError err
            )
            {
            Error = err;
            }

        EvalError WhatsWrong()
            {
            return Error;
            }

        virtual void Explain
            (
            DiagOutput & out
            );

    private:
        EvalError Error;
```

```
    };

void EvalEx::Explain
    (
    DiagOutput & out
    )
    {
    switch (Error)
        {
        case EVX_SYNTAX:
            out.DisplayMsg("Evaluator: expression syntax error",
                        DIAG_ERROR);
            break;
        case EVX_PARENTHESIS:
            out.DisplayMsg("Evaluator: missing parenthesis",
                        DIAG_ERROR);
            break;
        case EVX_DECIMAL:
            out.DisplayMsg("Evaluator: extra decimal point",
                        DIAG_ERROR);
            break;
        case EVX_INVCHAR:
            out.DisplayMsg("Evaluator: invalid character",
                        DIAG_ERROR);
            break;
        case EVX_NULLDATA:
            out.DisplayMsg("Evaluator: empty formula",
                        DIAG_WARNING);
            break;
        case EVX_NOVAR:
            out.DisplayMsg("Evaluator: variable not found",
                        DIAG_ERROR);
            break;
        case EVX_OVERFLOW:
            out.DisplayMsg("Evaluator: token too long",
                        DIAG_ERROR);
            break;
        default:
            out.DisplayMsg("Unknown Evaluator exception",
                        DIAG_FATAL);
        }
    }
```

APPLICATION

The *Evaluator* class and its associated types can be found in the files **eval-uatr.h** and **evaluatr.cpp**. Code for testing the class is in the module **tbe-val.cpp**.

CHAPTER 12

DATA COMPRESSION

Even with today's high-powered computers and multi-gigabyte hard drives, it always seems as if we have more information than space for keeping it. Data compression techniques can help, and this chapter implements the most popular compression algorithm of all: Huffman encoding.

COMPRESSION THEORY

Most of the data we generate is redundant. A text document, for example, largely consists of the same three dozen or so characters, but we're using a full eight bits to represent each character when five bits might do. And graphics information often contains strings of identical bytes representing areas filled with the same color.

Data compression is used to solve this problem by changing the representation of data. For example, *run-length encoding* replaces a string of identical characters with one copy of the character and a count. Run-length encoding works well for consistent data, such as bitmapped graphics images, but it isn't effective with less homogenous information, such as documents or database files.

A useful compression algorithm will convert an input string into a smaller form that can later be expanded into a copy of the original. No algorithm can perform this feat in every case; there will always be some piece of data that simply can't be compressed—and in a few rare cases, a compression algorithm may actually make data larger. The best algorithms minimize the chance of encountering an extreme case, and one of the most popular of these algorithms was developed by D.A. Huffman in 1952.

Huffman encoding uses a simple idea: Create a set of codes for which the shortest code represents the most common piece of data. Codes created by the Huffman algorithm require a file to be analyzed, counting bytes to determine their frequency. From the frequencies, the Huffman algorithm builds a table of codes used to compress the information. Including the table of codes with the compressed data allows the original file to be reconstructed.

To be most effective, Huffman encoding uses a variable-length code; no code is a prefix of any other, which makes decompression easier by allowing the extraction of the file bit-by-bit. The shortest codes are assigned to the most common characters, and infrequent characters receive longer codes. To create the codes, the Huffman algorithm creates a special binary tree—known as a *trie* (pronounced "try")—based on the byte frequencies of the original data.

A trie is a binary tree that has data only in its leaf nodes. Each internal trie node has two branches, designated 1 and 0, that correspond to the "greater than" and "less than" links in binary tree nodes. With the frequency counts in hand, the Huffman algorithm constructs a trie based on the frequencies of bytes.

The compression process begins by counting the bytes in the original data, storing these values in a frequency table. For example, the frequency counts for "A SIMPLE STRING TO BE ENCODED USING A MINIMAL NUMBER OF BITS" are shown in Table 12.1 (omitting letters with zero occurrence).

TABLE 12.1 THE FREQUENCY COUNTS FOR THE TEXT "A SIMPLE STRING TO BE ENCODED USING A MINIMAL NUMBER OF BITS"

LETTER	FREQ
A	3
B	3
C	1
D	2
E	5
F	1
G	2
I	6
L	2
M	4
N	5
O	3
P	1
R	2
S	4
T	3
U	2
space	11

The trie is constructed by sorting the values into order using the heap technique I presented in Chapter 2. Trie construction is done from the bottom up, working from the least common values to the most common. A trie for the frequencies in Table 12.1 is shown in Figure 12.1

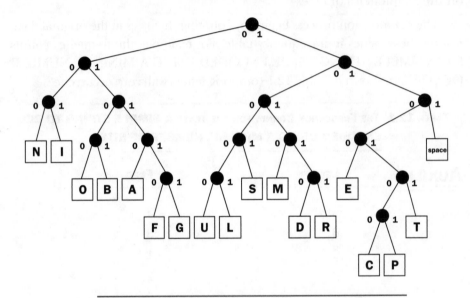

FIGURE 12.1 A TRIE FOR THE FREQUENCIES SHOWN IN TABLE 12.1.

Once you've counted characters and constructed a trie, encoding a file is a simple matter of following the tree from its root to the character being encoded. For example, whenever you store a letter *A*, you'll use the binary code 0110 by beginning at the root and following the left, right, right, and left branches in the tree.

To convert Huffman-encoded data to its original form, use the bits input to follow the tree to the compressed character. Let's look at decoding this sequence of encoded input bytes—110110100110100—using the above trie. The first bit takes us to the right; then we move right, left, right, and right again, reaching the terminal node containing *T.* Having found a character, we begin again at the root with a zero bit, moving to the right, then left, and right twice to find the letter *O.* The remaining bits take our algorithm to the *P* character, completing the word *TOP*. The trie ensures that the same sequence of bits always leads to the same character and that no two characters have the same encoding.

Compression using the Huffman algorithm is very effective on text files. For example, the test string "A SIMPLE STRING TO BE ENCODED USING A MINIMAL NUMBER OF BITS" can be shrunk from its original 480 bits (at 8 bits per character) to only 261 bits—a savings of more than 45 percent. Of course, when storing the compressed information for later expansion, perhaps in a file, you'll need to include a copy of the encoding table from which you can construct a decompression trie.

Auxiliary Types

The constructor for my *Huffman* class takes as input a pointer to a buffer and the number of bytes in that buffer. It then creates a *HuffEncoded* object using the preceding algorithm; a program can then access a pointer to the information and its code array, or the program can call a decompression routine that decodes the encoded data and returns a *HuffDecoded* object containing the expanded data. I also allow the creation of a *Huffman* object from a *HuffEncoded* structure; this allows a *HuffDecoded* object to be stored outside the program—usually in a disk file—and then retrieved into a new Huffman object for decoding.

Headers

I defined the constant *CSET_SZ* to define the number of characters in the resident set—in this case, 256 characters in an 8-bit ASCII character set. If encoding 16-bit UNICODE characters, you'll need to set *CSET_SZ* to 65536.

The header for encoded data contains the original length of the data, the length of the encoded data, and a pointer to a dynamically allocated memory buffer containing the compressed information.

```
struct HuffHdr
    {
    size_t        LenOrig;        // # of bytes in orig. data
    size_t        LenData;        // # of encoded bytes
    unsigned short Code[CSET_SZ]; // character codes

    // default constructor
    HuffHdr();

    // copy constructor
    HuffHdr
        (
        const HuffHdr & hdr
        );

    // assignment operator
    void operator =
        (
        const HuffHdr & hdr
        );
    };
```

I've defined *HuffHdr* as a *struct* so that its elements are easily accessed by the other compression classes. Its constructor and destructor serve to regularize assignments and copies.

```
// default constructor
HuffHdr::HuffHdr()
    {
    LenOrig = 0;
    LenData = 0;

    memset(Code,0,CSET_SZ * sizeof(unsigned short));
    }

// copy constructor
HuffHdr::HuffHdr
    (
    const HuffHdr & hdr
    )
    {
```

```
    LenData = hdr.LenData;
    LenOrig = hdr.LenOrig;

    memcpy(Code,hdr.Code,CSET_SZ * sizeof(unsigned short));
    }

// assignment operator
void HuffHdr::operator =
    (
    const HuffHdr & hdr
    )
    {
    LenData = hdr.LenData;
    LenOrig = hdr.LenOrig;

    memcpy(Code,hdr.Code,CSET_SZ * sizeof(unsigned short));
    }
```

The routines in this book use the *size_t* type, usually defined by your compiler as an unsigned *int*, for indicating the size of a block. Under a 16-bit operating system such as DOS or Win16, this approach limits these Huffman routines to processing a 64K block of information; under a 32-bit operating system such as Win32, the limit is 4 gigabytes.

The 16-bit limitation can be handled by using *huge* pointers and by redefining *size_t* as a 32-bit *unsigned long*, or by processing information in blocks of less than 64K bytes.

Compressed Data

My routines hold encoded information in a *void* buffer allocated in dynamic memory.

```
class HuffEncoded
    {
    friend
        class Huffman;

    public:
```

```
    // copy constructor
    HuffEncoded
        (
        const HuffEncoded & he
        );

    // destructor
    ~HuffEncoded();

    // assignment operator
    void operator =
        (
        const HuffEncoded & he
        );

    // get pointer to buffer
    const void * GetData();

    // get header
    HuffHdr GetHeader();

private:
    // default constructor
    HuffEncoded();

    // data elements
    char *  CompData; // buffer containing compressed data
    HuffHdr Hdr;      // encoding table and other data
    };
```

Each *HuffEncoded* object contains a header and a pointer to an associated block of memory, *CompData*, that is *Hdr.LenData* bytes long.

The default constructor creates an empty *HuffEncoded* object. The *Huffman* class is a friend of *HuffEncoded*; it's *Huffman*'s job to encode data into the *CompData* buffer. Therefore, this constructor is private so that new *HuffEncoded* objects can be created only by *Huffman*.

```
HuffEncoded::HuffEncoded()
    {
    CompData = NULL;
    }
```

The copy constructor and assignment operator duplicate an existing *HuffEncoded* object. The copy constructor is public so that programs can create copies of *HuffEncoded* objects created by a *Huffman* object.

```
HuffEncoded::HuffEncoded
    (
    const HuffEncoded & he
    )
    {
    Hdr = he.Hdr;

    if (he.CompData == NULL)
        CompData = NULL;
    else
        {
        CompData = new char [Hdr.LenData];

        if (CompData == NULL)
            throw HuffEx(HFX_ALLOC);

        memcpy(CompData,he.CompData,Hdr.LenData);
        }
    }

void HuffEncoded::operator =
    (
    const HuffEncoded & he
    )
    {
    if (CompData != NULL)
        delete [] CompData;

    Hdr = he.Hdr;

    if (he.CompData == NULL)
        CompData = NULL;
    else
        {
        CompData = new char [Hdr.LenData];

        if (CompData == NULL)
            throw HuffEx(HFX_ALLOC);
```

```
        memcpy(CompData,he.CompData,Hdr.LenData);
        }
    }
```

The destructor automatically deletes any memory allocated to *CompData*.

```
HuffEncoded::~HuffEncoded()
    {
    if (CompData != NULL)
        delete [] CompData;
    }
```

Two inline interrogation functions return the *CompData* pointer and header. Note that *GetData* returns a *const* pointer; data stored in a *HuffEncoded* object can be read, but the interrogation functions prevent it from being modified.

```
inline const void * HuffEncoded::GetData()
    {
    return (const void *)CompData;
    }

inline HuffHdr HuffEncoded::GetHeader()
    {
    return Hdr;
    }
```

Decompressed Data

When your program asks a *Huffman* object to decompress its information, it returns a *HuffDecoded* object.

```
class HuffDecoded
    {
    friend
        class Huffman;

    public:
```

```
    // copy constructor
    HuffDecoded
        (
        const HuffDecoded & hd
        );

    // destructor
    ~HuffDecoded();

    // assignment
    void operator =
        (
        const HuffDecoded & hd
        );

    // get pointer to buffer
    const void * GetData();

    // get size of buffer
    size_t      GetLen();

private:
    // constructor
    HuffDecoded();

    // data elements
    char * Data;
    size_t DataLen;
};
```

The *Data* pointer references a buffer containing *DataLen* bytes of decompressed data.

```
HuffDecoded::HuffDecoded()
    {
    Data    = NULL;
    DataLen = 0;
    }
```

Following the design of *HuffEncoded*, the primary constructor for *HuffDecoded* is private, to be used only by a *Huffman* object.

The *HuffDecoded* copy constructor, assignment operator, and destructor also work much like their counterparts in *HuffEncoded*.

```
HuffDecoded::HuffDecoded
    (
    const HuffDecoded & hd
    )
    {
    DataLen = hd.DataLen;

    if (hd.Data == NULL)
        Data = NULL;
    else
        {
        Data = new char [DataLen];

        if (Data == NULL)
            throw HuffEx(HFX_ALLOC);

        memcpy(Data,hd.Data,DataLen);
        }
    }

HuffDecoded::~HuffDecoded()
    {
    if (Data != NULL)
        delete [] Data;
    }

void HuffDecoded::operator =
    (
    const HuffDecoded & hd
    )
    {
    if (Data != NULL)
        delete [] Data;

    DataLen = hd.DataLen;

    if (hd.Data == NULL)
        Data = NULL;
    else
```

```
        {
        Data = new char [DataLen];

        if (Data == NULL)
            throw HuffEx(HFX_ALLOC);

        memcpy(Data,hd.Data,DataLen);
        }
    }
```

Two interrogation functions provide read-only access to the uncompressed information and its length.

```
inline const void * HuffDecoded::GetData()
    {
    return (const void *)Data;
    }

inline size_t HuffDecoded::GetLen()
    {
    return DataLen;
    }
```

HUFFMAN CLASS

The *Huffman* class is the meat of my compression library; it creates *HuffEncoded* objects from input data and makes *HuffDecoded* objects when asked to decode compressed information.

```
class Huffman
    {
    public:
        // compression constructor
        Huffman
            (
            const void * info,
            size_t bytes
```

```
            );

        // construct from compressed data
        Huffman
            (
            const HuffHdr & hdr,
            const char *    bytes
            );

        // copy constructor
        Huffman
            (
            const Huffman & huff
            );

        // assignment operator
        void operator =
            (
            const Huffman & huff
            );

        // get encoded data
        HuffEncoded GetEncoded();

        // get decoded data
        HuffDecoded GetDecoded();

    protected:
        // data elements
        HuffEncoded Data; // encoded data
    };
```

Compression

In essence, a *Huffman* object is a shell around its internal *HuffEncoded* object. The first constructor creates a new *HuffEncoded* object from an input buffer of a given length.

```
Huffman::Huffman
    (
```

```
const void * info,
size_t bytes
)
{
// allocate data space
char * edata = new char [bytes + 1];

if (edata == NULL)
    throw HuffEx(HFX_ALLOC);

// allocate code table
unsigned short * code = new unsigned short [CSET_SZ];

if (code == NULL)
    throw HuffEx(HFX_ALLOC);

// allocate code len table
unsigned short * clen = new unsigned short [CSET_SZ];

if (clen == NULL)
    throw HuffEx(HFX_ALLOC);

// allocate frequency table
size_t * freq = new size_t [CSET_SZ * 2];

if (freq == NULL)
    throw HuffEx(HFX_ALLOC);

// allocate heap
size_t * heap = new size_t [CSET_SZ];

if (heap == NULL)
    throw HuffEx(HFX_ALLOC);

// allocate link array
int * link = new int [CSET_SZ * 2];

if (link == NULL)
    throw HuffEx(HFX_ALLOC);

// clear work areas
memset(code,0,sizeof(unsigned short) * CSET_SZ);
memset(clen,0,sizeof(unsigned short) * CSET_SZ);
```

```
memset(freq,0,sizeof(size_t) * CSET_SZ * 2);
memset(heap,0,sizeof(size_t) * CSET_SZ);
memset(link,0,sizeof(int)    * CSET_SZ * 2);

// count frequencies
const unsigned char * iptr = (const unsigned char *)info;
size_t i;

for (i = 0; i < bytes; ++i)
    {
    ++freq[size_t(*iptr)];
    ++iptr;
    }

// create trie using heap
size_t n = 0;

for (i = 0; i < CSET_SZ; ++i)
    {
    if (freq[i])
        {
        heap[n] = i;
        ++n;
        }
    }

for (i = n; i > 0; --i)
    HeapAdjust(freq,heap,n,i);

size_t temp;

while (n > 1)
    {
    --n;
    temp    = heap[0];
    heap[0] = heap[n];

    HeapAdjust(freq,heap,n,1);

    freq[CSET_SZ + n] = freq[heap[0]] + freq[temp];
    link[temp]        =  CSET_SZ + n;
    link[heap[0]]     = -CSET_SZ - n;
```

```
        heap[0]                 =  CSET_SZ + n;

        HeapAdjust(freq,heap,n,1);
        }

link[CSET_SZ + n] = 0;

// generate codes
size_t j, k, x, maxx = 0, maxi = 0;
int l;

for (k = 0; k < CSET_SZ; ++k)
    {
    if (!freq[k])
        {
        code[k] = 0;
        clen[k] = 0;
        }
    else
        {
        i = 0;
        j = 1;
        x = 0;
        l = link[k];

        while (l)
            {
            if (l < 0)
                {
                x +=  j;
                l  = -l;
                }

            l   = link[l];
            j += j;
            ++i;
            }

        code[k] = (unsigned short)x;
        clen[k] = (unsigned char)i;

        if (x > maxx)
```

```
                    maxx = x;

            if (i > maxi)
                maxi = i;
            }
        }

    // make sure longest codes fit in unsigned short-bits
    if (maxi >= (sizeof(unsigned short) * 8))
        throw HuffEx(HFX_OVERFLOW);

    // encode data
    size_t mask;        // mask for extracting bits
    size_t nout =  0;   // number of bytes output
    char   bout =  0;   // byte of encoded data
    int    bit  = -1;   // count of bits stored in bout
    iptr = (const unsigned char *)info;

    // watch for one-value file!
    if (maxx == 0)
        {
        edata[0] = char(*iptr);
        nout = 1;
        goto done;
        }

    for (j = 0; j < bytes; ++j)
        {
        // start copying at first bit of code
        mask = 1 << (clen[(*iptr)] - 1);

        // copy code bits
        for (i = 0; i < clen[(*iptr)]; ++i)
            {
            if (bit == 7)
                {
                // store full output byte
                edata[nout] = bout;
                ++nout;
                bit  = 0;
                bout = 0;
                }
            else
```

```
        {
        // move to next bit
        ++bit;
        bout <<= 1;
        }

    if (code[(*iptr)] & mask)
        bout |= 1;

    mask >>= 1;
    }

++iptr;
}


// output any incomplete bytes
bout <<= (7 - bit);
edata[nout] = bout;
++nout;

// yes, a label!
done:

// store all information
Data.CompData   = edata;
Data.Hdr.LenOrig = bytes;
Data.Hdr.LenData = nout;

// store codes with len marker bits
for (i = 0; i < CSET_SZ; ++i)
    Data.Hdr.Code[i] |= (unsigned short)
                    (code[i] | (1 << clen[i]));

// remove work areas
delete [] code;
delete [] clen;
delete [] freq;
delete [] heap;
delete [] link;
}
```

The constructor begins by allocating work space and creating a frequency count; it then creates an indirect heap based on these frequencies.

The heap itself is a set of index links that show the organization of the heap, and it is built using the *HeapAdjust* utility function.

```
static void HeapAdjust
    (
    size_t * freq,
    size_t * heap,
    int      n,
    int      k
    )
    {
    int j;

    —heap;

    int v = heap[k];

    while (k <= (n / 2)) // loop invariant!
        {
        j = k + k;

        if ((j < n) && (freq[heap[j]] > freq[heap[j+1]]))
            ++j;

        if (freq[v] < freq[heap[j]])
            break;

        heap[k] = heap[j];
        k = j;
        }

    heap[k] = v;
    }
```

Chapter 4 explains the heap algorithm, which I customized as a specific algorithm in the case of *Huffman*.

From the heap, the constructor creates a sequence of codes in the *code* array, with the length of each code stored in the corresponding elements of the *clen* array. This is done by defining a set of linked lists in the *link* array, based on the trie structure built from frequency information.

Once the trie is built, the program generates codes by following the nodes of the trie from character to root.

The constructor proceeds to encode the information by copying encoded bits into *Data.CompData*. Then information on codes and sizes is stored in the *Data.Hdr* record. Because I need the lengths of the codes to decode the message, I store the length as the high-order bit of the code. In theory, the code for any given character will be no more than a dozen bits or so; thus, there is plenty of room to store an extra bit to mark the length of each code, saving me from having to store both the *code* and the *clen* arrays.

A program would call the *GetEncoded* function to retrieve the compressed information from a *Huffman* object.

```
inline HuffEncoded Huffman::GetEncoded()
    {
    return Data;
    }
```

The header and associated data could then be stored in a file, from which a program could later extract them for decompression. A *Huffman* object can be constructed from compressed data using the following constructor:

```
Huffman::Huffman
    (
    const HuffHdr & hdr,
    const char *    bytes
    )
    {
    if (bytes == NULL)
        throw HuffEx(HFX_NULLDATA);

    Data.Hdr     = hdr;
    Data.CompData = new char [Data.Hdr.LenData];

    if (Data.CompData == NULL)
        throw HuffEx(HFX_ALLOC);
```

```
    memcpy(Data.CompData,bytes,Data.Hdr.LenData);
    }
```

Decompression

To decode compressed information, call the *GetDecoded* function.

```
HuffDecoded Huffman::GetDecoded()
    {
    size_t i, j, n, mask;
    unsigned long k, t;
    char * cptr;
    char * dptr;
    char   c;
    HuffDecoded dec;

    // allocate output array
    dec.Data = new char [Data.Hdr.LenOrig];

    if (dec.Data == NULL)
        throw HuffEx(HFX_ALLOC);

    // handle decompression of one-value file
    if (Data.Hdr.LenData == 1)
        {
        memset(dec.Data,Data.CompData[0],Data.Hdr.LenOrig);
        dec.DataLen = Data.Hdr.LenOrig;
        return dec;
        }

    // allocate heap
    unsigned long * heap = new unsigned long [CSET_SZ];

    if (heap == NULL)
        throw HuffEx(HFX_ALLOC);

    // allocate code table
    unsigned short * code = new unsigned short [CSET_SZ];

    if (code == NULL)
```

```
        throw HuffEx(HFX_ALLOC);

// allocate code len table
unsigned short * clen = new unsigned short [CSET_SZ];

if (clen == NULL)
    throw HuffEx(HFX_ALLOC);

// initialize work areas
memset(heap,0,CSET_SZ * sizeof(unsigned long));

for (i = 0; i < CSET_SZ; ++i)
    {
    // extract lengths by finding leftmost bit
    mask = 0x8000;
    clen[i] = (sizeof(unsigned short) * 8) - 1;
    code[i] = Data.Hdr.Code[i];

    while (1)
        {
        if (code[i] & mask)
            {
            // clear marker bit and exit
            code[i] &= (unsigned short)(~mask);
            break;
            }

        // next bit to right
        mask >>= 1;
        --clen[i];
        }
    }

// allocate output character buffer
char * outc = new char [CSET_SZ];

if (outc == NULL)
    throw HuffEx(HFX_ALLOC);

// create decode table in trie heap
char * optr = outc;

for (j = 0; j < CSET_SZ; ++j)
```

```
        {
        (*optr) = char(j);
        ++optr;

        if (code[j] | clen[j])
            {
            k = 0;
            mask = 1 << (clen[j] - 1);

            for (i = 0; i < clen[j]; ++i)
                {
                k = k * 2 + 1;

                if (code[j] & mask)
                    ++k;

                mask >>= 1;
                }

            heap[j] = k;
            }
        }

    // sort outc based on heap
    for (i = 1; i < CSET_SZ; ++i)
        {
        t = heap[i];
        c = outc[i];
        j = i;

        while ((j) && (heap[j-1] > t))
            {
            heap[j] = heap[j - 1];
            outc[j] = outc[j - 1];
            —j;
            }

        heap[j] = t;
        outc[j] = c;
        }

    // find first character in table
    for (j = 0; heap[j] == 0; ++j) ;
```

```
// decode data
k    = 0;
i    = j;
mask = 0x80;
n    = 0;
cptr = Data.CompData;
dptr = dec.Data;

while (n < Data.Hdr.LenOrig)
    {
    k = k * 2 + 1;

    if ((*cptr) & mask)
        ++k;

    while (heap[i] < k)
        ++i;

    if (k == heap[i])
        {
        (*dptr) = outc[i];
        ++dptr;
        ++n;
        k = 0;
        i = j;
        }

    // move to next bit
    if (mask > 1)
        mask >>= 1;
    else
        {
        mask = 0x80;
        ++cptr;
        }
    }

// delete work area
delete [] heap;
delete [] code;
delete [] clen;

// store length of decoded data
```

```
dec.DataLen = Data.Hdr.LenOrig;

return dec;
}
```

GetDecoded constructs a trie from the code information stored in the header of the compressed data. Once the *code, clen,* and *heap* arrays have been allocated and loaded, *GetDecoded* proceeds to read the input data a bit at a time, following the heap-based trie to encoded characters. The function also keeps track of how many characters have been input and how many have been output to ensure that it decodes as many characters as were encoded.

Other Functions

Huffman also implements a copy constructor and assignment operator:

```
inline Huffman::Huffman
    (
    const Huffman & huff
    )
    {
    Data = huff.Data;
    }

inline void Huffman::operator =
    (
    const Huffman & huff
    )
    {
    Data = huff.Data;
    }
```

EXCEPTION TYPES

The *Huffman* classes throw exceptions of type *HuffEx*, based on the enumerated type *HuffError*.

```
enum HuffError
    {
    HFX_ALLOC,
    HFX_NULLDATA,
    HFX_OVERFLOW
    };

// exception objects
class HuffEx : public ExceptionBase
    {
    public:
        HuffEx
            (
            HuffError err
            )
            {
            Error = err;
            }

        HuffError WhatsWrong()
            {
            return Error;
            }

        virtual void Explain
            (
            DiagOutput & out
            );

    private:
        HuffError Error;
    };
```

The *HuffEx::Explain* function displays appropriate error messages.

```
void HuffEx::Explain
    (
    DiagOutput & out
    )
    {
    switch (Error)
        {
```

APPENDIX A

THE TESTBED APPLICATION

Following is the code for the the Testbed application:

TESTBED.H

```
#define IDM_EXIT          9999
#define IDM_COPY          9001

#define IDM_RAND_GEN      1000
#define IDM_RAND_TABLE    1001

#define IDM_SETS_BASIC    2000
#define IDM_SETS_CHARSET  2001
#define IDM_SETS_LIMITED  2002
#define IDM_SETS_OBJECT   2003
```

```
#define IDM_TREE_BINARY      3000
#define IDM_TREE_REDBLACK    3001
#define IDM_TREE_HEAP        3002

#define IDM_CONT_LISTS       4000
#define IDM_CONT_STACKQ      4001
#define IDM_CONT_DICTIONARY  4002

#define IDM_MATH_POLY        5000
#define IDM_MATH_MATRIX      5001
#define IDM_MATH_SPARSEMAT   5002

#define IDM_APPL_COMP        6000
#define IDM_APPL_EVAL        6001
#define IDM_APPL_FUZZY       6002
```

TBDEF.H

```
//==========================================================
//   Testbed Application for C++ Templates and Tools
//        tbdef.h    v1.00
//
//        Common type definitions and function prototypes.
//
//        Copyright 1995 by Scott Robert Ladd
//==========================================================

#include "strstrea.h"

//-----------------
// type definitions
//-----------------

enum ErrorType
    {
    ET_CRASH,
    ET_ERROR,
    ET_WARNING
    };
```

```
//-------------------------------
// external function prototypes
//-------------------------------

int PASCAL WinMain
    (
    HANDLE instance,
    HANDLE prevInstance,
    LPSTR  commandLine,
    int    commandShow
    );

static BOOL InitApplication
    (
    HANDLE instance
    );

static BOOL InitInstance
    (
    HANDLE instance,
    int    commandShow
    );

long WINAPI _export MainWindow
    (
    HWND   thisWindow,
    UINT   message,
    WPARAM wordParam,
    LPARAM longParam
    );

void RunTest
    (
    WPARAM testid
    );

void TestRandGen
    (
    strstream & buffer
    );

void TestRandTable
    (
```

```
    strstream & buffer
    );

void TestSet
    (
    strstream & buffer
    );

void TestCharSet
    (
    strstream & buffer
    );

void TestLimitedSet
    (
    strstream & buffer
    );

void TestObjectSet
    (
    strstream & buffer
    );

void TestTreeBinary
    (
    strstream & buffer
    );

void TestTreeRedBlack
    (
    strstream & buffer
    );

void TestTreeHeap
    (
    strstream & buffer
    );

void TestContainerLists
    (
    strstream & buffer
    );
```

```
void TestContainerStackQ
    (
    strstream & buffer
    );

void TestContainerDictionary
    (
    strstream & buffer
    );

void TestMathPoly
    (
    strstream & buffer
    );

void TestMathMatrix
    (
    strstream & buffer
    );

void TestMathMatrix2
    (
    strstream & buffer
    );

void TestMathSparse
    (
    strstream & buffer
    );

void TestApplCompress
    (
    strstream & buffer
    );

void TestApplEvaluator
    (
    strstream & buffer
    );

void TestApplFuzzy
    (
    strstream & buffer
```

```
    );

void CopyBuffer
    (
    HWND wnd
    );

void ErrorMessage
    (
    const char * msg,
    ErrorType etype = ET_WARNING
    );
```

TESTBED.DEF

```
NAME        Testbed
DESCRIPTION 'Testbed'
EXETYPE     WINDOWS
PROTMODE
STUB        'WINSTUB.EXE'
CODE        PRELOAD MOVABLE DISCARDABLE
DATA        PRELOAD MOVABLE MULTIPLE
HEAPSIZE    8192
STACKSIZE   8192
```

TESTBED.RC

```
#include "windows.h"
#include "testbed.h"

TestbedIcon ICON "testbed.ico"

TestbedMenu MENU
    BEGIN
    POPUP "&Tools"
        BEGIN
```

```
        MENUITEM "&Random Numbers",          IDM_RAND_GEN
        MENUITEM "Random Value &Table",      IDM_RAND_TABLE
        END
    POPUP "&Sets"
        BEGIN
        MENUITEM "&Basic",                   IDM_SETS_BASIC
        MENUITEM "&Character",               IDM_SETS_CHARSET
        MENUITEM "&Bounded",                 IDM_SETS_LIMITED
        MENUITEM "&Object",                  IDM_SETS_OBJECT
        END
    POPUP "&Trees"
        BEGIN
        MENUITEM "&Binary",                  IDM_TREE_BINARY
        MENUITEM "&Red-Black",               IDM_TREE_REDBLACK
        MENUITEM "&Heap",                    IDM_TREE_HEAP
        END
    POPUP "&Containers"
        BEGIN
        MENUITEM "&Linked Lists",        IDM_CONT_LISTS
        MENUITEM "&Stacks and Queues",   IDM_CONT_STACKQ
        MENUITEM "&Dictionary",          IDM_CONT_DICTIONARY
        END
    POPUP "&Math"
        BEGIN
        MENUITEM "&Polynomials",             IDM_MATH_POLY
        MENUITEM SEPARATOR
        MENUITEM "&Matrices",                IDM_MATH_MATRIX
        MENUITEM "&Sparse Grids",            IDM_MATH_SPARSEMAT
        END
    POPUP "&Apps"
        BEGIN
        MENUITEM "&Compression",             IDM_APPL_COMP
        MENUITEM "&Evaluator",               IDM_APPL_EVAL
        MENUITEM "&Fuzzy Logic",             IDM_APPL_FUZZY
        END
    POPUP "&Utility"
        BEGIN
        MENUITEM "&Copy",                    IDM_COPY
        END
    MENUITEM "E&xit",                    IDM_EXIT
    END
```

TESTBED.CPP

```
//=============================================================
//   Testbed Application for C++ Templates and Tools
//       testbed.c    v1.00    20-Jan-1995
//
//       An application to test the class libraries presented
//       in my book C++ Templates and Tools.
//
//       Copyright 1995 by Scott Robert Ladd
//=============================================================

#include "windows.h"  // Windows definitions
#include "testbed.h"  // menu and control constants
#include "tbdef.h"    // types, prototypes, common includes
#include "diagwin.h"  // diagnostic display class for windows
#include "limits.h"   // limits of types
#include "string.h"   // C-style string functions
#include "strstrea.h" // strstream definitions
#include "iomanip.h"  // stream manipulators

//------------------------
// global data
//------------------------

// constants
const char * AppName = "Testbed";
const int    DisplayID = 1;
const DWORD  DisplayStyle = WS_CHILD |
                            WS_VSCROLL |
                            WS_HSCROLL |
                            ES_MULTILINE |
                            ES_READONLY |
                            ES_LEFT |
                            ES_AUTOHSCROLL |
                            ES_AUTOVSCROLL;

// variables
HANDLE ThisInstance;
HWND   Display;
```

```
DiagOutWin Diag(AppName);

#ifdef _MSC_VER
    #pragma warning(disable:4100)
#endif

#ifdef __TURBOC__
    #pragma argsused
#endif

//----------------------------------------------
//  WinMain -- program start and message loop
//----------------------------------------------

int PASCAL WinMain
    (
    HANDLE instance,
    HANDLE prevInstance,
    LPSTR  commandLine,
    int    commandShow
    )
    {
    MSG msg;

    if (prevInstance)
        {
        ErrorMessage("Testbed is already running!", ET_WARNING);
        return 0;
        }

    if (!InitApplication(instance))
        return 0;

    if (!InitInstance(instance, commandShow))
        return 0;

    while (GetMessage(&msg, NULL, NULL, NULL))
        {
        TranslateMessage(&msg);
        DispatchMessage(&msg);
        }

    return msg.wParam;
```

```
    }

//--------------------------
// initialize an application
//--------------------------

static BOOL InitApplication
    (
    HANDLE instance
    )
    {
    WNDCLASS wc;

    wc.style         = 0;
    wc.lpfnWndProc   = MainWindow;
    wc.cbClsExtra    = 0;
    wc.cbWndExtra    = 0;
    wc.hInstance     = instance;
    wc.hIcon         = LoadIcon(instance,"TestbedIcon");
    wc.hCursor       = LoadCursor(NULL, IDC_ARROW);
    wc.hbrBackground = GetStockObject(BLACK_BRUSH);
    wc.lpszMenuName  = "TestbedMenu";
    wc.lpszClassName = "TestbedWindowClass";

    return RegisterClass(&wc);
    }

//----------------------
// initialize an instance
//----------------------

static BOOL InitInstance
    (
    HANDLE instance,
    int commandShow
    )
    {
    HWND hWnd;

    // save the instance handle
    ThisInstance = instance;

    // create a window
```

```
hWnd = CreateWindow("TestbedWindowClass",
                    "Testbed",
                    WS_OVERLAPPEDWINDOW,
                    CW_USEDEFAULT, CW_USEDEFAULT,
                    CW_USEDEFAULT, CW_USEDEFAULT,
                    NULL, NULL,
                    instance, 0);

if (!hWnd)
    {
    ErrorMessage("Cannot create main window", ET_WARNING);
    return FALSE;
    }

ShowWindow(hWnd, commandShow);
UpdateWindow(hWnd);

// get size of client area
RECT area;

GetClientRect(hWnd,&area);

// create edit control
Display = CreateWindow("EDIT","",
                       DisplayStyle,
                       0, 0, area.right, area.bottom,
                       hWnd, (HMENU)DisplayID,
                       instance,0);

if (!Display)
    {
    ErrorMessage("Cannot create output window", ET_WARNING);
    return FALSE;
    }

ShowWindow(Display, SW_SHOW);
UpdateWindow(Display);

// set fixed-pitch font (9pt system) for edit control
LOGFONT dfont;

dfont.lfHeight        = 12;
dfont.lfWidth         = 0;
```

```
        dfont.lfEscapement      = 0;
        dfont.lfOrientation     = 0;
        dfont.lfWeight          = FW_DONTCARE;
        dfont.lfItalic          = FALSE;
        dfont.lfUnderline       = FALSE;
        dfont.lfStrikeOut       = FALSE;
        dfont.lfCharSet         = ANSI_CHARSET;
        dfont.lfOutPrecision    = OUT_DEFAULT_PRECIS;
        dfont.lfClipPrecision   = CLIP_DEFAULT_PRECIS;
        dfont.lfQuality         = DEFAULT_QUALITY;
        dfont.lfPitchAndFamily  = FIXED_PITCH | FF_DONTCARE;
        dfont.lfFaceName[0]     = 0; // default system font

        HFONT efont = CreateFontIndirect(&dfont);

        if (efont == NULL)
            {
            ErrorMessage("Cannot create system font", ET_WARNING);
            return FALSE;
            }

        SendMessage(Display,WM_SETFONT,(WPARAM)efont,0L);

        return TRUE;
        }

//----------------------
// Main window function
//----------------------

long WINAPI _export MainWindow
    (
    HWND    thisWindow,
    UINT    message,
    WPARAM  wordParam,
    LPARAM  longParam
    )
    {
    HFONT font;

    switch (message)
        {
        case WM_COMMAND:
```

```
    switch (wordParam)
        {
        case IDM_RAND_GEN:
        case IDM_RAND_TABLE:
        case IDM_SETS_BASIC:
        case IDM_SETS_CHARSET:
        case IDM_SETS_LIMITED:
        case IDM_SETS_OBJECT:
        case IDM_TREE_BINARY:
        case IDM_TREE_REDBLACK:
        case IDM_TREE_HEAP:
        case IDM_CONT_LISTS:
        case IDM_CONT_STACKQ:
        case IDM_CONT_DICTIONARY:
        case IDM_MATH_POLY:
        case IDM_MATH_MATRIX:
        case IDM_MATH_SPARSEMAT:
        case IDM_APPL_COMP:
        case IDM_APPL_EVAL:
        case IDM_APPL_FUZZY:
            RunTest(wordParam);
            break;

        case IDM_COPY:
            CopyBuffer(thisWindow);
            break;

        case IDM_EXIT:
            DestroyWindow(thisWindow);
            break;

        default:
            return DefWindowProc(thisWindow, message,
                            wordParam, longParam);
        }

    break;

case WM_SIZE:
    // resize edit control
    MoveWindow(Display,0,0,
            LOWORD(longParam),
            HIWORD(longParam),
```

```
                             TRUE);
                break;

          case WM_DESTROY:
                font = (HFONT)SendMessage(Display,WM_GETFONT,0,0L);
                DeleteObject(font);
                PostQuitMessage(0);
                break;

          default:
                return DefWindowProc(thisWindow, message,
                                        wordParam, longParam);
          }

    return 0L;
    }

//----------------------------------------
// framework for running test procedures
//----------------------------------------

void RunTest
    (
    WPARAM testid
    )
    {
    strstream buffer;

    HCURSOR cursor = SetCursor(LoadCursor(NULL,IDC_WAIT));

    try
        {
        switch (testid)
            {
            case IDM_RAND_GEN:
                TestRandGen(buffer);
                break;
            case IDM_RAND_TABLE:
                TestRandTable(buffer);
                break;
            case IDM_SETS_BASIC:
                TestSet(buffer);
                break;
```

```
case IDM_SETS_CHARSET:
    TestCharSet(buffer);
    break;
case IDM_SETS_LIMITED:
    TestLimitedSet(buffer);
    break;
case IDM_SETS_OBJECT:
    TestObjectSet(buffer);
    break;
case IDM_TREE_BINARY:
    TestTreeBinary(buffer);
    break;
case IDM_TREE_REDBLACK:
    TestTreeRedBlack(buffer);
    break;
case IDM_TREE_HEAP:
    TestTreeHeap(buffer);
    break;
case IDM_CONT_LISTS:
    TestContainerLists(buffer);
    break;
case IDM_CONT_STACKQ:
    TestContainerStackQ(buffer);
    break;
case IDM_CONT_DICTIONARY:
    TestContainerDictionary(buffer);
    break;
case IDM_MATH_POLY:
    TestMathPoly(buffer);
    break;
case IDM_MATH_MATRIX:
    TestMathMatrix(buffer);
    TestMathMatrix2(buffer);
    break;
case IDM_MATH_SPARSEMAT:
    TestMathSparse(buffer);
    break;
case IDM_APPL_COMP:
    TestApplCompress(buffer);
    break;
case IDM_APPL_EVAL:
    TestApplEvaluator(buffer);
    break;
```

```
            case IDM_APPL_FUZZY:
                TestApplFuzzy(buffer);
                break;
            default:
                buffer << "unknown test selection!";
            }
        }
    catch (ExceptionBase & ex)
        {
        ex.Explain(Diag);
        buffer << "\r\nPROGRAM ERROR! BUFFER MAY BE INCOMPLETE!";
        }

    // terminate buffer
    buffer << ends;

    // display buffer in edit control

SendMessage(Display,WM_SETTEXT,0,(LPARAM)(LPSTR)buffer.str());

    // restore cursor and set focus to edit window
    SetCursor(cursor);
    SetFocus(Display);
    }

//-----------------------------
// Copy buffer to the clipboard
//-----------------------------

void CopyBuffer
    (
    HWND wnd
    )
    {
    // open the clipboard
    if (OpenClipboard(wnd) == FALSE)
        {
        ErrorMessage("Cannot open clipboard", ET_WARNING);
        return;
        }

    // get the size of the edit buffer
    WORD bufsize = (WORD)SendMessage(Display,WM_GETTEXTLENGTH
```

```
                                    ,0,0L);

    if (bufsize == 0)  // if empty, nothing to copy
        return;

    // allocate a buffer
    HGLOBAL buffer = GlobalAlloc(GPTR,bufsize + 1);

    if (buffer == NULL)
        {
        ErrorMessage("Cannot allocate clipboard buffer",
                     ET_ERROR);
        return;
        }

    // get pointer to the buffer
    void FAR * bufptr = GlobalLock(buffer);

    if (bufptr == NULL)
        {
        ErrorMessage("Cannot lock clipboard buffer",
                     ET_ERROR);
        return;
        }

    // copy buffer contents to global memory
    SendMessage(Display,WM_GETTEXT,bufsize,
                (LPARAM)(LPSTR)bufptr);

    // unlock global memory
    GlobalUnlock(buffer);

    // load text into clipboard
    if (NULL == SetClipboardData(CF_TEXT,buffer))
        ErrorMessage("Cannot write to clipboard", ET_ERROR);

    // close the clipboard
    if (CloseClipboard() == FALSE)
        ErrorMessage("Cannot close clipboard", ET_ERROR);
    }

//---------------------------------------------
// Display an error message of given severity
```

```
//----------------------------------------------

void ErrorMessage
    (
    const char * msg,
    ErrorType etype
    )
    {
    UINT style;
    UINT sound;
    int response;
    char text[128];

    // copy message to output buffer
    strcpy(text,msg);

    // set values specific to error severity
    switch (etype)
        {
        case ET_CRASH:
            sound = MB_ICONSTOP;
            style = MB_OK;
            strcat(text," PROGRAM WILL TERMINATE!");
            break;
        case ET_ERROR:
            sound = MB_ICONEXCLAMATION;
            style = MB_YESNO;
            strcat(text,"Click 'Yes' to terminate program, "
                        "or 'No' to continue");
            break;
        case ET_WARNING:
            sound = MB_ICONASTERISK;
            style = MB_OK;
        }

    // match icon to sound
    style |= sound;

    // sound off and display message
    MessageBeep(sound);
    response = MessageBox(NULL,text,AppName,style);

    // check for termination
```

```
switch (etype)
    {
    case ET_ERROR:
        if (response == IDNO)
            break;
    case ET_CRASH:
        PostQuitMessage(1); // boom-boom
        // program should never reach this point!
    }
}
```

In addition, there are two files, testbed.ico and testbed.ide, used by the compiler to create the testbed program.

BIBLIOGRAPHY

Cormen, Thomas H., Charles E. Leiserson, and Ronald L. Rivest.
Introduction to Algorithms. McGraw-Hill, 1990.

Ellis, Margaret A., and Bjarne Stroustrup. *The Annotated C++ Reference
Manual.* Addison-Wesley, 1990.

Knuth, Donald E. *The Art of Computer Programming, Volume 1: Fundamental
Algorithms, 2nd Edition.* Addison-Wesley, 1973.

Knuth, Donald E. *The Art of Computer Programming, Volume 2:
Seminumerical Algorithms, 2nd Edition.* Addison-Wesley, 1981.

Knuth, Donald E. *The Art of Computer Programming, Volume 3: Sorting and
Searching.* Addison-Wesley, 1973.

Ladd, Scott Robert. *Applying C++*. M&T Books, 1990.

Ladd, Scott Robert. *C++ Components & Algorithms*, Second Edition. M&T Books, 1994.

Polk, Michael J., and Bill Zoellick. *File Structures: A Conceptual Toolkit*. Addison-Wesley, 1987.

Press, William A., Brian P. Flannery, Saul A. Teukolsky, and William T. Vetterling. *Numerical Recipes in C: The Art of Scientific Computing, Second Edition*. Cambridge, 1992.

Sedgewick, Robert. *Algorithms in C*. Addison-Wesley, 1990.

Stroustrup, Bjarne. *The C++ Programming Language, 2nd Edition*. Addison-Wesley, 1991.

Zadeh, Lotfi, and Janusz Kacprzyk. *Fuzzy Logic for the Management of Uncertainty*. Wiley, 1994.

Index

U

V

W

Z

About the Disk

The enclosed disk contains the complete source code from the book C++ TEMPLATES AND TOOLS. Each directory contains the code for a specific set of classes and templates:

COMPRESS	Huffman data compression (Chapter 12)
DICT	Dictionary and doubly-linked lists (Chapter 5)
GRIDS	Grid and sparse grids (Chapter 8)
LISTS	Linking lists, stacks, queues, and deques (Chapter 2)
MATRIX	Matrices (Chapter 9)
PARSING	Recursive-descent function parser (Chapter 11)
POLY	Polynomials (Chapter 10)
PQHEAPS	Priority queues and heaps (Chapter 4)
SETS	Bit sets (Chapter 6)
SIMPLE	Simple classes, exception classes, and random numbers (Chapter 1)
TESTBED	TESTBED application
TREES	Binary and red-black trees (Chapter 3)

All code has been tested with Borland C++ 4.5, and a Borland IDE file is included in the TESTBED directory. Testing was performed under Windows 3.1 and Windows/NT 3.5. Borland C++ generates incorrect code for the binary tree classes when the -Oe (Global Register Allocation) optimization option is in effect.

The author noted a trivial last-minute problem that could not be fixed on the enclosed disk. A conflict may occur with some of the identifiers RED and BLACK in the Red-Black Tree template; a simple search-and-replace changing RED to RB_RED and BLACK to RB_BLACK will solve the problem if it occurs.